fine Cooking
Pies & Crisps

fine Cooking
Pies & Crisps

Over 100 Sweet and Savory No-Fail Recipes

Editors and Contributors of *Fine Cooking*

The Taunton Press

The Taunton Press
Inspiration for hands-on living®

The Taunton Press, Inc.
63 South Main Street, PO Box 5506, Newtown, CT 06470-5506
e-mail: tp@taunton.com

Editor: Carolyn Mandarano
Copy editor: Valerie Cimino
Indexer: Barbara Mortenson
Jacket/Cover design: Kimberly Adis
Interior design: Kimberly Adis
Layout: Amy Griffin
Photographs: Scott Phillips ©The Taunton Press, Inc., except for p. 25 © Mark Ferri;
p. 39 © Ben Fink; pp. 53, 55, 56, 57, 59, and 164 © Alexandra Grablewski;
p. 91 by Martha Holmberg © The Taunton Press, Inc.; pp. 98, 109, 110, 111, and 112 © Colin Clark;
p. 146 © Mark Thomas; p. 165 © Pernille Pedersen; p. 180 © Judi Rutz

The following names/manufacturers appearing in *Fine Cooking Pies & Crisps* are trademarks:
Café du Monde®, Captain Morgan®, Cointreau®, Community Coffee®, Domino®, Eagle®,
Grand Marnier®, Grandma's®, Guinness®, Heath®, Honey Maid®, Kahlúa®, Knob Creek®,
Lyle's Golden Syrup®, Maker's Mark®, Microplane®, Nabisco®, Nilla®, Pepperidge Farm®,
Pop-Tarts®, Pyrex®, Skor®, Steen's®, Whole Foods Market℠.

Library of Congress Cataloging-in-Publication Data in Progress
ISBN 978-1-60085-826-0

Printed in the United States of America
10 9 8 7 6 5 4 3 2 1

contents

peach and blueberry galette
(recipe on p. 95)

fruit pies, crisps & cobblers

pineapple–macadamia nut tart

MAKES ONE 9-INCH TART;
SERVES 6 TO 8

FOR THE CRUST

- ½ cup macadamia nuts, toasted
- ¼ cup granulated sugar
- 4½ oz. (1 cup) unbleached all-purpose flour
- Kosher salt
- 4 oz. (½ cup) chilled unsalted butter, cut into ½-inch pieces
- 1 large egg, lightly beaten

FOR THE FILLING

- ¾ cup macadamia nuts
- ¼ cup granulated sugar
- 1 large egg, at room temperature
- 2 oz. (4 Tbs.) unsalted butter, at room temperature
- 1½ Tbs. unbleached all-purpose flour
- 1 Tbs. light or dark rum
- ¼ tsp. pure vanilla extract

FOR THE TOPPING

- 1 Tbs. unbleached all-purpose flour
- 1 medium fresh pineapple (about 3½ lb.), peeled, cut lengthwise into quarters, cored, and cut crosswise into ⅛-inch-thick slices
- 3 Tbs. mild honey, such as clover
- 2 Tbs. light or dark rum

This sunny-looking stunner uses buttery, slightly sweet macadamia nuts for both the filling and the crust. If you like, serve it with a dollop of rum-spiked whipped cream and toasted coconut flakes.

MAKE THE CRUST

1. In a food processor, pulse the nuts and sugar until finely chopped, 12 to 15 one-second pulses. Be careful not to overprocess; you want to keep some of the crunchy nut texture. Add the flour and ¼ tsp. salt and pulse to combine. Add the butter and pulse just until the dough resembles coarse sand and starts to gather into clumps, about eight 1-second pulses. Drizzle the egg evenly over the mixture and pulse just until blended in, five or six 1-second pulses. Do not overmix.

2. Turn the dough out onto a piece of plastic wrap and shape it into a disk (it will be very sticky). Wrap it tightly and chill for at least 2 hours or overnight.

3. Using your fingers, press the dough evenly into the bottom (not the sides) of a 9½-inch fluted tart pan with a removable bottom. If the dough sticks to your fingers, dip them in water. Freeze the crust for 20 minutes.

MAKE THE FILLING

1. In a food processor, grind the macadamia nuts until they resemble coarse sand. Add the remaining filling ingredients and process until completely smooth, about 2 minutes.

2. Position a rack in the center of the oven and heat the oven to 375°F.

3. Using a small offset spatula, spread the filling over the bottom of the tart shell, leaving a ¼-inch border, and then sprinkle with the flour. Working from the outside in and leaving a ¼-inch border, arrange the pineapple tightly in overlapping concentric circles over the filling. (Each circle should overlap the previous circle by ½ inch.) Use larger pieces of pineapple for the outer circles and smaller pieces as you work your way toward the center. If necessary, trim pieces to fit. You may not need all of the pineapple, but it's better to use more rather than less, since it will shrink as it bakes.

continued on p. 6

how to assemble a top-notch tart

Press the dough into the bottom of the pan only. It will rise up the sides as it bakes to form an edge. Dip your fingers in water if the dough gets too sticky; it works better than flour.

Spread the filling to ¼ inch from the edge so the sides of the tart can rise properly.

Tightly arrange the pineapple slices so that each circle overlaps the previous circle by ½ inch. This prevents gaps from forming as the pineapple bakes and shrinks slightly. Use larger pieces of pineapple for the outer circles and smaller pieces for the inner ones.

continued from p. 4

Make Ahead

The tart can be made 1 day ahead of serving. Cover with plastic and store at room temperature.

4. Bake the tart, rotating the pan after 20 minutes, until the crust is light golden brown, 30 to 35 minutes. If the edges brown too quickly, cover them with foil.

5. Meanwhile, combine the honey and rum in a small saucepan. Cook over medium-high heat until just slightly reduced, 1 to 2 minutes. Remove from the heat.

6. Brush half of the honey syrup over the pineapple topping, taking care not to move the pineapple slices. Continue to bake the tart until the crust is deep golden brown, 5 to 15 minutes more.

7. Transfer the tart to a rack and brush a bit more syrup on the top (you may not use it all). It's fine if the tart looks liquidy in the center; it will thicken and firm up as it cools. Let cool completely and serve.
—Dabney Gough

how to prep a pineapple

Many stores sell trimmed and cored fresh pineapples. These are fine if you're pressed for time, but you'll get better flavor if you start with a whole pineapple. Trimming it isn't difficult.

Using a chef's knife, slice ½ inch off the top and bottom of the pineapple and rest it on a cut end. Slice the rind off in strips, removing as many of the eyes as possible.

With a paring knife, cut around and remove any remaining eyes.

Quarter the pineapple lengthwise, trim the core from each quarter, and slice according to the recipe instructions.

mixed berry tarts with lemony filling

- **1 recipe Buttery Shortbread Pastry Dough (recipe on p. 8)**
- **½ cup heavy cream**
- **1 cup Lemon Curd (recipe on p. 8)**
- **1 cup each fresh raspberries, blueberries, and black-berries or boysenberries (rinsed, picked over, and dried), placed in separate bowls**

Make Ahead

The lemon curd can be made ahead and stored, covered, for up to a week in the refrigerator. You can combine the lemon curd and whipped cream and hold the filling for about 2 hours in the fridge. The shells can be baked a day ahead (store the cooled shells in an airtight container); fill them shortly before serving. The baked shells also freeze well; thaw before filling.

You can decorate these delicious tarts with berries before serving them, or set out dishes of berries and let guests garnish their own tarts with the berries of their choice.

1. Have ready eight 4¾-inch fluted tart pans with removable bottoms.

2. Working quickly, shape the dough into an 8-inch log and divide it into eight equal pieces. On a lightly floured surface, roll a piece of dough into a 5-inch round. Gently press the dough into a tart pan. Repeat with the remaining dough. Put the tarts on a baking sheet and chill in the refrigerator for 15 minutes. Meanwhile, heat the oven to 400°F.

3. Cut out eight roughly 6-inch-square pieces of foil and spray one side lightly with nonstick cooking spray. Line each tart with a square of foil, oiled side down, being sure to gently fold the foil over the top edge of the tart. Place a handful of pie weights, raw rice, or dried beans into each lined tart. Transfer the tarts (still on the baking sheet) to the oven and bake until the crust turns golden brown and starts to pull away from the sides of the pans, 25 to 30 minutes. (Check the color by carefully lifting up the foil on a few of the tarts.) Let the tarts cool on the baking sheet on a rack for 5 minutes. Carefully remove the lining and weights. Let cool completely on the baking sheet on the rack.

4. In a medium bowl, whip the cream to soft peaks. Add the lemon curd and gently fold together with a rubber spatula until combined. Divide the mixture among the pastry shells and smooth the filling with a spatula or the back of a spoon. The filling should be no higher than the edge of the tart shell. Carefully remove the outer rings and bottoms of the tart shells (use a metal spatula for the bottoms) and arrange the tarts on a large platter. Top each tart with a mixture of raspberries, blueberries, and blackberries and serve immediately.
—*Janie Hibler*

PER SERVING: 560 CALORIES | 8G PROTEIN | 51G CARB | 38G TOTAL FAT | 23G SAT FAT | 10G MONO FAT | 2G POLY FAT | 205MG CHOL | 340MG SODIUM | 3G FIBER

continued on p. 8

continued from p. 7

buttery shortbread pastry dough

**MAKES ENOUGH DOUGH FOR
1 SINGLE PIE CRUST, 8 MINI
TARTS, OR 12 TURNOVERS**

- **9** oz. (2 cups) unbleached all-purpose flour
- **7** oz. (14 Tbs.) chilled unsalted butter, cut into 1-inch pieces
- **1** large egg, lightly beaten
- **2** Tbs. granulated sugar
- **1** Tbs. chilled heavy cream
- **2** tsp. fresh lemon juice
- **1** tsp. table salt

This versatile dough can be used for everything from tarts to turnovers. The dough is quite soft, but all the butter in the recipe makes it forgiving and easy to work with. When baked, the crust is very tender—almost like a shortbread cookie.

1. In a food processor, combine the flour, butter, egg, sugar, cream, lemon juice, and salt and pulse until the dough starts gathering together in big clumps.

2. Turn the dough out onto a countertop and gather it together. Shape the dough as directed in the recipe.

lemon curd

MAKES ABOUT 1¾ CUPS

- **3** large eggs
- **⅔** cup granulated sugar
- **½** cup fresh lemon juice (from about 2 large lemons)
- **3** oz. (6 Tbs.) unsalted butter
- **1** Tbs. finely grated lemon zest

This recipe makes more than you need for the tarts, but once you taste this lemon curd, the leftovers will disappear before you know it.

In a medium bowl, whisk the eggs until well blended. Combine the sugar, lemon juice, butter, and lemon zest in a small (1- to 2-quart) saucepan. Gently heat over medium-low heat until the butter has melted. Don't let the mixture come to a boil. Remove the pan from the heat and whisk the lemon mixture into the beaten eggs. Pour the mixture back into the saucepan and cook gently over medium-low heat, stirring constantly with the whisk, until the mixture thickens and reaches at least 160°F, about 5 minutes. Again, don't let the mixture boil. Let the lemon curd cool briefly before transferring it to a heat-proof container. Press a piece of plastic wrap onto the surface of the curd and poke a few holes in it with the tip of a knife—this will keep a skin from forming on the curd. Refrigerate until completely chilled. The curd will continue to thicken as it cools. It will keep, covered, in the refrigerator for up to 1 week.

raspberry-peach cobbler with cornmeal topping

SERVES 8 TO 10

FOR THE COBBLER DOUGH

- 7½ oz. (1⅔ cups) unbleached all-purpose flour
- ⅓ cup granulated sugar or packed light brown sugar
- 1 Tbs. baking powder
- ¼ tsp. table salt
- 3 oz. (6 Tbs.) chilled unsalted butter, cut into 10 pieces
- ¼ cup finely ground cornmeal
- ¾ cup chilled sour cream

TO FINISH THE COBBLER

- 4 cups sliced ripe peaches (cut into 1-inch-thick wedges)
- 4 cups fresh raspberries
- ½ to ¾ cup granulated sugar, plus 1½ Tbs. for sprinkling on top
- 2 Tbs. unbleached all-purpose flour
- ½ tsp. finely grated lemon zest
- Pinch of table salt

Make Ahead

The cobbler will stay warm at room temperature for 1 to 1½ hours.

Cornmeal adds a bit of crunch to the biscuit topping in this cobbler that's bursting with juicy peaches and ripe raspberries.

MAKE THE DOUGH

1. Position a rack in the center of the oven and heat the oven to 350°F.

2. In a food processor, combine the flour, sugar, baking powder, and salt. Pulse briefly to blend the ingredients, about 10 seconds. Add the butter pieces and pulse until they are the size of small peas, five to seven one-second pulses.

3. Dump the mixture into a large mixing bowl. Add the cornmeal and stir until evenly dispersed. Add the sour cream. Using a rubber spatula, gently smear the ingredients together until the flour is evenly moistened and the dough begins to form large, soft, moist clumps. Bring the dough together into an 8-inch log. Divide the dough into ten roughly equal round pieces. Refrigerate the pieces in the bowl while preparing the fruit.

ASSEMBLE AND BAKE THE COBBLER

1. Put the peaches and raspberries in a large bowl. Gently toss with the sugar (use ½ cup for very ripe, sweet fruit and ¾ cup for fruit that's not perfectly ripe and sweet), flour, lemon zest, and salt, making sure to mix everything evenly.

2. Pile the fruit into a 9x13-inch glass baking dish, scraping in any remaining juices or sugar from the bowl, and spread evenly. Remove the pieces of dough from the refrigerator and arrange them randomly on top of the filling, leaving spaces between the pieces. Don't be tempted to flatten the dough—the large pieces are important for proper and even baking of the filling and topping. Sprinkle the remaining 1½ Tbs. of granulated sugar evenly over the cobbler.

3. Bake until the filling is bubbling and the topping is browned, 50 to 60 minutes. Let sit for about 20 minutes to allow the juices to settle. You can serve this cobbler hot or warm, with lightly sweetened whipped cream or vanilla ice cream, if you like.

—Abigail Johnson Dodge

PER SERVING: 310 CALORIES | 4G PROTEIN | 50G CARB | 10G TOTAL FAT | 7G SAT FAT | 2G MONO FAT | 0.5G POLY FAT | 30MG CHOL | 190MG SODIUM | 5G FIBER

cranberry-pear tart in a walnut shortbread crust

MAKES ONE 9-INCH TART;
SERVES 8 TO 12

FOR THE WALNUT SHORTBREAD CRUST

- **1 large egg yolk**
- **1 Tbs. half-and-half**
- **½ tsp. pure vanilla extract**
- **6¾ oz. (1½ cups) unbleached all-purpose flour**
- **3 Tbs. granulated sugar**
- **½ tsp. table salt**
- **4 oz. (½ cup) chilled unsalted butter, cut into ½-inch dice**
- **⅓ cup walnuts, toasted and finely chopped**

FOR THE CRANBERRY-PEAR FILLING

- **3 large ripe pears, such as Anjou or Bartlett**
- **2 cups fresh cranberries, picked through, rinsed, and dried**
- **1 Tbs. brandy**
- **⅔ cup granulated sugar**
- **2 tsp. unbleached all-purpose flour**
- **½ tsp. ground cardamom**
- **½ tsp. ground ginger**
- **¼ tsp. ground cinnamon**
- **⅛ tsp. ground allspice**
- **⅛ tsp. table salt**

Cranberries steal the show in this festive tart. Their delightful tartness is a natural complement to the sweetness of fruits such as pears and apples. When fresh cranberries show up on supermarket shelves in early fall, stock up on a few bags. Fresh cranberries will last upwards of a month in the fridge and up to a year in the freezer.

MAKE THE CRUST

1. Position a rack near the center of the oven and heat the oven to 400°F.

2. In a small bowl, mix the egg yolk, half-and-half, and vanilla. Put the flour, sugar, and salt in a food processor; pulse until combined. Add the butter and pulse until the butter pieces are no longer visible. With the processor running, add the yolk mixture in a steady stream and then pulse until the moisture is fairly evenly dispersed, 10 to 20 seconds. Transfer the mixture to a bowl. Using your hands, mix in the chopped walnuts to distribute them evenly. The dough will be a mealy, crumbly mass.

3. Pour the crumb mixture into a 9½-inch round fluted tart pan with a removable bottom. Starting with the sides of the pan, firmly press the crumbs against the pan to create a crust about ¼ inch thick. Press the remaining crumbs evenly against the bottom of the pan. Prick the bottom of the crust all over with a fork and freeze for 10 minutes. Bake until the sides just begin to darken and the bottom is set, about 15 minutes. Transfer to a cooling rack. Reduce the oven temperature to 350°F.

MAKE THE FILLING

1. Peel the pears, quarter them lengthwise, core, and cut crosswise into ¼-inch-thick slices.

2. In a food processor, coarsely chop the cranberries. In a medium bowl, mix the pears, cranberries, and brandy. In a small bowl, mix the sugar, flour, cardamom, ginger, cinnamon, allspice, and salt; add to the cranberry-pear mixture, tossing to combine. Spoon the filling into the parbaked crust, leveling the filling and packing it down slightly with the back of a spoon.

FOR THE BUTTERY BROWN SUGAR STREUSEL

- 1¾ oz. (⅓ cup plus 1 Tbs.) unbleached all-purpose flour
- ¼ cup packed light brown sugar
- ⅛ tsp. table salt
- 1 oz. (2 Tbs.) unsalted butter, melted
- ¼ tsp. pure vanilla extract

Make Ahead

The tart will keep, covered and at room temperature, for 2 to 3 days.

MAKE THE STREUSEL AND BAKE

1. In a small bowl, mix the flour, brown sugar, and salt. Add the melted butter and vanilla. Combine with your fingers until the mixture begins to clump together in small pieces when pressed. Sprinkle the streusel over the filling, breaking it into smaller pieces if necessary.

2. Bake until the fruit is tender when pierced with a fork and the streusel and the edges of the crust are golden brown, about 50 minutes. If the tart begins to get overly brown at the edges, cover with foil. Let the tart cool on a rack until it's just barely warm before serving.
—*Nicole Rees*

PER SERVING: 300 CALORIES | 3G PROTEIN | 44G CARB | 12G TOTAL FAT | 7G SAT FAT | 3G MONO FAT | 2G POLY FAT | 45MG CHOL | 150MG SODIUM | 3G FIBER

rustic red raspberry turnovers

MAKES 12 PETITE TURNOVERS

- 1 recipe Buttery Shortbread Pastry Dough (recipe on p. 8)
- 4 tsp. granulated sugar; more as needed
- 1 Tbs. unbleached all-purpose flour
- ½ tsp. ground cinnamon
- ¼ tsp. ground nutmeg
- 8 to 10 oz. (2 cups) fresh red raspberries, rinsed, picked over, and air-dried or patted dry with paper towels
- 1 to 2 Tbs. whole milk

If you're lucky enough to have a "pick-your-own" farm close by, opt for fresh-picked raspberries, but if supermarket raspberries are all you can find, you can use them and still get fabulous results.

1. Divide the pastry in half. Pat each half into roughly a square shape about 1 inch thick, wrap each in plastic, and chill for 20 minutes.

2. Line a rimmed baking sheet with parchment. On a lightly floured surface, using a floured rolling pin, roll out one square of the pastry into a 9x14-inch rectangle. If the dough is too sticky, dust it too with a little flour. Cut the dough into six rounds, each about 4 inches in diameter. Remove the excess dough from around the rounds and discard or save for another use. Run a metal spatula under each round to separate it from the counter.

3. In a large bowl, stir together the sugar, flour, cinnamon, and nutmeg. Add the raspberries and gently toss to coat. Taste and add more sugar if the fruit seems tart.

4. Put a heaping tablespoon of raspberries (3 to 6 berries, depending on their size) in a single layer on one half of each dough round. Press gently to flatten the berries a bit. Dampen the pastry edges with a little water and carefully fold the other side of the dough over the berries to make a half-moon. Press the edges of the dough together with your fingers or the tines of a fork. If any small cracks formed in the dough, pinch them together as best you can with damp fingers. Use a spatula to transfer the turnovers to the baking sheet.

5. Repeat this process with the remaining half of the pastry dough and the rest of the berries. When all the turnovers are assembled, refrigerate for at least 15 minutes and up to 4 hours. Meanwhile, position a rack in the middle of the oven and heat the oven to 400°F.

6. When ready to bake, brush the tops of the turnovers (but not the edges or they will get too brown) with the milk and sprinkle with sugar. Bake until golden brown, 20 to 25 minutes. Transfer to a rack to cool. Serve warm or at room temperature. *—Janie Hibler*

PER SERVING: 230 CALORIES | 3G PROTEIN | 22G CARB | 14G TOTAL FAT | 9G SAT FAT | 4G MONO FAT | 0.5G POLY FAT | 55MG CHOL | 200MG SODIUM | 2G FIBER

forming the turnovers

Put 3 to 6 berries in a single layer on one half of each dough round. Fold over the other side of the dough to make a half moon, then press the edges of the dough together.

classic apple pie

MAKES ONE 9-INCH DOUBLE-
CRUST PIE; SERVES 8 TO 10

- **1½** **to 1¾ lb. Cortland apples
(about 4 medium)**
- **1** **lb. Granny Smith apples
(about 2½ medium)**
- **2** **tsp. fresh lemon juice**
- **⅔** **cup packed light brown sugar**
- **¼** **cup plus 1 Tbs. granulated
sugar**
- **3** **Tbs. cornstarch**
- **½** **tsp. ground cinnamon; more
to taste**
- **¼** **tsp. kosher salt**
- **⅛** **tsp. ground nutmeg**
- **1** **large egg white**
- **2** **tsp. unsalted butter, at room
temperature, plus 1 Tbs.
chilled unsalted butter cut
into small (¼-inch) cubes**
- **4** **to 6 Tbs. unbleached all-
purpose flour**
- **1** **recipe Flaky Pie Pastry
(recipe on p. 18)**

For best results, bake this pie at least a few hours before you plan to cut into it; otherwise, the filling may be soupy. With time, the fruit reabsorbs the juices, and the pie will cut like a charm.

Position two oven racks in the lower third of the oven and heat the oven to 400°F.

MAKE THE FILLING

1. Peel the apples, cut each in half from top to bottom, remove the cores with a melon baller, and trim the ends with a paring knife. Lay the apples, cut side down, on a cutting board. Cut the Cortland apples crosswise into ¾-inch pieces and then halve each piece diagonally. Cut the Granny Smith apples crosswise into ¼-inch slices, leaving them whole. Put the apples in a large bowl and toss with the lemon juice.

2. Combine the brown sugar, ¼ cup of the granulated sugar, corn-starch, cinnamon, kosher salt, and nutmeg in a small bowl. (Don't add this to the fruit yet.)

3. In a small dish, lightly beat the egg white with 1 tsp. water. Set aside.

ASSEMBLE THE PIE

1. Butter a 9-inch ovenproof glass (Pyrex®) pie plate, including the rim, with the 2 tsp. of softened butter.

2. Rub 2 to 3 Tbs. of flour into the surface of a pastry cloth, forming a circle about 15 inches across, and also into a rolling pin stocking. If you don't have a pastry cloth, rub the flour into a large, smooth-weave, cotton kitchen towel and use a floured rolling pin. Roll one of the disks of dough into a circle that's about 15 inches across and ⅛ inch thick. Lay the rolling pin across the upper third of the dough circle; lift the pastry cloth to gently drape the dough over the pin and then roll the pin toward you, wrapping the remaining dough loosely around it. Hold the rolling pin over the near edge of the pie plate. Allowing for about a 1-inch overhang, unroll the dough away from you, easing it into the contours of the pan. If the dough isn't centered in the pan, gently adjust it and then lightly press it into the pan. Take care not to stretch the dough. If it tears, simply press it back together—the dough is quite forgiving.

3. Brush the bottom and sides of the dough with a light coating of the egg white wash (you won't need all of it). Leaving a ¼-inch overhang, cut around the edge of the dough with kitchen shears.

4. Combine the sugar mixture with the apples and toss to coat well. Mound the apples in the pie plate, rearranging the fruit as needed to make the pile compact. Dot the apples with the 1 Tbs. chilled butter cubes.

Cortland and Granny Smith apples have different textures. To help them cook evenly and retain their shape, cut the Cortlands into ¾-inch-thick chunks and the Granny Smiths into ¼-inch-thick slices.

5. Rub another 2 to 3 Tbs. flour into the surface of the pastry cloth and stocking. Roll the remaining dough into a circle that's ⅛ inch thick and about 15 inches across. Use the rolling pin to move the dough. As you unroll the dough, center it on top of the apples. Place your hands on either side of the top crust of the pie and ease the dough toward the center, giving the dough plenty of slack. Leaving a ¾-inch overhang, trim the top layer of dough around the rim of the pie plate. Fold the top layer of dough under the bottom layer, tucking the two layers of dough together. Press a lightly floured fork around the edge of the dough to seal it, or flute the edge of the dough with lightly floured fingers.

6. Lightly brush the top with cold water and sprinkle the surface with the remaining 1 Tbs. sugar. Make steam vents in the dough by poking the tip of a paring knife through it in a few places; it's important to vent well so that the steam from the cooking apples won't build up and crack the top of the crust.

BAKE THE PIE

1. Cover the rim of the pie with aluminum foil bands. This will prevent the edge of the crust from overbrowning.

2. Place a rimmed baking sheet or an aluminum foil drip pan on the oven rack below the pie to catch any juices that overflow during baking. Set the pie on the rack above.

3. Bake until the top and bottom crusts are golden brown and the juices are bubbling, 60 to 75 minutes; to thicken, the juices must boil, so look for the bubbles through the steam vents or through cracks near the edges of the pie and listen for the sound of bubbling juices. During the last 5 minutes of baking, remove the foil bands from the edges of the pie. Cool the pie for at least 3 hours and up to overnight before serving.

4. Store the pie at room temperature for up to 1 day. For longer storage, cover with aluminum foil and refrigerate for up to 5 days; reheat before serving in a 325°F oven until warmed through, about 20 minutes.
—Carole Walter

PER SERVING: 460 CALORIES | 4G PROTEIN | 60G CARB | 23G TOTAL FAT | 10G SAT FAT | 7G MONO FAT | 3.5G POLY FAT | 30MG CHOL | 230MG SODIUM | 2G FIBER

continued on p. 18

continued from p. 17

flaky pie pastry

**MAKES ENOUGH DOUGH FOR
ONE 9-INCH DOUBLE-CRUST
PIE**

10½ oz. (2 ⅓ cups) unbleached
       all-purpose flour

   1 Tbs. granulated sugar

   ¾ tsp. table salt

   ½ tsp. baking powder

   4 oz. (½ cup) chilled unsalted
       butter, cut into ½-inch cubes

   4 oz (½ cup) chilled vegetable
       shortening, cut into ½-inch
       pieces

   5 to 6 Tbs. ice water; more as
       needed

1. Put the flour, sugar, salt, and baking powder in a food processor fitted with a steel blade. Chill for 20 to 30 minutes.

2. Pulse the dry ingredients together for a few seconds to blend. With the processor off, add half of the butter and half of the shortening. Pulse 5 times and then process for 5 seconds. Add the remaining butter and shortening and pulse again 5 times, then process for 5 seconds. You should have a mixture of both large and small crumbs. Empty the mixture into a large mixing bowl.

3. Drizzle 1 Tbs. of the ice water around the edge of the bowl, letting it trickle into the crumbs. Flick the moistened crumbs toward the center with a table fork, rotating the bowl as you work. Repeat with the remaining 4 Tbs. ice water, 1 Tbs. at a time. As you add the water, the crumbs should begin to form larger clusters. Once you've added 5 Tbs. water total, take a handful of crumbs and squeeze them gently; they should hold together. If they easily break apart, the mixture needs more water: add the remaining Tbs., 1 tsp. at a time, checking the consistency after each addition. If the crumbs still fail to hold together, you can add additional water, but do so sparingly.

4 steps to flaky dough

You want a mixture of both large and small crumbs. The large pieces give you a flaky pastry; the small pieces make it tender.

Add the water slowly and sparingly, drizzling it around the side of the bowl. Too much water will toughen the crust.

Use a fork to "fluff" the crumbs with the liquid. Don't stir or mash the crumbs because this compacts the mixture and results in a tough dough.

Test whether you've added enough water by gently squeezing a handful of crumbs; if they don't hold together, the mixture needs more water.

4. Gather a handful of the crumbly dough and press it against the side of the bowl to form a small mass, flouring your hand as needed to prevent excessive sticking. Increase the size of this mass by pressing it into more of the crumbly mixture until you've used up about half of the total mixture in the bowl. Make a second mass of dough with the remaining crumbs. If some of the crumbs on the bottom of the bowl need more moistening, add a few drops of water.

5. Form the two masses of dough into balls, dust them with flour, and flatten them into 4- to 5-inch disks. Pat the disks to release any excess flour. Score the tops lightly with the side of your hand to create a tic-tac-toe pattern. With cupped hands, rotate each disk on the work surface to smooth the edges of the disks. Wrap each in plastic wrap. Chill at least 30 minutes before using.

Tips for Rolling Dough

• **Cool pie dough rolls best.** Dough that's too cold will crack when it's rolled; if too warm, it will stick to the rolling surface. Test your dough's firmness by pressing the disk with your fingers; they should leave a slight imprint.

• **Roll from the center out.** Set the pin in the middle of the dough and roll away from you; return to the center and roll toward you. Rolling back and forth repeatedly will toughen the dough. For the same reason, don't flip the dough over.

• **Give the dough a quarter turn frequently.** This helps ensure even thickness.

• **Prevent sticking by reflouring.** Lightly reflour the rolling surface and pin, if necessary, to prevent sticking. Don't sprinkle flour on the dough, however, or you risk toughening it.

• **Ease up on the rolling pin.** As you approach the edge of the dough, ease up on the rolling pin; otherwise, the edges will get too thin.

freeform pear tarts
with almond and cinnamon

MAKES 4 TARTS

- ¼ cup granulated sugar

- ¼ tsp. ground cinnamon

- 1 sheet frozen puff pastry (9¾-inch square), thawed overnight in the refrigerator

  Flour, for dusting

- 2 Tbs. almond paste (from a can or tube)

- 4 tsp. sour cream

- 2 small firm-ripe pears (preferably Bartlett), peeled, cored, and cut into 12 wedges each

The tarts are delicious served warm and topped with vanilla ice cream.

1. Position a rack in the center of the oven and heat the oven to 425°F.

2. Line a baking sheet with parchment. Combine the sugar and cinnamon in a small bowl. Unroll or unfold the puff pastry on a lightly floured surface. Pinch any creases together and then smooth them out with your fingertips. Cut the pastry sheet into four equal squares and transfer them to the lined baking sheet.

3. Roll 1½ tsp. of almond paste into a small ball, flatten it slightly with the palm of your hand, and put it in the center of one puff pastry square. Drop 1 tsp. of sour cream on top. Sprinkle about 1½ tsp. of the cinnamon sugar over the sour cream. Arrange 4 pear wedges in the center of the puff pastry, two leaning away from the center one way and two leaning the other way. Sprinkle with another 1½ tsp. of the cinnamon sugar. Repeat with the remaining three puff pastry squares and filling ingredients—you won't need all of the sliced pears.

4. Fold the corners of the puff pastry over the pears until the tips are just touching but not overlapping and press the dough against the pears. (The tarts won't look pretty now, but they'll be beautiful once they bake and puff up.) Bake until puffed and golden brown on the edges, 22 to 27 minutes. Let cool. Any juices that leak onto the baking sheet will harden to a candy-like consistency, so break off and discard these bits before serving. *—Gale Gand*

PER SERVING: 380 CALORIES | 5G PROTEIN | 47G CARB | 19G TOTAL FAT | 5G SAT FAT | 10G MONO FAT | 2G POLY FAT | 5MG CHOL | 300MG SODIUM | 4G FIBER

forming the tarts

Arrange four pear slices in the center of a puff pastry square, sprinkle with cinnamon sugar, and then bring the pastry edges together so they touch but don't overlap. This allows the puff pastry tips to "blossom" while baking.

What Is Almond Paste?

Made with finely ground blanched almonds and sugar, almond paste is commonly used in cake batters and pastry fillings. It's also the base ingredient in marzipan (which is made by adding hot sugar syrup and light corn syrup to almond paste). In this recipe, almond paste provides a subtle, perfumy almond flavor that marries perfectly with the sweetness of the pears. You'll find cans or tubes of almond paste in most grocery stores.

rhubarb–brown sugar crumble

SERVES 6 TO 8

1 Tbs. unsalted butter, at room temperature, for the baking dish

FOR THE TOPPING

4½ oz. (1 cup) unbleached all-purpose flour

1 cup lightly packed light brown sugar

½ cup old-fashioned oats

½ tsp. ground cinnamon

¼ tsp. kosher salt

4 oz. (½ cup) chilled unsalted butter, cut into small pieces

FOR THE FILLING

7 cups ⅓-inch-thick sliced rhubarb (about 2 lb.)

1 cup lightly packed light brown sugar

¼ cup cornstarch

1 Tbs. fresh lemon juice

2 tsp. finely grated lemon zest (from 1 medium lemon, using a rasp-style grater)

¼ tsp. kosher salt

A generous amount of oatmeal streusel tops this crumble, providing a crunchy contrast to the tart, juicy filling.

Position a rack in the center of the oven and heat the oven to 350°F. Grease an 8x8-inch Pyrex baking dish with the softened butter.

MAKE THE TOPPING

In a food processor, combine the flour, brown sugar, oats, cinnamon, and salt and pulse several times to combine. Add the chilled butter and pulse until the mixture has the texture of coarse meal and clumps together when squeezed lightly, about 1 minute.

MAKE THE FILLING

1. Combine the rhubarb, brown sugar, cornstarch, lemon juice, lemon zest, and salt in a large bowl and stir with a spatula until evenly mixed. Transfer the rhubarb mixture to the baking pan, and sprinkle the topping evenly over the fruit; the pan will be very full, but the crumble will settle as it bakes.

2. Bake until the topping is lightly browned, the rhubarb is tender (probe in the center with a skewer to check), and the juices are bubbling thickly around the edges, 45 to 60 minutes. Transfer to a rack to cool to warm or room temperature and to allow the juices to thicken, at least 1 hour. —*Karen Barker*

PER SERVING: 430 CALORIES | 3G PROTEIN | 77G CARB | 14G TOTAL FAT | 8G SAT FAT | 3.5G MONO FAT | 0.5G POLY FAT | 35MG CHOL | 100MG SODIUM | 3G FIBER

strawberry-rhubarb pie

SERVES 8

FOR THE CRUST

- **12** oz. **(2 ⅔ cups)** unbleached all-purpose flour; more for rolling
- **2½** tsp. granulated sugar
- **¾** tsp. kosher salt
- **4** oz. **(½ cup)** chilled unsalted butter, cut into small pieces
- **4** oz. **(½ cup plus 1 Tbs.)** chilled vegetable shortening, cut into small pieces

FOR THE FILLING

- **4** cups ½-inch-thick sliced rhubarb (about 1¼ lb.)
- **1** lb. strawberries, hulled and sliced ½ inch thick (about 2½ cups)
- **1½** cups plus 2 Tbs. granulated sugar
- **¼** cup plus 1½ Tbs. quick-cooking tapioca
- **2** Tbs. fresh orange juice
- **1** tsp. finely grated orange zest
- **½** tsp. ground cinnamon
- **¼** tsp. ground cloves
- **¼** tsp. ground allspice
- **¼** tsp. kosher salt
- **1** oz. **(2 Tbs.)** chilled butter, cut into small pieces

FOR THE GLAZE

- **1** large egg yolk

Don't worry if the crust cracks slightly during baking; it only adds to the homemade look of the pie.

MAKE THE CRUST

1. In a food processor, add the flour, sugar, and salt, and pulse to combine. Add the butter and shortening and pulse until the mixture resembles coarse meal, about 1 minute. Transfer the mixture to a large bowl.

2. Fill a measuring cup with ½ cup very cold water. While tossing and stirring the flour mixture with a fork, add the water 1 Tbs. at a time until the dough just begins to come together in small clumps and holds together when you pinch a little between your fingers (you may need only ¼ cup of water).

3. Transfer the dough to a clean work surface and gather it together with your hands. Lightly knead the dough once or twice, divide it in half, and shape the halves into disks. Wrap the disks separately in plastic and refrigerate for at least 1 hour or up to 2 days.

MAKE THE FILLING

Position a rack in the center of the oven and heat the oven to 375°F. In a large mixing bowl, combine the rhubarb, strawberries, sugar, all the tapioca, orange juice, zest, cinnamon, cloves, allspice, and salt. Toss gently to mix well, and then let sit for at least 10 minutes and up to 30 minutes (while you roll out the bottom crust).

ASSEMBLE THE PIE

1. If the dough was refrigerated for several hours or overnight, let it sit at room temperature until pliable, about 20 minutes. On a lightly floured surface, roll out one of the dough disks into a ⅛-inch-thick circle, 12 to 13 inches in diameter, and transfer it to a 9-inch Pyrex pie plate. Pour the filling into the pie shell and dot the top with the chilled butter. In a small bowl, beat the egg yolk with 1 tsp. water. Brush the edges of the pie shell with some of the egg glaze.

continued on p. 24

continued from p. 23

2. Roll out the second dough disk the same way and set it over the fruit filling to form a top crust. Press the edges of the dough together to seal the crust, trim the overhang to ½ inch, and fold it under. Flute or crimp the dough all around. Brush the top crust with the remaining egg glaze (you won't need all of it). Cut four 1- to 1½-inch-long steam vents in the top crust.

3. Set the pie on a foil-lined rimmed baking sheet and bake until the pastry is golden brown and the fruit juices bubble thickly out of the pie, 70 to 80 minutes. Transfer to a rack and let cool completely before serving, about 4 hours. —*Karen Barker*

PER SERVING: 630 CALORIES I 6G PROTEIN I 87G CARB I 29G TOTAL FAT I 13G SAT FAT I 9G MONO FAT I 4.5G POLY FAT I 50MG CHOL I 150MG SODIUM I 4G FIBER

More about Rhubarb

Rosy red, sweet-tart rhubarb is a harbinger of spring, the first fruit to come into season. Though it's usually treated as a fruit and used mainly in desserts, rhubarb is technically a vegetable. The edible parts are the fleshy, celery-like stalks. In fact, the leaves are poisonous, which is why you'll never see them attached at the market.

When used in desserts, rhubarb needs a good amount of sugar to offset its tartness. The simplest way to cook rhubarb is to simmer it in a little liquid with sugar for a compote or a sauce. Rhubarb releases a lot of liquid as it cooks, so if you plan to use it in a pie or crumble, you'll need to add a thickener, such as tapioca or cornstarch.

Buying
Look for firm, crisp, unblemished stalks with a bright, intense red color. Choose thinner stalks, as larger ones can be overly stringy and tough.

Prepping
Trim off the ends and any bits of leaves still attached. Peel the fibrous exterior only if it's very tough. Cut rhubarb as you would celery, into slices or small dice depending on the recipe.

Storing
Wrap the stalks tightly in plastic and refrigerate them; they should stay crisp for up to 5 days. You can also freeze sliced or diced rhubarb in plastic bags for up to 6 months. Frozen rhubarb tends to release more liquid and doesn't hold its shape as well as fresh rhubarb, so use it where texture is not essential, such as in muffins.

peach, plum & apricot cobbler

SERVES 8

1 Tbs. unsalted butter, at room temperature, for the baking dish

FOR THE FILLING

4 lb. assorted ripe plums, peaches, apricots, and nectarines, rinsed and pitted (prick the skins of peaches and nectarines first)

½ cup packed light brown sugar

3 Tbs. unbleached all-purpose flour

½ tsp. grated orange zest

FOR THE TOPPING

4½ oz. (1 cup) unbleached all-purpose flour

½ cup ground, toasted almonds

½ cup granulated sugar

2½ tsp. baking powder

¼ tsp. salt

1 large egg

½ cup buttermilk

3 oz. (6 Tbs.) unsalted butter, melted and cooled

½ tsp. pure vanilla extract

2 Tbs. toasted sliced almonds

This cobbler is a terrific way to combine all the juicy summer stone fruits that are in season together. You can vary the exact mix based on what's available at your market.

Heat the oven to 375°F. Lightly butter a 9x13-inch baking dish.

MAKE THE FILLING

Cut the peaches and nectarines into ½-inch wedges. Cut the plums into ¾-inch wedges and apricots into quarters. In a medium bowl, toss the fruit with the brown sugar, flour, and orange zest until well blended. Pile the fruit into the prepared baking dish and spread evenly.

MAKE THE TOPPING

In a medium bowl, whisk together the flour, ground almonds, sugar, baking powder, and salt. Beat the egg into the buttermilk and add this to the flour mixture, along with the butter and vanilla extract. Gently stir just until the dry ingredients are moistened. Drop by spoonfuls onto the fruit filling, leaving about a 1-inch border of fruit. Sprinkle the toasted almond slices over the topping. Bake until the fruit is bubbling and the topping is browned (a pick will come out clean), 50 to 55 minutes. Serve warm or at room temperature. —*Abigail Johnson Dodge*

PER SERVING: 430 CALORIES | 7G PROTEIN | 70G CARB | 15G TOTAL FAT | 6G SAT FAT | 6G MONO FAT | 1G POLY FAT | 50MG CHOL | 260MG SODIUM | 6G FIBER

strawberry-blueberry cobbler with pecans and cinnamon

SERVES 8 TO 10

FOR THE DOUGH

- **7½ oz. (1⅔ cups) unbleached all-purpose flour**
- **⅓ cup granulated sugar or packed light brown sugar**
- **1 Tbs. baking powder**
- **¼ tsp. table salt**
- **3 oz. (6 Tbs.) chilled unsalted butter, cut into 10 pieces**
- **½ cup chopped toasted pecans**
- **¾ tsp. ground cinnamon**
- **¾ cup chilled sour cream**

FOR THE FILLING

- **4 cups hulled ripe strawberries, well rinsed and drained (small berries left whole, medium ones halved, and large ones quartered)**
- **4 cups ripe blueberries, well rinsed, picked over, and drained**
- **½ to ¾ cup granulated sugar**
- **2 Tbs. unbleached all-purpose flour**
- **Pinch of table salt**
- **2 tsp. minced fresh ginger**
- **1 tsp. pure vanilla extract**
- **1½ Tbs. granulated, turbinado, or demerara sugar (optional)**

Because not all berries are perfectly ripe and sweet, the fruit filling recipe calls for a range of granulated sugar. Start by tossing your berries with ½ cup of sugar, then add more to taste.

MAKE THE DOUGH

1. Position a rack in the center of the oven and heat the oven to 350°F.

2. In a food processor, combine the flour, sugar, baking powder, and salt. Pulse briefly to blend the ingredients. Add the butter pieces and pulse until they are the size of small peas, five to seven 1-second pulses.

3. Dump the mixture into a large mixing bowl. Add the pecans and cinnamon and stir until evenly dispersed. Add the sour cream. Using a rubber spatula, gently smear the ingredients together until the flour is evenly moistened and the dough begins to form large, soft, moist clumps. Bring the dough together into an 8-inch-long log. Divide the log into 10 roughly equal round pieces. Refrigerate the pieces in the bowl while preparing the fruit.

MAKE THE FILLING

Put the berries into a large bowl. Toss with the granulated sugar, flour, and salt. Add the ginger and vanilla and toss gently.

ASSEMBLE AND BAKE THE COBBLER

1. Pile the fruit into a 9x13-inch Pyrex (or similar) baking dish, scraping in any remaining juices or sugar from the bowl, and spread evenly. Remove the pieces of the dough from the refrigerator and arrange them randomly on top of the filling, leaving spaces between the pieces. Don't be tempted to flatten the dough—the large pieces are important for proper and even baking of the filling and topping. If desired, sprinkle a little granulated, turbinado, or demerara sugar evenly over the cobbler.

2. Bake until the filling is bubbling and the topping is browned, 50 to 60 minutes. Let sit for about 20 minutes to allow the juices to settle. You can serve this cobbler hot or warm (it will stay warm at room temperature for 1 to 1½ hours). Serve with lightly sweetened whipped cream or vanilla ice cream, if you like. —*Abigail Johnson Dodge*

PER SERVING: 340 CALORIES | 5G PROTEIN | 48G CARB | 15G TOTAL FAT | 7G SAT FAT | 4.5G MONO FAT | 2G POLY FAT | 30MG CHOL | 190MG SODIUM | 5G FIBER

apple crisp
with pecans and orange

SERVES 8

About 1 tsp. butter, at
room temperature, for
the baking dish

FOR THE TOPPING

4½ oz. (1 cup) unbleached all-
    purpose flour

⅓ cup old-fashioned rolled oats

¼ cup plus 2 Tbs. lightly packed
   light brown sugar

¼ cup plus 2 Tbs. granulated
   sugar

½ tsp. ground cinnamon

¼ tsp. kosher salt

4 oz. (½ cup) chilled unsalted
   butter, cut into 8 pieces

1 cup lightly toasted, coarsely
   chopped pecans

FOR THE FILLING

3 lb. Granny Smith apples
   (6 large or 8 medium),
   peeled, cored, and sliced
   ¼ inch thick

½ cup granulated sugar

2 Tbs. fresh orange juice (from
   1 orange)

1 Tbs. finely grated orange zest
   (from 1 orange)

1½ tsp. unbleached all-purpose
    flour

¾ tsp. ground cinnamon

⅛ tsp. kosher salt

*Be sure to use rolled oats (also
known as old-fashioned oats)
for this recipe. Instant oats
can't be substituted—when
precooked, they get soft, so
they will turn your baked dish
into lumpy mush.*

Position a rack in the center of
the oven and heat the oven to 350°F. Lightly butter a 9x9x2-inch pan
or other 10-cup ovenproof baking dish.

MAKE THE TOPPING

In a food processor, pulse the flour and the oats until the oats are
finely ground. Add the brown sugar, granulated sugar, cinnamon, and
salt and pulse until just combined. Add the butter and pulse in short
bursts until the mixture just starts to form crumbs and has a streusel-
like consistency. When squeezed together with light pressure, the
mixture should just clump. Add the pecans and pulse just to blend;
you don't want to chop the nuts further.

ASSEMBLE AND BAKE THE CRISP

1. In a large bowl, combine all of the filling ingredients and gently toss
until well combined. Transfer the mixture to the prepared baking dish.
Press down to compact slightly into an even layer. Sprinkle the topping
in a thick, even layer all over the filling.

2. Bake until the topping is golden brown, the juices are bubbling around
the edges, and the apples are soft when pierced with the tip of a knife,
55 to 60 minutes. Transfer to a rack to cool for 20 to 30 minutes before
serving. The crisp can be served warm or at room temperature, but it's
best served the day it's made. —*Karen Barker*

PER SERVING: 480 CALORIES | 4G PROTEIN | 70G CARB | 23G TOTAL FAT | 9G SAT FAT |
9G MONO FAT | 3.5G POLY FAT | 30MG CHOL | 60MG SODIUM | 6G FIBER

Make Ahead

You can make and
refrigerate the
topping up to 2 days
ahead, or freeze for
up to 2 months. Bring
to room temperature
before using.

gingerbread-pear cobbler

SERVES 12 TO 16

1 Tbs. unsalted butter, at room temperature, for the pan

FOR THE PEAR LAYER

5¼ lb. ripe pears (about 12 medium), peeled, cored, and cut into ⅛- to ¼-inch-thick slices (Bosc or Anjou pears work well)

¾ cup granulated sugar

2 Tbs. fresh lemon juice (from 1 lemon)

1½ tsp. minced lemon zest (from 1 lemon)

2 Tbs. minced crystallized ginger

1½ Tbs. unbleached all-purpose flour

1 oz. (2 Tbs.) unsalted butter, at room temperature, cut into small pieces

FOR THE GINGERBREAD BISCUIT LAYER

9 oz. (2 cups) unbleached all-purpose flour

5½ Tbs. granulated sugar

1 Tbs. ground ginger

2½ tsp. baking powder

2 tsp. ground cinnamon

¾ tsp. ground cloves

½ tsp. table salt

¼ tsp. baking soda

3 oz. (6 Tbs.) vegetable shortening

1¼ oz. (2½ Tbs.) unsalted butter, at room temperature

2 large eggs

6 Tbs. whole milk

⅓ cup molasses

¾ tsp. pure vanilla extract

Though best eaten warm from the oven—and even better with whipped cream or ice cream—this cobbler can be made a day ahead.

Position a rack in the center of the oven and heat the oven to 400°F. Lightly butter a 10x15x2-inch baking dish.

MAKE THE PEAR LAYER

In a large bowl, gently toss the sliced pears with the sugar, lemon juice, and lemon zest. Make sure the lemon juice completely coats the pears to keep them from browning. Sprinkle the crystallized ginger and flour over the top. Stir until evenly incorporated, breaking apart any ginger pieces that may be stuck together. Spread the pear mixture evenly in the bottom of the prepared pan and dot with the softened butter pieces.

MAKE THE BISCUIT LAYER

1. In a medium bowl, stir the flour, sugar, ginger, baking powder, cinnamon, cloves, salt, and baking soda with a fork. With the fork, work in the shortening and the softened butter until the size of small peas.

2. In a small bowl, whisk the eggs, milk, molasses, and vanilla. Make a well in the center of the dry ingredients and pour the egg mixture into the well. Stir just until the dry ingredients are completely blended. Dollop the batter by heaping tablespoonfuls onto the pears to create a cobbled effect, taking care to space the dollops about 1 inch apart. (Though the batter will cover only about half of the pear layer, don't spread it out. It will rise and spread to cover most of the pears as it bakes. If you run out of space to dollop the batter before it's all used, distribute what remains among the existing dollops.)

FOR THE TOPPING

½ **cup sliced almonds**

2 **Tbs. granulated sugar**

ADD THE TOPPING AND BAKE

Sprinkle the nuts and sugar evenly over the cobbler. Bake until the pears are tender and the topping is golden brown, 35 to 40 minutes. If needed, rotate the pan midway through the baking to allow the top to brown evenly. Let rest for at least 20 minutes before serving. Serve warm.

STORING

Once completely cool, wrap the cobbler in plastic and store it at room temperature for up to 24 hours. For longer storage, refrigerate for up to 1 week. To reheat, remove the plastic, cover loosely with foil, and set in a 300°F oven until warmed through, 20 to 25 minutes.
—*Julia M. Usher*

PER SERVING: 340 CALORIES | 4G PROTEIN | 57G CARB | 12G TOTAL FAT | 4.5G SAT FAT | 4G MONO FAT | 2G POLY FAT | 35MG CHOL | 170MG SODIUM | 5G FIBER

More about Molasses

True molasses is a by-product of sugar cane processing. Sugar cane juice is boiled, crystallized, and then centrifuged to separate the crystallized cane sugar from the liquid. That leftover liquid is molasses; it can be refined and processed as is, or it may be boiled up to two more times to produce different grades of sweetness and intensity. Three basic grades exist, but producers use several different terms to refer to them.

Light, mild, Barbados, or robust molasses has been boiled only once. It has a high sugar content and a mild flavor, and it can be used directly on foods as a syrup. Some brands of single-boil molasses haven't even had any sugar removed from them—they're simply refined sugar cane juice that's been reduced to a syrup. A widely distributed brand of this type is Grandma's® Original.

Dark, full, or cooking molasses has been boiled twice. It's slightly bitter and less sweet than single-boil molasses. It's typically used for baking and cooking.

Blackstrap molasses has been boiled three or more times. It has the deepest, most intense flavor of the three. It is generally used for animal feed, although some people prize it for its nutritional value.

The preservative sulphur dioxide is often added to molasses. It alters the flavor somewhat, so use unsulphured molasses when you can.

black- and blueberry pie with lemon-cornmeal crust

SERVES 8

FOR THE DOUGH

- **9 oz. (2 cups)** unbleached all-purpose flour; more as needed
- **⅓ cup** fine yellow cornmeal
- **1 Tbs.** granulated sugar
- **2 tsp.** finely grated lemon zest
- **1 tsp.** table salt
- **6 oz. (¾ cup)** chilled unsalted butter, cut into 10 pieces
- **2 oz. (4 Tbs.)** chilled vegetable shortening
- **1 Tbs.** fresh lemon juice combined with ¼ cup ice-cold water

FOR THE FILLING

- **⅔ cup plus 1 Tbs.** granulated sugar
- **⅓ cup** cornstarch
- **⅛ tsp.** ground allspice
- **⅛ tsp.** ground cinnamon
- **⅛ tsp.** table salt
- **5 cups (1 lb. 10 oz.)** room-temperature blueberries, washed, picked over, and drained on paper towels
- **2 cups (10½ oz.)** room-temperature blackberries, washed, picked over, and drained on paper towels
- **½ oz. (1 Tbs.)** chilled unsalted butter
- **1 oz. (2 Tbs.)** unsalted butter, melted

Blackberries paired with blueberries make a classic American pie. This recipe goes easy on the blackberries, since their more assertive flavor and seedy texture can easily overwhelm the blueberries.

MAKE THE DOUGH

1. In a large bowl, stir the flour, cornmeal, sugar, lemon zest, and salt. Using a pastry blender or two knives, begin to cut the butter into the flour. While the butter is still in large pieces, add the shortening to the bowl and continue to cut the fat into the flour until most pieces are the size of large peas.

2. With a big fork, stir in the lemon water, 1 to 2 Tbs. at a time, until the mixture looks shaggy but is moist enough to hold together when pressed. With well-floured hands, gently gather and press the dough into two equal disks, handling it only enough to make the edges of the disks reasonably smooth. Wrap the dough in plastic and chill for at least 1 hour, but preferably 2 to 4 hours, before rolling.

ROLL THE BOTTOM CRUST

Roll one disk of the dough out on a lightly floured surface into a 13-inch circle about ⅛ inch thick. Gently transfer the dough to a 9-inch metal, glass, or ceramic pie plate (fold the dough in half and unfold it into the pan). Don't stretch the dough as you line the pan, or it will spring back when baked. If necessary, trim the overhanging dough to 1 inch from the edge of the pan. Refrigerate until needed.

MAKE THE FILLING

In a large bowl, whisk ⅔ cup of the sugar with the cornstarch, allspice, cinnamon, and salt. Add the blueberries and blackberries and toss gently until thoroughly combined. Set aside.

FILL AND TOP THE PIE

1. Roll the second disk of dough out on a lightly floured surface into a 13-inch circle about ⅛ inch thick. Using a sharp knife or pizza cutter, cut the dough into ¾-inch-wide strips. Pour the fruit filling into the pastry-lined pie plate, being sure to include any dry ingredients remaining in the bowl. Lay five of the dough strips over the pie, parallel to each other and spaced evenly (use longer strips in the center of the pie and shorter strips near the edges). Carefully fold back the second and fourth strips a little past the center of the pie and lay a long strip of dough across the center of the pie, perpendicular to the other strips. Unfold the second and fourth strips over the perpendicular strip. Next, fold back the first, third, and fifth strips and lay a new strip across the pie, perpendicular to the folded strips. Unfold the three

continued on p. 32

continued from p. 31

Make Ahead

The dough can be made up to 2 days ahead and refrigerated or up to 2 months ahead and frozen.

strips over the new strip. Use this alternating technique to weave in three more strips (two go on the other side of the pie), completing the lattice top and evenly covering the pie. Trim the strips to overhang the pie by ¾ inch.

2. Roll the overhanging bottom dough and the strips together into a cylinder that rests on the edge of the pie pan. Crimp the edge. Cut the chilled 1 Tbs. butter into small pieces and dot over the open areas of the lattice. Freeze the assembled pie for about 15 minutes to relax the dough.

3. Meanwhile, position a rack in the center of the oven and set a foil-lined heavy-duty rimmed baking sheet on the rack. Heat the oven to 425°F. Just before baking, brush the lattice top with the melted butter and sprinkle with the remaining 1 Tbs. sugar. Put the pie on the heated baking sheet and bake for 15 minutes. Reduce the oven temperature to 375°F and bake until the fruit is bubbling consistently at the center of the pie, 60 to 80 minutes more. This is important—if it isn't bubbling near the center, it hasn't thickened yet. If the crust starts to get too brown, cover it loosely with foil during the last few minutes of the baking time.

4. Let the pie cool to just warm before serving. It can be stored at room temperature for up to 2 days. —*Nicole Rees*

PER SERVING: 480 CALORIES | 4G PROTEIN | 63G CARB | 24G TOTAL FAT | 13G SAT FAT | 7G MONO FAT | 2.5G POLY FAT | 50MG CHOL | 270MG SODIUM | 5G FIBER

how to make a lattice top

Fold back the second and fourth strips a little past the center of the pie and lay a long strip of dough across the center of the pie, perpendicular to the other strips. Unfold the second and fourth strips over the perpendicular strip.

Fold back the first, third, and fifth strips and lay a new strip across the pie, perpendicular to the folded strips. Unfold the three strips over the new strip.

Weave in three more strips using this alternating technique, completing the lattice top and evenly covering the pie.

Roll the overhanging bottom dough and the strips together into a cylinder that rests on the edge of the pie pan.

Crimp the edge.

peach and blueberry crisp
with spiced pecan topping

SERVES 6

2 oz. (4 Tbs.) unsalted butter, at room temperature; more for the pan

3 oz. (⅔ cup) unbleached all-purpose flour

½ cup packed light brown sugar

½ tsp. ground cinnamon

¼ tsp. table salt

⅔ cup coarsely chopped pecans

3 cups (about 1 lb.) room-temperature blueberries, washed, picked over, and drained on paper towels

3 medium peaches (about 1 lb.), halved, pitted, and sliced ½ inch thick

¼ cup granulated sugar

3 Tbs. cornstarch

¼ tsp. freshly ground nutmeg

Unlike most recipes for fruit crisp, which feed a large crowd, this one, baked in a 9x9-inch pan, is perfect for smaller households or gatherings.

1. Position a rack in the center of the oven and heat the oven to 375°F. Lightly butter a 9x9-inch metal or ceramic baking pan.

2. In a small bowl, combine the flour, brown sugar, cinnamon, and ⅛ tsp. of the salt. With your fingers, work the butter into the flour mixture until the mixture readily clumps together when pressed. Mix in the pecans.

3. In a large bowl, toss the blueberries and peaches. In a small bowl, combine the granulated sugar with the cornstarch, nutmeg, and the remaining ⅛ tsp. salt and toss this mixture with the fruit.

4. Spread the fruit into the prepared baking pan. Pressing the streusel into small lumps, sprinkle it over the fruit. Bake until the fruit is bubbling in the center and the topping is crisp and well browned, 45 to 50 minutes. Cool slightly and serve warm. —*Nicole Rees*

PER SERVING: 400 CALORIES | 4G PROTEIN | 61G CARB | 18G TOTAL FAT | 6G SAT FAT | 8G MONO FAT | 3.5G POLY FAT | 20MG CHOL | 105MG SODIUM | 5G FIBER

Buying and Storing Blueberries

You can judge some fruit with your nose, but not blueberries. Use your eyes first: Blueberries should have a lovely silvery white bloom over the dark blue. Look for pints free of small, purplish or greenish immature berries, a sign that they were picked before their peak. Then use the "heft" test: Berries should be plump and heavy. The surefire way of judging blueberries is to taste a few, because sweetness is variable even within the same pint.

At home, pick through them, discarding any squishy berries that may turn moldy and infect their healthy neighbors. Store the berries in the coldest part of the refrigerator, but not in a drawer, where it's too humid. To keep them dry, don't wash them until you're ready to use them. While fresh-picked blueberries will keep for up to 2 weeks in an airtight container, they can lose moisture during the second week and shrink slightly. For baking, this can work in your favor, because the flavor becomes concentrated.

To freeze blueberries, rinse them in a colander, dry thoroughly on paper towels, and then spread them on rimmed baking sheets in a single layer until frozen solid. Once frozen, put into plastic storage bags.

orange and brown butter tart

SERVES 8

FOR THE TART SHELL

- 5 oz. (1¼ cups) unbleached all-purpose flour
- 1 Tbs. granulated sugar
- Pinch of table salt
- 5 oz. (10 Tbs.) chilled unsalted butter, cut into small pieces
- 1 tsp. finely grated orange zest

FOR THE FILLING

- 3 Tbs. unsalted butter
- 2 cups whole milk
- 3 Tbs. cornstarch
- 2 large eggs
- ½ cup granulated sugar
- Pinch of kosher or table salt
- ¼ tsp. pure vanilla extract

FOR THE TOPPING

- 3 large navel or blood oranges, or a combination
- ½ cup orange marmalade
- 1 Tbs. orange liqueur, such as Cointreau®

Adding brown butter to this filling gives it a lovely nutty flavor, enhancing the sweetness of the oranges.

MAKE THE TART SHELL

1. In a food processor, pulse the flour, sugar, and salt a few times to combine. Add the butter and orange zest and pulse until the mixture resembles cornmeal, six to eight 1-second pulses. A teaspoon at a time, pulse in up to 1 Tbs. water until the dough just holds together in clumps. Press the dough together, shape into a 6-inch disk, and wrap in plastic. Refrigerate for 30 minutes.

2. Press the dough evenly into the bottom and sides of a 9½-inch fluted tart pan with a removable bottom—the dough sides should be ¼ to ⅜ inch thick. To smooth the bottom, cover with plastic wrap and press with a flat-bottom measuring cup or glass. Freeze the covered shell for 30 minutes. Meanwhile, position a rack in the center of the oven and heat the oven to 400°F.

3. Remove the plastic, line the dough with parchment, and fill with dry beans or pie weights. Bake the tart shell until the top edges are light golden, about 15 minutes. Carefully remove the parchment and beans, reduce the heat to 375°F, and continue to bake until the shell is golden all over, about 15 minutes. Cool on a rack.

MAKE THE FILLING

1. In a small saucepan, heat the butter over medium-high heat until it melts and the milk solids turn brown, swirling the pan occasionally for even browning, about 3 minutes. Immediately pour into a small heatproof bowl to stop the cooking.

2. In a medium bowl, whisk ¼ cup of the milk with the cornstarch. Whisk in the eggs.

3. In a medium saucepan, bring the remaining 1¾ cups milk, the sugar, and salt to a boil over medium heat. Take the pan off the heat, whisk about ¼ cup of the hot milk into the egg mixture, and then whisk the egg mixture into the hot milk. Return to medium heat and continue whisking until the filling boils and becomes very thick, 30 seconds to 1 minute. Off the heat, whisk in the brown butter and vanilla.

4. Spread the filling evenly in the tart shell and set aside at room temperature while you prepare the topping.

MAKE THE TOPPING

1. Using a sharp knife, trim off the peel and pith from the oranges. Halve the oranges lengthwise and then slice them thinly crosswise and remove any seeds. Arrange the orange slices on the top of the tart in concentric, slightly overlapping circles.

2. Stir the marmalade in a small saucepan over medium heat until melted, 30 to 60 seconds. Strain and then stir in the Cointreau. Brush enough of the mixture on the oranges to give them a shine (you may not need it all). Refrigerate for 1 hour before serving so the filling can set up. —*Joanne Weir*

PER SERVING: 430 CALORIES | 6G PROTEIN | 54G CARB | 22G TOTAL FAT | 13G SAT FAT | 6G MONO FAT | 1G POLY FAT | 110MG CHOL | 110MG SODIUM | 2G FIBER

continued on p. 38

continued from p. 37

how to cut oranges

Follow these steps to make slices or segments from any type of orange.

Cut off the top and bottom of the orange, slicing off enough to expose a circle of the orange's flesh.

With a paring knife, slice off a strip of peel from top to bottom. Try to get all of the white pith, but leave as much of the flesh as possible. Continue all the way around.

To make slices, cut the orange crosswise to the desired thickness.

To make segments, use a paring knife to cut on either side of each membrane, freeing the orange segment in between. Work over a bowl to catch the juice.

pear and brown sugar crisp

SERVES 6

FOR THE TOPPING

⅔ cup unbleached all-purpose flour

5 Tbs. unsalted butter, at room temperature

¾ cup rolled oats (instant or old-fashioned oatmeal)

½ cup firmly packed light brown sugar

Pinch of salt

FOR THE PEAR FILLING

3 lb. pears (about 6 large) such as Bosc or Bartlett, peeled, halved, and cored

1 Tbs. fresh lemon juice

2 tsp. pure vanilla extract

⅓ to ½ cup granulated sugar

½ tsp. ground cinnamon

Pinch of ground cloves

4½ tsp. cornstarch

Bosc and Bartlett pears are best in this crisp. Look for ones that are firm-ripe, or just at the beginning of the ripening window.

MAKE THE TOPPING

In a food processor, combine the flour, butter, oats, brown sugar, and salt; pulse until the mixture starts to hold together. Set aside.

MAKE THE FILLING

Heat the oven to 350°F. Cut the pears into pieces about 1 inch long by ½ inch thick. In a large bowl, mix the pears, lemon juice, vanilla, ⅓ cup of the sugar, the cinnamon, cloves, and cornstarch; toss to combine. Taste and add more sugar if you like.

BAKE THE CRISP

Pour the pear mixture into a 7x11-inch baking dish or individual ramekins. Cover with the topping. Turn the oven down to 325°F and bake the crisp until the top is golden brown and the pears are tender, 70 to 80 minutes. Serve warm or at room temperature. —*Frank McClelland*

PER SERVING: 420 CALORIES | 4G PROTEIN | 80G CARB | 11G TOTAL FAT | 6G SAT FAT | 3G MONO FAT | 1G POLY FAT | 25MG CHOL | 150MG SODIUM | 7G FIBER

custard tart with wine-poached grapes

SERVES 8

Sweet, citrusy custard and a nutty almond crust make a perfect backdrop for the tender poached grapes in this elegant dessert.

FOR THE CRUST

- 3½ oz. (7 Tbs.) chilled unsalted butter, cut into ½-inch pieces; more for the pan
- 3⅜ oz. (¾ cup) unbleached all-purpose flour
- ¼ cup toasted, slivered almonds
- ¼ cup granulated sugar
- ½ tsp. table salt
- 1 large egg yolk, chilled

FOR THE FILLING

- 2 large eggs
- 2 large egg yolks
- ½ cup granulated sugar
- 3 Tbs. fresh lime juice
- 3 Tbs. dry white wine, preferably Sauvignon Blanc
- ½ cup heavy cream

FOR THE TOPPING

- ½ cup dry white wine, preferably Sauvignon Blanc
- 2 Tbs. honey
- 2 Tbs. granulated sugar
- 1 Tbs. fresh lime juice
- 65 seedless red grapes (2¼ cups)

MAKE THE CRUST

1. Butter a 4x13½-inch rectangular fluted tart pan with a removable bottom. Combine the flour, almonds, sugar, and salt in a food processor and process until the almonds are finely chopped, about 40 seconds. Add the butter and pulse until the mixture resembles coarse meal, about 15 seconds. Add the egg yolk and process until moist clumps form. With lightly floured hands, press the dough evenly over the bottom and up the sides of the prepared tart pan. Freeze until firm, about 45 minutes.

2. Position a rack in the center of the oven, put a rimmed baking sheet on the rack, and heat the oven to 375°F. Bake the crust on the heated baking sheet until light golden on the bottom and golden brown on the edges, about 15 minutes. Cool completely.

MAKE THE FILLING

1. In a medium heavy-duty saucepan, whisk the eggs, yolks, sugar, lime juice, and white wine until well blended. Cook over medium-high heat, whisking frequently, until the mixture boils and thickens, about 3 minutes. Transfer the filling to a medium bowl and let cool until warm.

2. Whisk the cream into the filling and pour the mixture into the baked tart shell. Bake at 375°F until the filling begins to slightly puff and bubble around the edges, about 15 minutes. Let cool to room temperature.

MAKE THE TOPPING

In a medium heavy-duty saucepan, boil the wine, honey, sugar, and lime juice over medium heat until the mixture reduces to a thick syrup and begins to darken slightly, 4 to 5 minutes—you should have about ¼ cup. Reduce the heat to low, add the grapes, cover, and poach gently over low heat until tender, about 3 minutes. With a slotted spoon, transfer the grapes to a dinner plate. Continue to boil the poaching liquid until syrupy, about 1 minute. Randomly place the grapes on top of the tart, pressing slightly into the filling. Gently brush the glaze over the grapes. Let the tart cool completely at room temperature for at least 4 hours before serving. —*Jeanne Kelley*

PER SERVING: 390 CALORIES | 5G PROTEIN | 46G CARB | 21G TOTAL FAT | 11G SAT FAT | 7G MONO FAT | 1.5G POLY FAT | 180MG CHOL | 180MG SODIUM | 1G FIBER

a buyer's guide to grapes

Here's a quick roundup of the most common table grape varieties.

Red Flame grapes are sweet in flavor with a crunchy texture. They're ideal for both eating out of hand and cooking, as they keep their shape well and acquire a deeper flavor when heated.

Concord grapes have thick skins, juicy flesh, large seeds, and a strong strawberry-like flavor. They come in purple and white varieties and are ideal for juices and jellies.

Champagne grapes have delicate, sweet, pea-size berries that need gentle handling. These seedless grapes are not used in the homonymous French sparkling wine but are so named because they're thought to resemble tiny bubbles.

Green Thompson grapes are the top seller at the supermarket. Large and seedless, they have firm skins that make them very durable. Their mild flavor pairs well with citrus.

Muscat grapes usually have seeds and come in black and white varieties. Prized for their honey-floral flavor and perfume, they're used for both eating (they're delicious with cheese) and making wine.

Autumn Royal grapes have large, oval-shaped black berries. Sweet and straightforward, these seedless grapes pair well with salty foods like prosciutto and salted nuts.

ginger-apple crumb pie

SERVES 8 TO 12

FOR THE CRUST

5¾ oz. (1¼ cups) unbleached all-purpose flour

¼ tsp. table salt

1½ oz. (3 Tbs.) chilled vegetable shortening, cut into ½-inch dice

1½ oz. (3 Tbs.) chilled unsalted butter, cut into ½-inch dice

2½ to 3½ Tbs. very cold water

FOR THE TOPPING

4½ oz. (1 cup) unbleached all-purpose flour

⅓ cup granulated sugar

2 Tbs. firmly packed light brown sugar

1½ tsp. ground ginger

⅛ tsp. table salt

4 oz. (½ cup) chilled unsalted butter, cut into 8 pieces

FOR THE FILLING

3 lb. Braeburn or Gala apples (about 6 medium) peeled, cored, and cut into ¼-inch-thick slices

2 tsp. finely grated fresh ginger (use a rasp-style grater)

½ cup granulated sugar

3 Tbs. unbleached all-purpose flour

1 oz. (2 Tbs.) unsalted butter, cut into very small pieces

The crunchy ginger crumb topping on this pie provides a lovely contrast to the tender apples in the filling. As you cover the pie, keep the topping as clumpy as possible for the most satisfying texture.

MAKE THE CRUST

1. In a stand mixer bowl (or a large mixing bowl), whisk the flour and salt to blend. Add the shortening and butter. Starting on low speed and then shifting to medium, beat with the paddle attachment (or cut in by hand) until the largest pieces of fat are about the size of peas, 1 to 2 minutes. With the mixer running on low (or mixing by hand), sprinkle on 2½ Tbs. of the water and blend until the dough just comes together into clumps; if the dough is too dry to do this, add the remaining water 1½ tsp. at a time. With your hands, shape the dough into a 4-inch-wide disk. Wrap in plastic and refrigerate for at least 30 minutes.

2. Roll out the dough between two sheets of plastic wrap. (If the dough was chilled for more than 30 minutes, you may need to let it warm up at room temperature to become pliable.) Occasionally loosen and reapply the wrap and continue rolling until you have an 11- to 12-inch round that's about ⅛ inch thick. Remove the top sheet of plastic. Turn a standard 9-inch metal or glass pie plate (1¼ inches deep) upside down over the center of dough. Slip your hand under the plastic and turn the pie plate right side up. Slip the dough into the pan to fit snugly and carefully remove the plastic. Trim the dough overhang to about ¼ inch, fold it under to create a thicker edge, and flute the edge. Cover loosely with plastic and refrigerate for at least 30 minutes or until ready to use.

MAKE THE TOPPING

In a medium bowl, combine the flour, sugar, brown sugar, ground ginger, and salt. Whisk to blend. Add the butter and work it in well with your fingers until the mixture holds together in small clumps and there are very few fine grains left in the bowl. Refrigerate until ready to use.

FILL, TOP, AND BAKE THE PIE

1. Position an oven rack in the lower third of the oven and heat the oven to 425°F.

2. In a large bowl, toss the apples with the ginger, distributing the ginger as evenly as possible. Add the sugar and flour and toss to coat evenly.

continued on p. 44

continued from p. 42

Make Ahead

You can make the crust and topping several hours ahead and refrigerate them, covered.

3. Scrape the apple mixture into the shell and mound it slightly in the center. Dot with the butter. Top with the crumb topping, keeping it as clumpy (not sandy) as you can. Try to cover all the apples. If any crumbs roll off the pie, gather them up and reapply.

4. Put the pie on a foil-lined baking sheet. Bake for 20 minutes and then reduce the heat to 375°F. Bake until the apples are tender (a skewer inserted into the center of the pie will meet slight resistance) and the juices are bubbling around the edges, another 30 to 35 minutes; if the top starts to brown too quickly after about 20 minutes, cover the pie lightly with foil. Let cool on a rack for 3 to 4 hours to let the juices set.
—*Wendy Kalen*

PER SERVING: 410 CALORIES | 3G PROTEIN | 67G CARB | 16G TOTAL FAT | 9G SAT FAT | 5G MONO FAT | 1G POLY FAT | 35MG CHOL | 80MG SODIUM | 5G FIBER

peach cobbler with star anise

SERVES 8

1 Tbs. unsalted butter, at room temperature, for the baking dish

FOR THE PEACH FILLING

½ cup packed light brown sugar

1 Tbs. cornstarch

¼ tsp. (scant), freshly ground star anise

Pinch of table salt

3 lb. firm but ripe peaches (about 6 large), pitted

1 tsp. pure vanilla extract

FOR THE COBBLER TOPPING

4½ oz. (1 cup) unbleached all-purpose flour

⅓ cup fine cornmeal

⅓ cup packed light brown sugar

1½ tsp. baking powder

¼ tsp. table salt

Pinch of freshly ground star anise

2 oz. (4 Tbs.) chilled unsalted butter, cut into ¾-inch pieces

6 Tbs. heavy cream

Lightly sweetened whipped cream, for garnish (optional)

Star anise is usually sold in the supermarket spice section. To grind it, put the whole spice in a spice or coffee grinder.

Position an oven rack in the middle of the oven; heat the oven to 375°F. Lightly butter a 10-cup baking dish (10x2-inch round or 9x9-inch square).

MAKE THE FILLING

1. In a large bowl, mix the brown sugar, cornstarch, ground star anise, and salt until combined; break up any lumps.

2. Cut the peaches into 1-inch-wide wedges and cut each wedge in half crosswise. Add the peaches and vanilla to the dry ingredients and toss to coat the peaches evenly. Pour the fruit and its juices into the buttered baking dish, scraping the bowl of any sugar. Spread the fruit evenly.

MAKE THE TOPPING

1. In a food processor, combine the flour, cornmeal, brown sugar, baking powder, salt, and ground star anise. Pulse briefly to blend. Add the chilled butter pieces and pulse until they're the size of small peas. Pour the cream over the dough and pulse just until moist crumbs form. Dump the dough onto a lightly floured work surface. Gather the dough and press it to form a square that's 1 inch thick. Lightly flour the dough. Roll it out, flouring as needed, to a ½-inch-thick rectangle; it should measure about 5x9 inches. Cut the rectangle in half lengthwise, and cut each half into four pieces, each about 2¼x2½ inches.

2. Arrange the dough squares on top of the peaches, leaving spaces between each one. Bake until the filling is bubbling and the topping is nicely browned, about 40 minutes. The cobbler is best when served warm on the same day it's baked, preferably with a little lightly sweetened whipped cream on the side. —*Abigail Johnson Dodge*

PER SERVING: 310 CALORIES I 3G PROTEIN I 53G CARB I 10G TOTAL FAT I 6G SAT FAT I 3G MONO FAT I 1G POLY FAT I 30MG CHOL I 200MG SODIUM I 3G FIBER

fresh pear pie with dried cherries and brown sugar streusel

SERVES 8

FOR THE STREUSEL

- 4½ oz. (1 cup) unbleached all-purpose flour
- ½ cup old-fashioned rolled oats
- ½ cup packed light brown sugar
- ¼ tsp. table salt
- 4 oz. (½ cup) unsalted butter, melted

FOR THE FILLING

- 3 lb. ripe Anjou or Bartlett pears (5 or 6 medium), peeled and cored, cut lengthwise into 8 wedges and then crosswise into ½-inch slices (about 7 cups)
- 1½ Tbs. fresh lemon juice
- ⅔ cup granulated sugar
- 1⅛ oz. (¼ cup) unbleached all-purpose flour
- ¼ tsp. table salt
- ¼ tsp. ground cinnamon
- ⅛ tsp. freshly grated nutmeg
- ¾ cup dried tart cherries, coarsely chopped
- 1 blind-baked All-Butter Piecrust (recipe on the facing page)

A hint of spice lets the delicate flavor of the pears shine through, while the dried cherries are a welcome alternative to traditional raisins.

Position a rack in the center of the oven, set a heavy-duty rimmed baking sheet on the rack, and heat the oven to 350°F.

MAKE THE STREUSEL

In a medium bowl, combine the flour, oats, sugar, and salt. Using your fingers, blend the butter into the flour mixture. The mixture will be moist. Set aside.

MAKE THE FILLING

1. In a large bowl, toss the pears with the lemon juice. In a small bowl, whisk the sugar, flour, salt, cinnamon, and nutmeg. Add the sugar mixture to the pears and toss well to combine. Stir in the cherries.

2. Mound the filling into the piecrust. Sprinkle the streusel topping over the pear mixture, pressing the streusel between your fingers into small lumps as you sprinkle.

3. Put the pie on the heated baking sheet and bake until the pastry is golden brown and the filling is bubbly and thickened at the edges, 55 to 65 minutes. Rotate the pie halfway through baking, and if the pastry or streusel browns before the filling has thickened, loosely cover the top or edges of the pie as needed with a pie shield or a sheet of aluminum foil. Transfer to a rack and cool completely before serving. The pie can be stored at room temperature for up to 2 days.
—Nicole Rees

PER SERVING: 630 CALORIES | 7G PROTEIN | 101G CARB | 24G TOTAL FAT | 15G SAT FAT | 6G MONO FAT | 1G POLY FAT | 60MG CHOL | 260MG SODIUM | 7G FIBER

all-butter piecrust

MAKES ONE 9-INCH PIECRUST

- **6 oz. (1⅓ cups) unbleached all-purpose flour**
- **1 tsp. granulated sugar**
- **⅜ tsp. table salt**
- **4 oz. (½ cup) chilled unsalted butter, preferably European style, cut into ¾-inch pieces**
- **3 to 4 Tbs. ice water**

Make Ahead

This pie dough can be made ahead and refrigerated overnight or frozen (before or after rolling) for up to 3 months. Simply transfer the dough to the refrigerator the night before you plan to make a pie, and it'll be ready to go.

MAKE THE DOUGH

1. Put the flour, sugar, and salt in a medium bowl and stir with a rubber spatula or a fork to combine. Add the butter to the bowl. Rub the chilled chunks of butter between your fingertips, smearing the butter into the flour to create small (roughly ¼-inch) flakes of fat.

2. Drizzle 3 Tbs. ice water over the flour mixture. Stir with the spatula or fork, adding 1 Tbs. more water if necessary, until the mixture forms a shaggy dough that's moist enough to hold together when pressed between your fingers.

3. With well-floured hands, gently gather and press the dough together, and then form it into a disk with smooth edges. Wrap the dough in plastic and chill for at least 1 hour, but preferably 2 to 4 hours, before rolling.

ROLL THE DOUGH

1. Let the chilled dough sit at room temperature to soften slightly—it should be cold and firm but not rock hard. Depending on how long the dough was chilled, this could take 5 to 20 minutes. When ready to roll, lightly flour the countertop or other surface (a pastry cloth, silicone rolling mat, or parchment on a counter also works great) and position the rolling pin in the center of the dough disk. Roll away from you toward 12 o'clock, easing the pressure as you near the edge to keep the edge from becoming too thin. Return to the center and roll toward 6 o'clock. Repeat toward 3 and then 9 o'clock, always easing the pressure at the edges and picking up the pin rather than rolling it back to the center.

2. Continue to "roll around the clock," aiming for different "times" on each pass until the dough is 13 to 14 inches in diameter and about ⅛ inch thick. Try to use as few passes of the rolling pin as possible. After every few passes, check that the dough isn't sticking by lifting it with a bench knife (dough scraper). Reflour only as needed—excess flour makes a drier, tougher crust. Each time you lift the dough, give it a quarter turn to help even out the thickness.

LINE THE PIE PLATE

1. Gently transfer the dough to a 9-inch pie plate, preferably metal, by folding it in half and unfolding it into the plate. Do not stretch the dough as you line the pan, or it will spring back when baked. Gently lift the outer edges of the dough to give you enough slack to line the sides of the pan without stretching the dough.

continued on p. 48

continued from p. 47

2. Trim the overhanging dough to 1 inch from the edge of the pan. Roll the dough under itself into a cylinder that rests on the edge of the pan.

3. To crimp the edge, have one hand on the inside of the edge and one hand on the outside, and use the index finger of the inside hand to push the dough between the thumb and index finger of the outside hand to form a U or V shape. Repeat around the edge of the pie plate, creating a crimped edge whose individual flutes are about 1 inch apart. As you are going along, if you notice that the edge is not perfectly symmetrical and that the amount of dough you'll have to crimp seems sparse in places, take a bit of trimmed scrap, wet it with a drop or two of water, and attach it to the sparse area by pressing it firmly into place.

4. Prick the sides and bottom of the crust all over with a fork. Refrigerate until firm, about 1 hour or overnight. This will relax the dough and help prevent the edges from caving in.

BLIND BAKE THE CRUST

1. Position a rack in the center of the oven and heat the oven to 425°F. Line the chilled piecrust with foil and fill it with dried beans or pie weights. Bake for 15 minutes; remove the foil and the beans or weights. Reduce the oven temperature to 375°F.

2. Bake until the bottom looks dry but is not quite done and the edges are light golden, 5 to 7 minutes more. —*Nicole Rees*

Blind-Baking Basics

Blind baking means baking an empty piecrust before adding a filling. Here's what you need to know.

Why blind bake?
Blind baking gives the crust a head start, allowing it to firm up before the filling is added. This prevents the crust from getting soggy. Dried beans or pie weights help it keep its shape. Without them, the crust will rise and puff on the bottom or slide down the sides under the weight of the crimped edge.

How long?
In recipes where the filling doesn't need further cooking or cooks for a short period of time, such as cream pies or fruit tarts, the crust is usually blind baked until cooked through and golden brown. But in recipes where the pie cooks for a while after adding the filling, it's best to blind bake the crust just partway so it won't overcook as it continues to bake with the filling.

Remember to chill
Don't be tempted to skip chilling a crust before blind baking it. Piecrusts baked right after shaping are warm enough for the butter to melt quickly in the oven, causing the edge to sink or even slump over the edge of the pie pan.

how to make the crust

Rub the chilled chunks of butter between your fingertips, smearing the butter into the flour to create small flakes of fat.

Stir until the mixture forms a shaggy dough that holds together when pressed between your fingers.

Gather and press the dough together, forming it into a disk with smooth edges.

Roll out the chilled dough on a lightly floured surface, rolling from the center out, until you reach the desired size and thickness.

Line the pan with the dough, lifting the outer edges of the dough to help line the sides of the pan without stretching the dough.

Once the overhanging dough has been trimmed, roll the dough under itself so that it rests on the edge of the pan.

Crimp the edge of the dough. Position one hand on the inside of the edge and one hand on the outside; use the index finger of the inside hand to push the dough between the thumb and index finger of the outside hand to form a U shape.

Before baking, line the chilled piecrust with foil and fill it with dried beans or pie weights.

Bake until the bottom looks dry but not quite done and the edges are light golden.

brown sugar and brandy pear turnovers

MAKES 4 TURNOVERS

2 Tbs. chopped dried cranberries

2 Tbs. brandy or Cognac

2 Tbs. unsalted butter

1 Tbs. packed dark brown sugar

1 lb. ripe pears (like Anjou, Comice, or Bartlett), cut into 12-inch chunks

Pinch of salt

2 tsp. fresh lemon juice

1 sheet (about 9 oz.) frozen puff pastry, thawed

2 Tbs. heavy cream (optional)

With frozen puff pastry, these turnovers take just minutes to prepare and can bake while you're enjoying dinner.

1. Heat the oven to 425°F. Put the cranberries and brandy or Cognac in a small bowl and let soak while you prepare the other ingredients.

2. Melt the butter in a wide, heavy-based skillet over medium-high heat. Add the brown sugar and cook, stirring, until the mixture is bubbly, about 2 minutes. Add the pears and salt. Continue cooking over medium-high heat until most of the pears' liquid has been released and cooked off, 4 to 5 minutes. Add the cranberries and brandy and keep cooking and stirring until the pears are just surrounded by a syrupy glaze, about another 3 minutes. Add the lemon juice and stir to blend. Spread the filling in a thin layer on a plate or baking dish and chill in the freezer while you roll the dough.

3. On a lightly floured surface, roll the dough to a 12-inch square and cut it into four even squares. Put one-quarter of the filling into the center of a square, dab the edges of the dough lightly with water, fold over to make a triangle, and press the edges together very firmly to seal. Transfer to a parchment-lined or nonstick baking sheet. Repeat with the other turnovers. Cut two or three 1-inch slashes in each turnover for steam to vent. Brush the tops of the turnovers with the cream, if using. Bake until they're deep golden brown on the top and bottom and the pastry no longer seems doughy in the center, 18 to 22 minutes. Let the turnovers cool for a few minutes and then serve warm.

—*Martha Holmberg*

ginger-spice cranberry-apple streusel pie

SERVES 8

FOR THE STREUSEL

- 4½ oz. (1 cup) unbleached all-purpose flour
- ¾ cup packed light brown sugar
- ½ cup chopped lightly toasted walnuts
- ¼ tsp. table salt
- 3 oz. (6 Tbs.) unsalted butter, melted

FOR THE FILLING

- 4 tart baking apples, such as Granny Smith or Pink Lady (1½ to 2 lb.)
- 6 oz. fresh or thawed frozen cranberries (1¾ cups)
- ¾ cup plus 6 Tbs. granulated sugar
- 1 oz. (3½ Tbs.) unbleached all-purpose flour
- 1 Tbs. finely chopped crystallized ginger
- ¼ tsp. ground cardamom
- ¼ tsp. ground cinnamon
- 1 blind-baked All-Butter Piecrust (recipe on p. 47)

Tart apples and cranberries are tempered with a nutty, sweet streusel and a hint of cardamom.

Position a rack in the center of the oven, set a heavy-duty rimmed baking sheet on the rack, and heat the oven to 350°F.

MAKE THE STREUSEL

In a medium bowl, combine the flour, sugar, walnuts, and salt. Using your fingers, blend the butter into the flour mixture. Set aside.

MAKE THE FILLING

1. Peel, quarter, and core each apple. Cut each quarter lengthwise into ¼-inch-thick slices and then cut each slice crosswise at ¼-inch intervals to make tiny rectangles. In a food processor, pulse the cranberries with ¾ cup of the sugar until coarsely chopped. In a large bowl, combine the remaining 6 Tbs. sugar with the flour, ginger, cardamom, and cinnamon, breaking up ginger clumps with your fingers. Toss in the cranberry mixture and apples.

2. Mound the filling into the piecrust. Sprinkle the streusel topping over the apple mixture, pressing the streusel between your fingers into small lumps as you sprinkle.

3. Put the pie on the heated baking sheet and bake until the streusel is deeply browned and the filling is bubbling vigorously at the edges of the pie, 65 to 75 minutes. Check every 20 minutes, and if the pastry edge or the streusel browns before the filling is done, loosely cover the top or edges of the pie as needed with aluminum foil.

4. Transfer to a rack and cool completely before serving. The pie can be stored at room temperature for up to 2 days. *—Nicole Rees*

PER SERVING: 610 CALORIES | 6G PROTEIN | 94G CARB | 25G TOTAL FAT | 13G SAT FAT | 6G MONO FAT | 4.5G POLY FAT | 55MG CHOL | 190MG SODIUM | 4G FIBER

brandied apricot-almond slab pie

MAKES 1 LARGE PIE; SERVES 10

Slab pies are like giant Pop-Tarts® designed to feed a crowd. As the pie cools, the filling—made with both fresh and dried apricots—firms up enough that the slices can be eaten out of hand.

FOR THE DOUGH

- **15** oz. (3⅓ cups) unbleached all-purpose flour
- **3** Tbs. granulated sugar
- **½** tsp. kosher salt
- **9** oz. (1 cup plus 2 Tbs.) chilled unsalted butter, cut into 18 pieces
- **1½** oz. (3 Tbs.) chilled vegetable shortening, cut into 3 pieces
- **⅓** cup cold water

FOR THE FILLING

- **10½** oz. (about 2 cups) dried apricots, coarsely chopped
- **⅔** cup granulated sugar
- **⅔** cup dry white wine
- **⅓** cup orange juice
- **12** oz. fresh apricots (about 6 small), pitted and sliced
- **1¼** tsp. fresh lemon juice
- **1** cup sliced almonds, toasted
- **1½** Tbs. brandy
- **¼** tsp. pure almond extract

FOR ASSEMBLY

- **1** large egg yolk
- **½** cup confectioners' sugar, sifted
- **1½** Tbs. heavy cream or whole milk
- **½** tsp. pure vanilla extract

MAKE THE DOUGH

1. Put the flour, sugar, and salt in a food processor. Add the butter and vegetable shortening and pulse until the mixture resembles coarse meal, 10 to 12 pulses. Sprinkle ⅓ cup cold water over the mixture and pulse until the dough just starts to come together, 8 to 10 pulses more. If the mixture seems dry, add more water 1 tsp. at a time. Do not overprocess.

2. Turn the dough out onto a clean work surface, and gather it into a rectangle that's about 8x12 inches. Flatten slightly, wrap in plastic, and refrigerate for at least 2 hours and up to 3 days.

MAKE THE FILLING

1. In a heavy-based 4-quart saucepan, combine the dried apricots, sugar, wine, orange juice, and ⅔ cup water. Simmer over medium-low heat, stirring often, until the apricots are very tender and can be mashed with a wooden spoon, 40 to 45 minutes. Add more water if the apricots are still not soft after most of the liquid has evaporated. The mixture should get thick and syrupy; don't let it scorch. Add the fresh apricots and lemon juice and cook, stirring often, until very soft, about 10 minutes. Mash the mixture with a wooden spoon or potato masher so that it has a thick, jam-like consistency. Remove from the heat.

continued on p. 54

continued from p. 53

2. Stir ¾ cup of the almonds, the brandy, and almond extract into the apricot mixture. Cool to room temperature and set aside. (The filling can be made, covered, and refrigerated up to 2 days ahead.)

ASSEMBLE AND BAKE THE PIE

1. Position a rack in the center of the oven and heat the oven to 375°F. Line a large rimmed baking sheet with parchment. In a small bowl, beat the egg yolk with 1 tsp. water.

2. On a lightly floured surface with a lightly floured rolling pin, roll the dough into a ⅛-inch-thick, 12x18-inch rectangle. Be sure to loosen the dough several times and reflour underneath so that it doesn't stick. Trim the dough into an 11x16-inch rectangle and transfer it to the baking sheet. Turn the baking sheet so that a long side faces you, and brush the edges of the dough with the egg wash. Spread the apricot filling evenly over the bottom half of the dough, leaving a ½-inch bor-der. Fold the top half of the dough over the filling, pressing along the edges to secure the sides. Press lightly along the edges with the back of a fork to seal. Brush egg wash all over the top of the dough. Using a paring knife, cut five small steam vents in the dough at about 3-inch intervals.

3. Bake until the pie is golden brown, 55 minutes. Transfer to a rack to cool completely.

4. In a small bowl, mix the confectioners' sugar, cream, and vanilla extract to form a smooth glaze that's just fluid enough to drizzle. With a spoon, drizzle the glaze over the top of the pie and immediately sprinkle with the remaining ¼ cup almonds. Allow to set for at least 2 hours before serving.

5. When ready to serve, use a serrated knife to cut the pie. The pie is best eaten the day it's made, but it will keep for 1 day, well wrapped, at room temperature. —*Karen Barker*

PER SERVING: 650 CALORIES | 9G PROTEIN | 81G CARB | 32G TOTAL FAT | 15G SAT FAT | 10G MONO FAT | 3.5G POLY FAT | 80MG CHOL | 65MG SODIUM | 5G FIBER

To seal the filled pie, press the fork down gently, just enough to create a good bond (and a pretty crimped effect), but not so hard that it pushes through to the second layer of dough or pierces it, which may cause the filling to leak.

blackberry-apple turnovers

MAKES 12 TURNOVERS

FOR THE DOUGH

- 11¼ oz. (2½ cups) unbleached all-purpose flour
- 2 Tbs. granulated sugar
- ½ tsp. kosher salt
- 6 oz. (¾ cup) chilled unsalted butter, cut into 12 pieces
- 6 oz. chilled cream cheese, cut into 6 pieces
- ½ cup heavy cream

FOR THE FILLING

- 6 oz. (1¼ cups) blackberries, rinsed, picked over, drained, and halved
- 1 large Pink Lady apple, peeled, cored, cut into ¼-inch dice
- ½ cup light brown sugar
- 1 Tbs. unbleached all-purpose flour
- ½ tsp. ground allspice
- ¼ tsp. kosher salt

FOR ASSEMBLY

- 1 large egg yolk

  Granulated sugar

Cup a dough square in one hand to create a triangular pocket. Fill the dough with your other hand, pull the corners up to form a triangle, and pinch to seal.

With a dense crispness and a high sugar-to-acid ratio, Pink Lady apples are ideal for these pies. Even when tender, they hold their shape and retain some firmness, for a nice contrast to the juicy, collapsed berries.

MAKE THE DOUGH

1. Put the flour, sugar, and salt in a food processor. Add the butter and cream cheese and pulse until the mixture resembles coarse meal, 8 to 10 pulses. Add the cream and pulse, pausing to scrape the bowl once or twice, just until the dough starts to come together, 8 to 10 pulses more. Do not overprocess. Turn the dough out onto a clean work surface, gather it together, and pat it into a rectangle. Wrap it in plastic and refrigerate for at least 2 hours and up to 3 days.

2. When ready to bake, position racks in the bottom and top thirds of the oven and heat the oven to 400°F. Line two large rimmed baking sheets with parchment.

3. On a lightly floured surface with a lightly floured rolling pin, roll the dough into a 13x18-inch rectangle. Loosen the dough and reflour underneath. Trim the edges to form a 12x16-inch rectangle, cut the dough into twelve 4-inch squares, and put six squares on each baking sheet.

MAKE THE FILLING

In a medium bowl, lightly toss the blackberries, apple, brown sugar, flour, allspice, and salt until combined.

ASSEMBLE AND BAKE THE TURNOVERS

1. In a small bowl beat the egg yolk with 1 tsp. water. Brush the outer edges of each dough square with egg wash. Spoon 2 rounded Tbs. of the filling into the center of each square. Bring the points together into a triangular shape, pressing to seal the edges. Brush the tops with egg wash and sprinkle with ½ tsp. granulated sugar. With a paring knife, cut a steam vent in the center of the top crust of each turnover.

3. Bake until the turnovers are browned and the filling is bubbling, 25 to 30 minutes, swapping and rotating the baking sheets' positions about halfway through baking. (Don't worry if juice leaks out.)

4. Transfer the baking sheets to racks and cool for 5 minutes. Loosen the turnovers with an offset spatula and cool completely on the sheets. The turnovers are best the day they're made. —*Karen Barker*

PER SERVING: 350 CALORIES | 4G PROTEIN | 38G CARB | 21G TOTAL FAT | 13G SAT FAT | 5G MONO FAT | 1G POLY FAT | 75MG CHOL | 125MG SODIUM | 2G FIBER

rustic fig and
raspberry mini crostatas

MAKES 10 CROSTATAS

FOR THE DOUGH

7½ oz. (1⅔ cups) unbleached all-purpose flour

3¾ oz. (¾ cup) whole-wheat flour

¼ cup plus ½ Tbs. granulated sugar

1 tsp. ground cinnamon

½ tsp. kosher salt

9 oz. (1 cup plus 2 Tbs.) chilled unsalted butter, cut into small pieces

3 Tbs. cold water

FOR THE FILLING

12 oz. small fresh figs (preferably Brown Turkey), quartered (about 2 cups)

6 oz. fresh raspberries (1½ cups), rinsed, picked over, and drained

⅓ cup plus 2 Tbs. granulated sugar

3 Tbs. plus 1 tsp. honey

1 Tbs. fresh thyme, coarsely chopped

2 tsp. finely grated orange zest

3 Tbs. plus 1 tsp. graham cracker crumbs

1 oz. (2 Tbs.) chilled unsalted butter, cut into 10 thin slices

1½ Tbs. heavy cream

An inspired combination of figs, raspberries, fresh thyme, orange zest, and honey makes these Italian-style pies an unexpected change from the familiar.

MAKE THE DOUGH

1. Put the flours, sugar, cinnamon, and salt in a food processor. Add the butter and pulse in short bursts until the mixture resembles coarse meal. Add 3 Tbs. cold water and pulse. If the mixture seems dry, add water 1 Tbs. at a time, pulsing until the dough just starts to come together. Do not overprocess. Turn the dough out onto a clean work surface, gather it together, and portion it into ten 2½-oz. rounds. Flatten them into disks, wrap individually in plastic, and refrigerate for at least 2 hours and up to 3 days.

2. When ready to bake, position racks in the bottom and top thirds of the oven and heat the oven to 400°F. Line two large rimmed baking sheets with parchment.

3. On a lightly floured surface with a lightly floured rolling pin, roll each dough disk into a 5 ½-inch round that's about ⅛ inch thick. Put five rounds on each baking sheet.

MAKE THE FILLING

In a medium bowl, lightly toss the figs, raspberries, ⅓ cup of the sugar, the honey, thyme, and orange zest until combined.

ASSEMBLE AND BAKE THE CROSTATAS

1. Sprinkle each round of dough with 1 tsp. graham cracker crumbs, leaving a ½-inch border. Put a generous ¼ cup of the fig mixture in the center of each dough round, mounding the fruit. Top each tart with a butter slice.

2. Fold the edges of the dough over some of the fruit to create a 1-inch rim, leaving the center exposed. Work your way around, pleating the dough as you go. With a pastry brush, brush the crust of each crostata with cream and sprinkle the crusts and filling with the remaining 2 Tbs. sugar.

3. Bake until the crostatas are golden brown, 30 to 35 minutes, swapping and rotating the baking sheets' positions about halfway through baking.

4. Transfer the baking sheets to racks to cool for about 5 minutes. Then loosen the crostatas with an offset spatula and cool completely on the sheets. The crostatas are best the day they're made.
—Karen Barker

PER SERVING: 450 CALORIES | 5G PROTEIN | 55G CARB | 25G TOTAL FAT | 15G SAT FAT | 6G MONO FAT | 1G POLY FAT | 65MG CHOL | 75MG SODIUM | 4G FIBER

fried peach pies

FOR THE DOUGH

11¼	oz. (2½ cups) unbleached all-purpose flour
2½	tsp. granulated sugar
¾	tsp. kosher salt
4½	oz. (9 Tbs.) chilled unsalted butter, cut into 16 pieces
¼	cup plus 3 Tbs. whole milk
1	tsp. fresh lemon juice

FOR THE FILLING

1	lb. 2 oz. firm-ripe peaches (2 large), peeled, pitted, and cut into ½-inch dice (2½ cups)
1⅓	cups granulated sugar
2	tsp. fresh lemon juice
⅛	tsp. kosher salt
½	Tbs. cornstarch
1½	Tbs. hot pepper jelly
1⅛	tsp. ground cinnamon
	Pinch plus ⅛ tsp. cayenne
	Peanut or canola oil, for frying

Fried hand pies are a southern tradition; this one makes the most of summer peaches.

MAKE THE DOUGH

1. Put the flour, sugar, and salt in a food processor. Add the butter and pulse until the mixture resembles coarse meal, 8 to 10 pulses. Add the milk and lemon juice and pulse until the dough just starts to come together, 8 to 10 pulses more. Do not overprocess. Turn the dough out onto a clean work surface, gather it into a rectangle, and flatten slightly. Wrap it in plastic and refrigerate for at least 2 hours and up to 3 days.

2. Line a rimmed baking sheet with parchment. On a lightly floured surface with a lightly floured rolling pin, roll out the dough until it's ⅛ inch thick. Cut the dough with a 4-inch round cookie cutter into 12 circles. (If necessary, gather the scraps and reroll once.) Shingle the dough on the prepared baking sheet. Refrigerate.

MAKE THE FILLING

1. Prepare an ice bath by filling a large bowl with several inches of ice water. Set a smaller metal bowl in the water.

2. In a heavy-based 3-quart saucepan, combine the peaches with ⅓ cup of the sugar, the lemon juice, and salt. Cook over medium-low heat until the peaches have softened and released some of their juices, about 5 minutes.

3. In a small bowl, combine the cornstarch with 1 Tbs. cold water. Add the slurry to the peach mixture and cook over medium-low heat until thickened, about 1 minute. Add the hot pepper jelly, ⅛ tsp. cinnamon, and a pinch of cayenne. Remove from the heat and stir to blend. Transfer the mixture to the bowl in the ice bath and cool.

ASSEMBLE THE PIES

Brush the perimeter of each dough round with water. Put a rounded tablespoon of filling in the center of each round. Fold the dough in half to form a half-moon shape and pinch the edges together to seal. Refrigerate, covered, for at least 15 minutes and up to 24 hours before frying.

FRY THE PIES

1. Combine the remaining 1 cup sugar, 1 tsp. cinnamon, and ⅛ tsp. cayenne in a shallow bowl and reserve.

2. Have ready a large rimmed baking sheet lined with paper towels. Fill a 10-inch skillet (preferably cast iron) with ½ inch of oil. Clip a candy thermometer to the side of the pan, making sure it doesn't touch the bottom. Heat the oil to 365°F and fry the pies in two batches until golden brown, 1 to 1½ minutes per side. With a slotted spoon, remove the pies from the pan, drain on the paper-towel-lined baking sheet, and then dredge in the cinnamon-sugar. Serve warm or at room temperature. These pies are best the day they're made. —*Karen Barker*

PER SERVING: 270 CALORIES | 3G PROTEIN | 47G CARB | 9G TOTAL FAT | 5G SAT FAT | 2.5G MONO FAT | 1G POLY FAT | 20MG CHOL | 75MG SODIUM | 1G FIBER

The lemon juice in the pastry helps produce a flaky, tender crust. Gluten, responsible for tough pastry, develops when flour is combined with liquids. The addition of an acid inhibits this process.

More about Peaches

During the last weeks of June, white peaches and the early yellow varieties arrive in stores. These first peaches of the season are low in acid and have a clear, sweet taste that makes them perfect for eating out of hand, but bakers should wait a month or so before they start rolling out their pie dough. Later varieties have a higher acid-to-sugar ratio, which gives the fruit more depth and complexity. Mid- to late-season peaches can stand up to stronger accompanying flavors and are the best choice for baking and using in desserts. In mid-August, start looking for the dark-fleshed Indian or blood peaches. Though usually smaller and not as juicy as their summer cousins, these peaches have a rich, almost berry-like flavor that's unsurpassed for cooking.

All peaches are classified as either freestone or cling. The flesh of a cling peach clutches at the stone of the fruit, while freestone varieties relinquish their seed more readily. You'll rarely find cling peaches at the market: Their firm flesh holds up well when cooked and is prized by commercial canners. The peaches you find at the grocery or farmers' market are almost always freestones.

Peach varieties are myriad and fleeting. Each variety in a geographic zone has a 2-week window, more or less, in the market. Depending on where you live, you'll find peaches with names like Red Haven, Elberta, O'Henry, Georgia Belle, and Sun Crest. Learn the names of your local varieties, if you can.

Choosing

A perfectly ripe peach should be firm and feel heavy in the palm of your hand. Look for the golden or creamy background color of the skin at the stem end of the peach. Don't be duped by a provocative blush color (varieties are being developed that are nearly 90 percent blush). The background color of the skin is all-important.

Size is crucial, too. Bigger is better when it comes to peaches. Bigger peaches seem to be sweeter and more fully developed in flavor. Sniff the peach you're considering: You can smell the nectar in a riper peach.

Prepping

When preparing peaches for cooking, remove the skin while keeping as much flesh as possible. The best way to do this is to quickly blanch peaches before you peel them. To blanch, bring a large pot of water to a boil. While the water heats, cut an X into the bottom of each peach. Drop the peaches into the boiling water and cook just until the skin begins to loosen, 30 to 60 seconds. Drain the peaches and then plunge into cold water to stop them from cooking further. The peel should slip off.

To slice a peach, run a small knife from stem to tip, cutting right through to the pit. Turn the peach in your hand, making one cut after another, and let the slices fall into a bowl. Once exposed to the air, peach flesh tends to turn brown quickly. To keep the color bright, sprinkle the slices with a bit of lemon juice.

Storing

Supermarket peaches are smaller, picked greener, and stored longer than those found at farmers' markets. But if imperfect peaches may be all that's available, you can ripen peaches in a brown paper bag or a ripening bowl.

If you've picked firm, ripe fruit with good background color at the stem end, the peaches will soften in 3 or 4 days. They'll keep in the refrigerator for a couple of days longer. Don't wash peaches until you're ready to use them or they're likely to develop mold.

blackberry-peach cobbler with buttermilk biscuits

SERVES 6 TO 8

FOR THE TOPPING

- 2   Tbs. turbinado (raw) sugar
- 2   tsp. finely grated orange zest
- 4½ oz. (1 cup) unbleached all-purpose flour
- ⅓   cup granulated sugar
- 2   tsp. baking powder
- ½   tsp. table salt
- 2½ oz. (5 Tbs.) chilled unsalted butter, cut into 5 pieces
- ⅓   cup finely ground cornmeal
- ½   cup buttermilk
- 1   tsp. pure vanilla extract

FOR THE FILLING

- 1   oz. (2 Tbs.) unsalted butter
- ½   cup granulated sugar
- 1   Tbs. cornstarch
- ½   tsp. ground cardamom
-     Pinch of table salt
- ¼   cup fresh orange juice
- 2   lb. ripe peaches, halved, pitted, and cut into 1-inch-thick slices
- 2   cups blackberries, rinsed, picked over, and drained

Use a nonreactive skillet, such as stainless steel or enamel-lined cast iron, for this cobbler. Because cast iron is a reactive, porous cooking surface, it can lend a metallic taste to the finished cobbler and can even discolor lighter-colored fruit.

The secret to this cobbler's bright flavor is fresh orange juice in the filling and orange-scented sugar on the biscuit topping. Use a light hand when mixing the biscuit dough, or the topping will be tough.

Position a rack in the center of the oven and heat the oven to 375°F.

MAKE THE TOPPING

1. In a small ramekin, mix the turbinado sugar and the orange zest until blended and set aside.

2. In a food processor, combine the flour, sugar, baking powder, and salt. Pulse briefly to blend, about 10 seconds. Add the butter pieces and pulse until they are the size of small peas, 8 to 10 one-second pulses.

3. Transfer the mixture to a medium bowl. Stir in the cornmeal with a spatula. Gently stir in the buttermilk and vanilla until the dough is evenly moistened and begins to form large, soft clumps; don't over-mix or the biscuits will be tough. Refrigerate.

MAKE THE FILLING

1. Melt the butter in a 10-inch nonreactive, ovenproof skillet (8- to 10-cup capacity) over medium-low heat. Add the sugar, cornstarch, cardamom, and salt and cook, stirring, until the sugar begins to melt, about 2 minutes. Whisking constantly, add the orange juice and bring to a boil.

2. Add the peaches and cook, stirring gently, until just barely tender, about 3 minutes. Add the blackberries and gently toss until the berries are hot, about 1 minute. Remove from the heat.

ASSEMBLE AND BAKE

1. Spread the fruit into a relatively even layer. Using a 3-Tbs. scoop or a soupspoon, drop the topping in about eight mounds onto the filling, leaving space between them. With your fingers, distribute the orange-sugar evenly over the biscuits.

2. Bake until the filling is bubbling and a toothpick inserted in a biscuit comes out clean, 25 to 30 minutes. Let sit for about 5 minutes to allow the filling to settle and thicken before serving.

—Abigail Johnson Dodge

PER SERVING: 330 CALORIES | 4G PROTEIN | 56G CARB | 11G TOTAL FAT | 7G SAT FAT | 3G MONO FAT | 0.5G POLY FAT | 25MG CHOL | 390MG SODIUM | 4G FIBER

classic tarte tatin

SERVES 6

FOR THE DOUGH

5⅝ oz. (1¼ cups) unbleached all-purpose flour

1 tsp. granulated sugar

¾ tsp. fine sea salt

3 oz. (6 Tbs.) chilled unsalted butter, cut into ½-inch pieces

1 large egg beaten with 1 Tbs. cold water

FOR THE TART

5 to 7 firm Granny Smith apples

4 oz. (½ cup) unsalted butter

¾ cup granulated sugar

Crème fraîche, for serving (optional)

A heavy-duty ovenproof skillet works best for this recipe; avoid using cast iron, which tends to get too hot and burn the apples.

MAKE THE DOUGH

1. Put the flour, sugar, and salt in a food processor and pulse a few times to mix. Add the butter and pulse until coarsely mixed into the flour. Add the egg mixture in three additions, pulsing after each. Continue pulsing until you have a soft, shaggy dough that holds together when pinched.

2. Turn the dough out onto a work surface and gather it into a ball. Wrap in plastic and refrigerate for about 1 hour.

3. Between two pieces of waxed paper or parchment, roll the dough into a circle that's about ⅛ inch thick and 11 inches wide. Prick the dough all over with a fork, then cover and refrigerate. (The dough can be refrigerated overnight or frozen for up to 2 months.)

PREPARE THE APPLES

1. Peel, core, and quarter 4 of the apples.

2. Put the butter in a heavy-based 10-inch ovenproof skillet over medium heat. When melted, use a pastry brush to coat the sides of the skillet with butter. Cover the butter with the sugar and cook just until the sugar is evenly moistened, about 1 minute. Remove the pan from the heat.

3. Lay the apple wedges in the skillet with their rounded sides down or against the side of the skillet. Build concentric circles, packing the apples in a snug single layer—it's fine if there are gaps. Peel, core, and quarter as many of the remaining apples as you need to fill in any gaps. If necessary, cut the pieces smaller to make it easier to wedge them in. The gap-filling pieces of apple will form a haphazard second layer, but they'll shrink as they cook, and you'll be able to nudge the pieces into the newly widening gaps.

4. Put the pan over medium to medium-high heat and cook until the apples begin to bubble, about 2 minutes. Continue cooking until the apple juices are mostly boiled away and the caramel is a deep golden color, 15 to 20 minutes. Adjust the heat and reposition the skillet as needed for even cooking. The heat shouldn't be too low (the apples will get mushy) or too high (you'll burn the caramel). As the apples shrink, gently nudge the top layer of apples into the gaps.

5. While the apples cook, position a rack in the center of the oven and heat the oven to 375°F. Line a rimmed baking sheet with foil.

6. When the apples are done, transfer the skillet to the baking sheet and let it sit for a few minutes so the caramel can settle down. Meanwhile, let the dough sit at room temperature until pliable.

BAKE THE TARTE TATIN

1. Place the dough on top of the fruit and tuck in the overhang. Bake until the pastry is golden, 25 to 20 minutes. Let the tart rest on the baking sheet until the bubbling caramel quiets down, 3 to 5 minutes. Gently run a table knife around the edges of the pan to loosen any apples stuck to the sides.

2. Cover the skillet with a large serving platter—preferably one with a rim—and cover your hands with oven mitts. Carefully invert the tart onto the platter and remove the skillet. If some apples have stuck to the pan, use the table knife to lift them off and gently press them back onto the tart.

3. Let the tart cool for at least 15 minutes before cutting it into wedges. Serve with crème fraîche on the side, if using. While the tart is best warm, it can also be served at room temperature. —*Dorie Greenspan*

PER SERVING: 510 CALORIES | 4G PROTEIN | 63G CARB | 28G TOTAL FAT | 17G SAT FAT | 7G MONO FAT | 1.5G POLY FAT | 105MG CHOL | 310MG SODIUM | 2G FIBER

plum cobbler with honey and lavender biscuits

SERVES 6 TO 8

FOR THE TOPPING

- 6 oz. (1⅓ cups) unbleached all-purpose flour
- ⅓ cup granulated sugar
- 1¾ tsp. baking powder
- ¼ tsp. table salt
- 3 oz. (6 Tbs.) chilled unsalted butter, cut into 5 pieces
- 1 tsp. chopped dried lavender
- ½ tsp. finely grated lemon zest
- 7 Tbs. heavy cream

FOR THE FILLING

- ⅔ cup mild honey (such as clover)
- 1 tsp. chopped dried lavender
- 2½ lb. ripe plums (about 12), halved and pitted, each half cut into 3 wedges
- 1 Tbs. cornstarch
- Pinch of table salt

The tender biscuits that top this skillet cobbler come together in a food processor in minutes. Use a mild honey in the filling so it doesn't overpower the plums.

Position a rack in the center of the oven and heat the oven to 375°F.

MAKE THE TOPPING

1. In a food processor, combine the flour, sugar, baking powder, and salt. Pulse briefly to blend. Add the cold butter and pulse into ½-inch pieces, 5 to 7 pulses. Add the lavender and lemon zest and pulse briefly to combine. Pour the cream over the top and pulse just until moist crumbs form, 8 to 10 pulses.

2. Turn the mixture out onto a work surface and gently knead until the dough comes together. Lightly flour the dough and roll it into a 5x9-inch rectangle. Cut the rectangle in half lengthwise, and cut each half into four equal pieces. Wrap in plastic and refrigerate. (The dough may be made up to 6 hours ahead.)

MAKE THE FILLING

1. Put the honey and lavender in a 10-inch nonreactive, ovenproof skillet (8- to 10-cup capacity). Bring to a boil over medium-low heat.

2. In a large bowl, toss the plums with the cornstarch and salt until evenly coated. Add to the boiling honey mixture and cook, stirring gently, until the plums release some juice and the sauce has thickened, about 6 minutes. Remove from the heat.

ASSEMBLE AND BAKE

Spread the fruit into a relatively even layer. Arrange the dough pieces on top of the fruit, leaving spaces between them. Bake until the filling is bubbling and the topping is nicely browned, 30 to 40 minutes. Let sit for about 15 minutes to allow the filling to settle and thicken before serving. —*Abigail Johnson Dodge*

PER SERVING: 380 CALORIES | 4G PROTEIN | 64G CARB | 14G TOTAL FAT | 9G SAT FAT | 4G MONO FAT | 0.5G POLY FAT | 40MG CHOL | 190MG SODIUM | 3G FIBER

> **Use dried, edible organic lavender to make this biscuit topping (not the lavender used to make scented sachets). It can be found at Whole Foods Market℠, natural food stores, and specialty markets.**

lattice-topped mixed berry pie

MAKES ONE 9-INCH PIE

FOR THE CRUST

6	oz. (¾ cup) chilled unsalted butter
6½	oz. (1½ cups) unbleached all-purpose flour
3½	oz. (¾ cup) cake flour
¼	tsp. table salt
¼	tsp. baking powder
4½	oz. (½ cup plus 1 Tbs.) chilled cream cheese
3	Tbs. heavy cream
1	Tbs. cider vinegar

FOR THE FILLING

1½	cups blueberries, rinsed, picked over, and dried well
1½	cups raspberries, rinsed, picked over, and dried well
1	cup blackberries, rinsed, picked over, and dried well
½	to 1 cup granulated sugar (depending on desired sweetness)
¼	cup unbleached all-purpose flour
1	Tbs. fresh lemon juice
	Pinch of freshly grated nutmeg
	Pinch of salt

FOR THE GLAZE

2	Tbs. whole milk
1	Tbs. turbinado or granulated sugar

The technique for "prefabbing" the lattice top (made off the pie and then added on and trimmed before baking) makes the cream cheese pie dough easier to work with.

MAKE THE DOUGH

1. Cut the butter into ¾-inch cubes. Wrap them in plastic and freeze until hard, at least 30 minutes. Put the all-purpose flour, cake flour, salt, and baking powder in a metal bowl and freeze for at least 30 minutes.

2. Put the cold flour mixture in a food processor and process for a few seconds to combine.

3. Cut the cold cream cheese into three or four pieces and add it to the flour mixture. Process for 20 seconds (the mixture should resemble fine meal). Add the frozen butter cubes and pulse until none of the butter pieces is larger than a pea, about five 3-second pulses. (Toss with a fork to see it better.)

4. Add the cream and vinegar and pulse in short bursts until the dough starts to come together (which will take a minute or two); the dough will still look crumbly but if you press it between your fingers, it should become smooth. Turn it out onto a clean work surface. Gather and press the dough together to form a unified mass.

5. Cut the dough in half and put each half on a large piece of plastic wrap. Loosely cover the dough with the plastic. Using the wrap as an aid (to avoid warming the dough with your bare hands), shape half of the dough into a flat disk and the other into a flat rectangle. Wrap each tightly in the plastic and refrigerate for at least 45 minutes and up to 24 hours.

MAKE THE LATTICE TOP

1. Remove the rectangle of dough from the refrigerator; if it's very firm, let it sit at room temperature until it's pliable enough to roll, 10 to 15 minutes. Roll it out between two sheets of parchment to a rectangle slightly larger than 9x14 inches. Remove the top sheet of parchment. Trim the dough to an exact 9x14-inch rectangle. Cut 12 strips that are 14 inches long and ¾ inches wide. If the dough gets soft, slide the parchment and dough onto a baking sheet and chill briefly before continuing.

2. On a parchment-lined baking sheet, arrange 6 strips horizontally, setting them ¾ inch apart; these will be the "bottom" strips (the other 6 will be your "top" strips). Fold back every other bottom strip halfway, starting with the strip closest to you. Lay one top strip vertically, slightly right of center.

continued on p. 68

continued from p. 66

3. Unfold the folded strips and fold back the other three strips. Lay a second top strip ¾ inch to the left of the first. Now fold back alternating strips on the right, starting at the top. Lay another top strip ¾ inch to the right of the center strip; unfold the folded strips. Repeat left and right with the rest of the strips.

4. Dab a little water between the strips where they overlap, pressing gently to seal. Cover the lattice loosely with plastic and put the baking sheet in the fridge while you make your filling and roll out the bottom crust.

ASSEMBLE THE PIE

1. Remove the disk of dough from the fridge; if it's very firm, let it sit at room temperature until it's pliable enough to roll, 10 to 15 minutes.

2. Toss all the filling ingredients together in a large bowl until well blended.

3. Set the dough between two sheets of parchment. Roll it out to a 13-inch round that's ⅛ inch thick, occasionally loosening and reapplying the parchment.

4. Remove one piece of parchment and flip the dough into a standard 9-inch glass pie pan (it should be 1¼ inches deep and hold 4 cups of liquid). Fit the dough into the pan and carefully peel off the plastic. Trim the dough so there's a ¾-inch overhang. Fold the overhang underneath itself to create an edge that extends about ¼ inch beyond the rim of the pie pan.

5. Pile the filling into the bottom crust. Remove the lattice top from the fridge and put your palm under the parchment at the center of the lattice. Lift the paper and invert the lattice onto the filling.

6. Trim the crust, leaving a ½-inch margin from the edge of the pie plate. Press the edges together, fold them under, and use your thumb and index fingers to pinch-crimp a fluted edge.

BAKE THE PIE

1. Lightly cover the assembled pie with plastic wrap and refrigerate for 1 hour. After 30 minutes of chilling, set an oven rack on the lowest rung and put a foil-lined baking stone or baking sheet on it. Heat the oven to 425°F.

2. When the pie has chilled for 1 hour, brush the lattice with the milk and sprinkle on the sugar.

3. Set the pie directly on the baking stone or sheet. Bake until the juices are bubbling all over (the bubbles should be thick and slow near the pan edges), 40 to 50 minutes. After the first 15 minutes, cover the rim with foil or a pie shield. If the lattice starts to darken too much in the last 10 minutes of baking, cover it loosely with a piece of foil that has a vent hole poked in the center.

4. Let the pie cool on a rack until the juices have thickened, 3 hours.
—Abigail Johnson Dodge

blackberry grunt

SERVES 6

FOR THE BERRIES

- 6 cups blackberries, rinsed, picked over, and drained
- ¾ cup granulated sugar
- 1 Tbs. grated lemon zest

FOR THE DUMPLING DOUGH

- 4½ oz. (1 cup) unbleached all-purpose flour
- 2 Tbs. granulated sugar
- 1 tsp. baking powder
- ½ tsp. baking soda
- ⅛ tsp. salt
- 2 Tbs. unsalted butter, melted
- ½ cup buttermilk; more as needed
- 1 Tbs. granulated sugar mixed with ½ tsp. ground cinnamon

  Vanilla ice cream, for garnish (optional)

This old-fashioned dessert is essentially a stovetop cobbler; it's called a grunt supposedly because of the sound the berries make as they simmer. You can substitute blueberries for the blackberries, if you like.

1. In a deep 10-inch skillet that has a tight-fitting lid, combine the berries, sugar, ⅓ cup water, and zest.

2. In a bowl, stir together the flour, sugar, baking powder, baking soda, and salt. Stir in the melted butter. Add enough of the buttermilk to form a soft, sticky dough that's slightly wetter than a biscuit dough.

3. Meanwhile, bring the berry mixture to a boil over high heat, stirring once or twice. Reduce to a simmer and, using a soupspoon, spoon the dough over the fruit, creating about 8 small dumplings. Sprinkle the dumplings with the cinnamon-sugar mixture. Cover the skillet tightly with the lid or foil and steam over medium-low heat, without uncovering, until the dumplings are set and the surface is dry when touched with a fingertip, about 15 minutes. (If you're not sure if the dumplings are done, you can gently break one open with a fork.) Try not to remove the lid (which would let steam escape) before 15 minutes, and if the dumplings need further cooking, quickly return the lid. Serve immediately, spooning the warm grunt (it will be fairly liquid) into small bowls. Garnish with vanilla ice cream, if you like. —*John Ash*

PER SERVING: 320 CALORIES | 4G PROTEIN | 67G CARB | 5G TOTAL FAT | 3G SAT FAT | 1G MONO FAT | 1G POLY FAT | 10MG CHOL | 10MG SODIUM | 8G FIBER

apple–brown butter jalousie

MAKES ONE 6X14-INCH
PASTRY; SERVES 8

1¼ to 1½ lb. Granny Smith
    apples (about 3 medium),
    peeled, halved lengthwise,
    cored, and cut crosswise into
    ½-inch-thick slices

¼   cup packed light or dark
    brown sugar

3   Tbs. granulated sugar

1   tsp. fresh lemon juice

¾   tsp. ground cinnamon

¼   tsp. kosher salt

    Pinch freshly grated
    nutmeg

3   Tbs. unsalted butter

1   vanilla bean, split and seeds
    scraped out with the back of
    a knife (reserve the seeds)

1   large egg

1   sheet frozen packaged puff
    pastry (Pepperidge Farm®
    brand), thawed overnight
    in the fridge or according to
    package instructions

    Flour, for rolling out the
    dough

1   tsp. demerara, turbinado, or
    granulated sugar

    Crème fraîche, lightly sweet-
    ened whipped cream, or
    vanilla ice cream, for serving
    (optional)

For this pastry, the fruit filling shouldn't be very juicy or the bottom crust will become soggy. The solution is to precook the apples and reduce their juices. The filling can be made and stored in a covered container in the refrigerator for up to 2 days.

MAKE THE FILLING

1. In a large bowl, toss the apples with the brown sugar, granulated sugar, lemon juice, cinnamon, salt, and nutmeg.

2. In a 12-inch skillet, melt the butter over medium heat until the milk solids turn golden brown, 1 to 2 minutes. Remove from the heat, add the vanilla seeds, and stir. Carefully add the apple mixture to the skillet; with a heatproof rubber spatula, scrape all the sugar and spices from the bowl into the skillet. Stir the apples to coat them with the butter and then spread them in a fairly even layer. Return the pan to medium heat and cook, stirring gently with the spatula every few minutes (try not to break the apple slices), until the apples are tender but not mushy (taste one) and still hold their shape, and the juices have cooked down to a fairly thick, brown, bubbling syrup, 10 to 13 minutes. Scrape the apples into a wide shallow dish or onto a baking sheet to cool completely before assembling the jalousie.

ASSEMBLE THE JALOUSIE

1. Line a large rimmed baking sheet with parchment. In a small bowl, make an egg wash by beating the egg with 1 Tbs. water until well combined.

2. Unfold the puff pastry dough on a floured surface, and gently pinch together any seams that have split. With a floured rolling pin, roll the dough into a 12x14-inch rectangle. With a sharp knife, cut the rectangle in half lengthwise to form two 6x14-inch rectangles. Use a long spatula to help you move one of the dough rectangles onto the parchment-lined baking sheet.

3. Use a pastry brush to brush a 1-inch border of egg wash around the perimeter of the dough. (Save the remaining egg wash.) Arrange the fruit in a 4-inch-wide strip down the length of the dough. (I like to shingle the apple slices in a thick herringbone pattern down the length of the dough; you may need to make a double layer of apples.) Some syrupy apple juices will likely remain in the dish; spoon 2 to 3 Tbs. over the apples. If some of the liquid seeps onto the egg-washed border, don't worry about it.

4. Lightly dust the remaining piece of puff pastry with flour and then gently fold it in half lengthwise; don't crease the fold. Using a sharp knife, cut 1½-inch-long slashes at 1-inch intervals along the folded side of the dough; leave at least a 1-inch border on the remaining

continued on p. 72

continued from p. 71

Make Ahead

The jalousie is best served the day it's made, but it will keep, wrapped well in aluminum foil, for 3 days. You can reheat it in a 325°F oven for 5 minutes before serving.

three sides. Do not unfold the dough. Using a long spatula, gently lift the folded strip and position it over the fruit-filled dough rectangle, matching up the straight edges.

5. Gently unfold the top piece of dough and stretch it over the filling, matching the straight edges all the way around the perimeter of the dough. Press the edges gently with your fingertips to seal the dough, and then, with a fork, very gently crimp the edges of the dough all the way around the pastry.

BAKE THE JALOUSIE

1. Chill the assembled jalousie for 15 to 20 minutes. Meanwhile, position a rack in the lower third of the oven and heat the oven to 400°F.

2. Right before baking, brush the top of the jalousie with a very light coating of the remaining egg wash (you won't need it all) and sprinkle with the demerara, turbinado, or granulated sugar.

3. Bake for 15 minutes and then rotate the baking sheet. Continue baking until the pastry is puffed, deep golden brown on top and light golden brown on the bottom—use a spatula to gently lift the jalousie so you can peek underneath—another 10 to 15 minutes. Immediately transfer the jalousie from the baking sheet to a wire rack to cool for at least 45 minutes. (Instead of trying to move the hot jalousie with a spatula, lift the parchment to move the jalousie to the rack and then carefully slide the paper out from under the pastry.)

4. Serve the jalousie slightly warm with crème fraîche, lightly sweetened whipped cream, or vanilla ice cream, if you like. —*Kim Masibay*

PER SERVING: 250 CALORIES | 3G PROTEIN | 30G CARB | 13G TOTAL FAT | 5G SAT FAT | 6G MONO FAT | 1G POLY FAT | 25MG CHOL | 190MG SODIUM | 1G FIBER

how to make a jalousie

Cut the large dough rectangle in half lengthwise.

Arrange the fruit in a strip down the length of one dough half.

Slash along the folded side of the other dough half.

Unfold the dough over the filling.

rustic apple-cinnamon tart

MAKES 1 LARGE TART; SERVES 8

FOR THE DOUGH

6¾ oz. (1½ cups) unbleached all-purpose flour

2 tsp. granulated sugar

½ tsp. table salt

5½ oz. (11 Tbs.) chilled, unsalted butter

1 large egg yolk

3 Tbs. whole milk

FOR THE FILLING

4 cups peeled, thinly sliced apples

¼ cup granulated sugar; more as needed

1 Tbs. unbleached all-purpose flour

1 tsp. pure vanilla extract

½ tsp. ground cinnamon

Big pinch of table salt

1 large egg, beaten well

2 Tbs. turbinado sugar

When you don't want to fuss with a pie, this freeform tart baked on a baking sheet is the perfect solution. Feel free to use pears instead of apples.

MAKE AND ROLL THE DOUGH

1. Combine the flour, sugar, and salt in a stand mixer fitted with a paddle attachment (or if mixing by hand, in a medium bowl). Cut the butter into ½-inch cubes and add them to the flour. On low speed, mix the butter and flour until the flour is no longer white and holds together when you clump it with your fingers, 1 to 2 minutes. If there are still lumps of butter larger than the size of peas, break them up with your fingers. Run a spatula along the bottom of the bowl to loosen anything stuck to the bowl. (If mixing by hand, mix with a pastry cutter or two forks until the butter is mixed into the flour as above.)

2. In a small bowl, mix the egg yolk and milk and add them to the flour mixture. On low speed, mix until the dough just comes together, about 15 seconds; the dough will be somewhat soft. (If mixing by hand, add the yolk mixture to the flour and mix gently with a fork until the liquid is well distributed.) The dough will still look crumbly and dry. Dump the dough onto a clean counter and work it with the heel of your hand, pushing and smearing it away from you and gathering it up with a bench scraper and repeating until the dough comes together and is pliable.

3. Turn the dough out onto a sheet of plastic wrap, press it into a flat disk, wrap it in the plastic, and let it rest in the refrigerator for 15 to 20 minutes (or up to 4 days) before rolling it out.

4. Position a rack in the center of the oven and heat the oven to 350°F. Line a heavy-duty rimmed baking sheet with parchment. Remove the dough from the refrigerator; if the dough is very firm, let it sit at room temperature until it's pliable enough to roll, 10 to 15 minutes. On a floured surface, roll the dough into a round that's 13 to 14 inches in diameter. It's all right if the edges are a little ragged. If you can't get a roughly round shape, trim the dough so that it's a rough circle and roll the trimmed scraps back into the dough. Transfer the dough round to the baking sheet and put it in the refrigerator while you prepare the filling.

continued on p. 74

continued from p. 73

ASSEMBLE AND BAKE THE TART

1. Put the apples in a large bowl. Toss the fruit with the ¼ cup granulated sugar. Taste the fruit; if it's more tart than you like, add up to 2 Tbs. more sugar. Add the flour, vanilla, cinnamon, and salt and toss until everything is evenly mixed.

2. Remove the dough from the refrigerator and let it sit at room temperature for about 5 minutes to keep it from cracking when you assemble the tart. Heap the apple mixture in the center of the dough round. Using your fingertips, fold the edges of the dough over some of the apples to create a rim about 2 inches wide. Work your way all around, pleating the dough as you go.

3. Using a pastry brush, brush the pleated dough evenly with the beaten egg. Sprinkle the turbinado sugar directly on the dough and fruit.

4. Bake the tart until the pleats of dough are completely golden brown without a trace of pale, unbaked dough, about 55 minutes. (It's all right if some of the juices escape from the tart and seep onto the pan.) Transfer to a rack and let cool. The tart may be baked up to 6 hours ahead of serving.

5. When cool enough to handle, use a spatula to transfer the tart to a serving plate or cutting board. Slice it and serve it warm or at room temperature. *—Joanne Chang*

PER SERVING: 315 CALORIES | 4G PROTEIN | 38G CARB | 17G TOTAL FAT | 10G SAT FAT | 5G MONO FAT | 1G POLY FAT | 81MG CHOL | 192MG SODIUM | 2G FIBER

pineapple-ginger brown sugar crisp

½ cup packed dark brown sugar

2¼ oz. (½ cup) unbleached all-purpose flour

¼ cup old-fashioned rolled oats (not quick-cooking or instant)

2 oz. (4 Tbs.) unsalted butter, cut into ¼-inch pieces

Pinch of freshly grated nutmeg

Kosher salt

1 large pineapple (about 4¼ lb.), peeled, cored, cut lengthwise into eighths, then crosswise into ½-inch pieces

1 Tbs. fresh lime juice

1 Tbs. finely grated fresh ginger

1 Tbs. cornstarch

Fruit crisps usually showcase apples or stone fruit, but they're just as good, if not better, made with pineapple. As it bakes, the pineapple releases much of its moisture, so the crisp comes out extra juicy and full of sweet-tart flavor. Serve with vanilla ice cream.

1. Position a rack in the center of the oven and heat the oven to 375°F.

2. Combine the brown sugar, flour, oats, butter, nutmeg, and ⅛ tsp. salt in a medium bowl. Using your fingers, rub in the butter until it's about the size of small peas and the mixture resembles coarse, crumbly breadcrumbs; it should hold together when squeezed. Refrigerate, uncovered, while you make the filling.

3. Put the pineapple in a large bowl. In a small bowl, combine the lime juice, ginger, and a pinch of salt and whisk to blend. Stir the lime mixture into the pineapple. Sprinkle the cornstarch over the pineapple and stir again.

4. Transfer the pineapple to a 9x9-inch baking dish and sprinkle the crumb mixture evenly over the top. Cover with foil and bake for 20 minutes. Remove the foil and continue to bake until the fruit is bubbling around the edges and the top is golden brown and crisp, about 15 minutes more. Let cool for at least 15 minutes before serving.

—Dabney Gough

PER SERVING: 210 CALORIES | 2G PROTEIN | 40G CARB | 6G TOTAL FAT | 3.5G SAT FAT | 1.5G MONO FAT | 0G POLY FAT | 15MG CHOL | 25MG SODIUM | 2G FIBER

pluot-blueberry skillet cobbler
with coconut dumplings

SERVES 6 TO 8

FOR THE TOPPING

1	13.5- to 14-oz. can coconut milk
9	oz. (2 cups) unbleached all-purpose flour
½	cup granulated sugar
1½	tsp. baking powder
½	tsp. table salt
1	large egg
1	large egg yolk
4	oz. (½ cup) unsalted butter, melted and cooled slightly

FOR THE FILLING

2¼	lb. ripe pluots, halved and pitted, each half cut into 3 wedges
¾	cup granulated sugar
2½	Tbs. cornstarch
¼	tsp. table salt
1	oz. (2 Tbs.) unsalted butter
2	cups blueberries, rinsed, picked over, and dried
1	Tbs. dark rum (optional)
¼	cup toasted, shredded sweetened coconut

> Don't sprinkle the toasted, shredded coconut over the dumplings until they're done baking or it will burn.

The pluot—a cross between a plum and an apricot—is a perfect flavor partner for the ripe summer blueberries in this dumpling-topped cobbler. A dash of dark rum adds yet another layer of flavor to the filling; it's optional but highly recommended.

Position a rack in the center of the oven and heat the oven to 375°F.

MAKE THE TOPPING

1. In a large saucepan, boil the coconut milk over medium heat, stirring occasionally, until reduced to ¾ cup, about 15 minutes. Set aside to cool completely.

2. In a large bowl, whisk the flour, sugar, baking powder, and salt until well blended.

3. In a medium bowl, whisk the reduced coconut milk, egg, and yolk until well blended. Add the coconut mixture and the melted butter to the flour mixture; gently fold together with a spatula. Refrigerate.

MAKE THE FILLING

1. In a large bowl, toss the pluots, sugar, cornstarch, and salt with a spatula.

2. In a 10-inch nonreactive, ovenproof skillet (8- to 10-cup capacity), melt the butter over medium-low heat. Add the pluot mixture, scraping the bowl clean. Cook, stirring, until the fruit begins to give off some juice and the liquid is boiling, about 3 minutes. Add the blueberries and rum, if using. Gently toss until the berries are hot, about 1 minute. Remove from the heat.

ASSEMBLE AND BAKE

Spread the fruit into a relatively even layer. Using a 2-Tbs. scoop, drop the topping randomly onto the filling. The topping will almost cover the fruit. Bake until the filling is bubbling and the topping is golden brown, 40 to 50 minutes. Sprinkle with the toasted coconut and let sit for at least 30 minutes to allow the filling to settle and thicken before serving. *—Abigail Johnson Dodge*

PER SERVING: 580 CALORIES | 7G PROTEIN | 80G CARB | 28G TOTAL FAT | 20G SAT FAT | 5G MONO FAT | 1G POLY FAT | 85MG CHOL | 310MG SODIUM | 4G FIBER

apple-cranberry crisp

1 Tbs. unsalted butter, at room temperature, for the pan

3 pounds apples (4 to 5 medium-large), such as Braeburn, Gala, Rome, or Honeycrisp

½ teaspoon ground cinnamon

2¼ cups fresh cranberries

1 teaspoon finely grated orange zest

1 tablespoon unsalted butter

3 tablespoons fresh orange juice

Pinch of table salt

1 cup granulated sugar

Pecan Topping (recipe below)

A crunchy pecan topping plays up the fall flavor combination of cran-berries and apples. Using a combination of apple varieties delivers an unexpected range of textures and tart-sweet flavors.

1. Heat the oven to 375°F. Butter the sides only of a 9x9-inch baking pan.

2. Peel, quarter, and core the apples. Cut each apple quarter cross-wise into ¾-inch-thick slices. Put them in a large bowl, sprinkle on the cinnamon, and toss until evenly coated. Combine the cranberries and orange zest in a food processor and pulse until the cranberries are finely chopped, scraping down the sides with a rubber spatula as needed.

3. Add the cranberries to the apples and toss to combine. Put the butter, orange juice, and salt in a small microwaveable dish or a small pan. Heat in the microwave or over medium-low heat until the butter melts, about 1 minute. Swirl to blend and pour the mixture over the apples. Toss to coat. Add the sugar and toss to coat again. Pour the apple mixture into the prepared pan and spread it evenly. Sprinkle the topping evenly on top of the apples.

4. Line a heavy-duty rimmed baking sheet with foil. Set the pan on the sheet and bake until the juices are bubbling on the sides; the top is golden brown, crisp, and hard; and the apples in the center are tender when pierced with a fork, 60 to 70 minutes (rotate the pan for even browning, if necessary). If the top starts to get too brown after 45 min-utes, cover it loosely with aluminum foil. Let cool on a rack for at least 30 minutes to let the juices thicken. Serve warm. —*Wendy Kalen*

PER SERVING: 520 CALORIES | 3G PROTEIN | 86G CARB | 21G TOTAL FAT | 9G SAT FAT | 8G MONO FAT | 3G POLY FAT | 35MG CHOL | 120MG SODIUM | 9G FIBER

pecan topping

5¾ ounces (1¼ cups) unbleached all-purpose flour

½ cup firmly packed light brown sugar

2 tablespoons granulated sugar

½ teaspoon ground cinnamon

¼ teaspoon table salt

4 oz. (½ cup) chilled unsalted butter, cut into ½-inch pieces

¾ cup pecans, coarsely chopped

Combine the flour, brown sugar, granulated sugar, cinnamon, and salt in a medium bowl. Rub in the butter with your fingertips until it's well blended and the mixture is clumpy but still a bit crumbly (it should hold together if you pinch it). Mix in the pecans. Refrigerate until ready to use.

bumbleberry pie

MAKES ONE 9-INCH PIE;
SERVES 6

- 1 recipe Buttery Shortbread Pastry Dough (recipe on p. 8)
- 1 cup strawberries, rinsed, picked over, and drained plus a small handful for garnish
- 1 cup blueberries, rinsed, picked over, and drained plus a small handful for garnish
- ¾ cup granulated sugar
- 3 Tbs. cornstarch
- Kosher salt
- 2 Tbs. unsalted butter
- 1½ Tbs. fresh lemon juice
- 1 cup red raspberries, rinsed, picked over, and drained plus a small handful for garnish
- 1 cup heavy cream
- 2 Tbs. confectioners' sugar
- ½ tsp. pure vanilla extract

There's no such thing as a bumbleberry—it's a name pioneer cooks gave to dishes made with a combination of berries.

1. Shape the dough into a 1-inch-thick disk, wrap in plastic, and refrigerate to firm a bit, 20 to 30 minutes. You want the dough to remain pliable enough to roll, but not so soft that it's sticky and difficult to move once it's rolled out. Lightly flour a clean surface and your rolling pin. Roll out the dough into a ⅛-inch-thick round. (Run a dough scraper under the dough after every few passes of the rolling pin to prevent sticking, and reflour the surface as necessary.) Lay the rolling pin in the center of the crust, fold the pastry over it, and transfer it to a 9-inch pie pan. Gently press the dough into the pan. Trim the overhang to about ½ inch. Fold the overhang under to build up the edge of the pastry; crimp to flute the edges. Prick the entire surface, including the sides, with a fork. Cover loosely and refrigerate for 30 minutes. Meanwhile, heat the oven to 400°F.

2. Apply a light coating of nonstick cooking spray to one side of a piece of aluminum foil that's slightly larger than the diameter of the pie pan. Line the pan with the foil, oiled side down, going up and over the edges, and fill with pie weights, raw rice, or dried beans. Set the pie pan on a baking sheet and bake for 20 minutes. Carefully remove the foil and pie weights and bake until the crust is golden brown, about another 15 minutes. Transfer the pie crust to a rack and let cool while you make the filling.

3. Hull the strawberries and slice them ¼ inch thick. Combine the 1 cup blueberries, sugar, cornstarch, ¼ teaspoon salt, and ⅔ cup water in a medium-size saucepan. Set the pan over medium heat and bring to a boil, stirring frequently. Cook, stirring constantly, until the mixture turns deep purple, thickens, and becomes translucent instead of cloudy looking, 1 to 2 minutes once the mixture begins bubbling. Remove from the heat and stir in the 1 cup strawberries, butter, and lemon juice. Sprinkle the 1 cup raspberries over the bottom of the pie crust and pour the filling over the top. Refrigerate until firm, about 4 hours. The pie can be made to this stage up to 12 hours in advance.

4. Just before serving, whip the cream to medium-firm peaks with the confectioners' sugar and the vanilla and mound on top of the filling. Scatter the remaining berries over the whipped cream for garnish. Serve immediately. *—Janie Hibler*

PER SERVING: 750 CALORIES | 7G PROTEIN | 77G CARB | 47G TOTAL FAT | 29G SAT FAT | 13G MONO FAT | 2G POLY FAT | 175MG CHOL | 470MG SODIUM | 4G FIBER

vanilla-fig skillet cobbler with spiced shortbread topping

SERVES 6 TO 8

FOR THE TOPPING

5⅝ oz. (1¼ cups) unbleached all-purpose flour

½ cup finely ground toasted hazelnuts

½ tsp. baking powder

¼ tsp. ground cinnamon

¼ tsp. ground ginger

¼ tsp. table salt

⅛ tsp. ground nutmeg

Pinch of ground cloves

Pinch of ground white pepper (optional)

4 oz. (½ cup) unsalted butter, at room temperature

½ cup firmly packed light brown sugar

3 large egg yolks

1 tsp. pure vanilla extract

FOR THE FILLING

½ cup granulated sugar

2 tsp. unbleached all-purpose flour

¼ tsp. table salt

2 oz. (4 Tbs.) unsalted butter, cut into 4 pieces

2 Tbs. fresh lemon juice

1 tsp. finely grated lemon zest

1 vanilla bean (about 5 inches long), halved lengthwise, seeds scraped out

2 lb. firm-ripe fresh figs, trimmed and halved (or quartered if large)

Toasted hazelnuts and warm spices give the cookie-like topping on this cobbler a deep, rich flavor that's reminiscent of linzer cookies.

MAKE THE TOPPING

1. In a medium bowl, combine the flour, hazelnuts, baking powder, cinnamon, ginger, salt, nutmeg (freshly ground is best), cloves, and white pepper (if using). Whisk until well blended.

2. In a stand mixer fitted with the paddle attachment, beat the butter and sugar on medium-high speed until light, 3 to 5 minutes. Add the egg yolks and vanilla and beat until well blended, about 1 minute. Add the flour mixture and mix on medium-low speed until well blended, about 1 minute.

3. Lay a large piece of plastic wrap on the counter. Scrape the dough onto the plastic. Using the plastic as an aid, shape the dough into a 7½-inch-long log. Wrap in the plastic and refrigerate until firm, about 4 hours or up to 2 days.

4. Cut the chilled dough into ten ¾-inch-thick slices, wrap, and refrigerate until ready to bake the cobbler.

MAKE THE FILLING

1. Position a rack in the center of the oven and heat the oven to 375°F.

2. Put the sugar, flour, and salt in a 10-inch nonreactive, ovenproof skillet (8- to 10-cup capacity) and whisk until well blended. Add 1 cup water and the butter, lemon juice, lemon zest, and vanilla bean halves and seeds. Cook over medium-low heat, stirring occasionally, until the butter melts and the sugar dissolves, about 2 minutes. Increase the heat to medium and boil, whisking constantly, until thickened, about 1 minute. Cover and set aside off the heat to steep for at least 30 minutes and up to 2 hours.

3. Return the syrup to a boil over medium-low heat. Add the figs and cook, tossing gently, until very hot and beginning to release their juice, 3 to 5 minutes. Remove from the heat.

To scrape out the sticky seed pulp from a vanilla bean, use the back of the knife, not the blade. This way you won't shave inedible strands of the bean pod into the seeds as you scrape.

ASSEMBLE AND BAKE

1. Spread the fruit into a relatively even layer. Arrange the topping slices randomly over the hot filling, leaving space between them.

2. Bake until the filling is bubbling and the topping is golden brown (a toothpick inserted into a few pieces should come out clean), 25 to 35 minutes. Let sit for about 30 minutes to allow the filling to settle and thicken before serving. —*Abigail Johnson Dodge*

PER SERVING: 480 CALORIES | 5G PROTEIN | 66G CARB | 24G TOTAL FAT | 12G SAT FAT | 9G MONO FAT | 1.5G POLY FAT | 115MG CHOL | 180MG SODIUM | 5G FIBER

lattice-top cherry pie

**MAKES ONE 9-INCH
LATTICE-TOP PIE; SERVES 8**

FOR THE DOUGH

- **6** oz. (¾ cup) chilled unsalted butter
- **6½** oz. (1 ½ cups) bleached all-purpose flour
- **3½** oz. (¾ cup) cake flour
- **¼** tsp. table salt
- **¼** tsp. baking powder
- **4½** oz. (½ cup plus 1 Tbs.) chilled cream cheese
- **3** Tbs. heavy cream
- **1** Tbs. cider vinegar

FOR THE FILLING

- **¾** cup plus 2 Tbs. granulated sugar
- **2½** Tbs. cornstarch
- **Pinch of table salt**
- **1½** pounds sour cherries, pitted (juices reserved), to equal 3½ cups
- **⅛** tsp. pure almond extract

FOR THE GLAZE

- **2** Tbs. whole milk
- **1** Tbs. turbinado or granulated sugar

This classic cherry pie filling uses sour cherries (not sweet cherries like Bings). During their brief season in early summer, sour cherries appear in some groceries and many farmers' markets.

MAKE THE DOUGH

1. Cut the butter into ¾-inch cubes. Wrap them in plastic and freeze until hard, at least 30 minutes. Put the all-purpose flour, cake flour, salt, and baking powder in a metal bowl and freeze for at least 30 minutes.

2. Put the cold flour mixture in a food processor and process for a few seconds to combine.

3. Cut the cold cream cheese into three or four pieces and add it to the flour mixture. Process for 20 seconds (the mixture should resemble fine meal). Add the frozen butter cubes and pulse until none of the butter pieces is larger than a pea, about five 3-second pulses. (Toss with a fork to see it better.)

4. Add the cream and vinegar and pulse in short bursts until the dough starts to come together (which will take a minute or two); the dough will still look crumbly but if you press it between your fingers, it should become smooth. Turn it out onto a clean work surface. Gather and press the dough together to form a unified mass.

5. Cut the dough in half and put each half on a large piece of plastic wrap. Loosely cover the dough with the plastic. Using the wrap as an aid (to avoid warming the dough with your bare hands), shape one half of the dough into a flat disk and the other into a flat rectangle. Wrap each tightly in the plastic and refrigerate for at least 45 minutes and up to 24 hours.

ROLL OUT THE BOTTOM CRUST

1. Remove the disk of dough from the fridge (keep the rectangle refrigerated); if it's very firm, let it sit at room temperature until it's pliable enough to roll, 10 to 15 minutes.

2. Set the dough between two sheets of plastic wrap sprinkled lightly with flour. Roll it out to a 13-inch round that's ⅛ inch thick, occasionally loosening and reapplying the plastic wrap.

3. Remove one piece of plastic and flip the dough into a standard

To keep the pie shell from getting soggy, pour in the fruit filling only after you've cut the strips of dough for the lattice.

9-inch metal pie pan (it should be 1¼ inches deep and hold 4 cups of liquid). Fit the dough into the pan and carefully peel off the plastic. Trim the dough so there's a ¾-inch overhang. Fold the overhang underneath itself to create an edge that extends about ¼ inch beyond the rim of the pie pan. Cover the dough-lined pie plate with plastic wrap and refrigerate for at least 30 minutes.

MAKE THE FILLING AND TOP THE PIE

1. In a medium bowl, stir the sugar, cornstarch, and salt. Stir in the cherries (along with any juices) and the almond extract. Let the mixture sit for 10 minutes.

2. Remove the rectangle of dough from the refrigerator and let it sit at room temperature until it's pliable enough to roll, 10 to 15 minutes. Roll the dough on a lightly floured surface to an 11x14-inch or larger rectangle (if it becomes an oval, that's fine); it should be no more than ⅛ inch thick.

3. Cut ten ¾-inch-wide strips lengthwise down the rectangle, using a ruler to measure and mark ¾-inch intervals and to cut a straight edge. If you want a crimped edge on the strips, use a fluted pastry wheel.

4. Stir the fruit filling a few times and scrape it into the pie shell. Make the lattice top as shown in the photos on p. 86.

BAKE THE PIE AND LET IT COOL

1. Lightly cover the assembled pie with plastic wrap and refrigerate for 1 hour. After 30 minutes of chilling, set an oven rack on the lowest rung and put a foil-lined baking stone or baking sheet on it. Heat the oven to 425°F.

2. When the pie has chilled for 1 hour, brush the lattice with the milk and sprinkle on the sugar.

3. Set the pie directly on the baking stone or sheet. Bake until the juices are bubbling all over (the bubbles should be thick and slow near the pan edges), 40 to 55 minutes. After the first 15 minutes, cover the rim with foil or a pie shield. If the lattice starts to darken too much in the last 10 minutes of baking, cover it loosely with a piece of foil that has a vent hole poked in the center.

4. Let the pie cool on a rack until the juices have thickened, 3 hours.
—*Rose Levy Beranbaum*

PER SERVING: 490 CALORIES | 5G PROTEIN | 62G CARB | 26G TOTAL FAT | 16G SAT FAT | 8G MONO FAT | 1G POLY FAT | 70MG CHOL | 180MG SODIUM | 2G FIBER

how to weave a lattice for a beautiful fruit pie

Arrange five strips of dough evenly over the filling, starting with a long strip for the center. Gently fold back every other strip (the second and fourth) to a little past the center.

Choose another long strip of dough, hold it perpendicular to the other strips, and set it across the center of the pie.

Unfold the two folded strips so they lie flat on top of the perpendicular strip. Now fold back the strips that weren't folded back last time (the first, third, and fifth ones).

Lay a strip of dough about ¾ inch away from the last one. Unfold the three folded strips. Fold back the original two strips, set a strip of dough ¾ inch from the last one, and unfold the two strips.

Repeat on the other side with the two remaining strips: fold back alternating strips, lay a strip of dough on top, and unfold. Remember to alternate the strips that are folded back to create a woven effect.

Trim the strips to a ½-inch overhang. Moisten the underside of each one with water and tuck it under the bottom crust, pressing to make it adhere. Crimp or flute the edges, if you like. Chill and bake the pie as directed.

Variations

Instead of cherry pie filling, choose one of those here. Note that baking and cooling times may be different than for the cherry pie.

rhubarb pie filling

¾   cup granulated sugar

4   tsp. cornstarch

1   tsp. finely grated lemon zest

Pinch of table salt

4   cups ½-inch pieces rhubarb
(about 1¼ pounds)

1. In a medium bowl, stir the sugar, cornstarch, lemon zest, and salt. Add the rhubarb and toss to coat. Let sit until the sugar is fully moistened, about 10 minutes.

2. Bake for 40 to 50 minutes; cool for 1 hour.

blueberry pie filling

½   cup granulated sugar

2   Tbs. cornstarch

2   tsp. finely grated lemon zest

2   Tbs. fresh lemon juice

Pinch of table salt

4   cups blueberries (2½ dry
pints or 1¼ pounds), rinsed,
picked over, and dried

1. In a medium bowl, stir the sugar, cornstarch, lemon zest, lemon juice, and salt. Add the blueberries and toss to coat.

2. Bake for 40 to 55 minutes; cool for 4 hours.

peach pie filling

2¾   pounds ripe but firm
peaches (about 8 medium)

1   Tbs. fresh lemon juice

⅔   cup turbinado or granulated
sugar

Pinch of table salt

4   tsp. cornstarch

¼   tsp. pure almond extract

1. Peel the peaches, then halve each, remove the pit, and slice each half into eight thin wedges; you should have 6 cups.

2. Put the peaches in a large bowl and sprinkle the lemon juice over them. Sprinkle on the sugar and salt and toss gently to mix. Let sit at room temperature for at least 30 minutes and up to 12 hours. Transfer the peaches to a colander suspended over a bowl to collect the juices; you should have almost 1 cup of liquid. (If the peaches sat for several hours, you'll have 1 to 1½ cups liquid.)

3. Pour the juices into a small, nonstick saucepan set over medium heat. Boil down the liquid, swirling but not stirring, until it's syrupy, about 10 minutes; it should reduce to ⅓ to ½ cup, depending on how much liquid you started with. Set aside to cool for 1 or 2 minutes.

4. Meanwhile, transfer the peaches to a bowl and toss them with the cornstarch and almond extract until all traces of cornstarch have disappeared. Pour the reduced peach juices over the peaches, tossing gently. (Don't worry if the liquid hardens on the peaches; it will dissolve during baking.)

5. Bake for 40 to 50 minutes; cool for 3 hours.

peach-ginger galette with hazelnuts

SERVES 8

This galette gets a zingy lift with fresh ginger. Serve it the day it's baked.

FOR THE GALETTE DOUGH

- 9 oz. (2 cups) unbleached all-purpose flour
- 3 Tbs. granulated sugar
- 1 tsp. ground ginger
- ½ tsp. table salt
- 5½ oz. (11 Tbs.) very chilled unsalted butter, cut into ½-inch pieces
- ⅓ cup very cold water

FOR THE HAZELNUT TOPPING

- ⅓ cup very coarsely chopped hazelnuts (with or without the skin)
- 1 Tbs. light brown sugar
- 1 tsp. unbleached all-purpose flour
- 1 Tbs. unsalted butter, melted

FOR THE PEACH FILLING

- 3 Tbs. cornstarch
- ⅓ cup packed light brown sugar
- ¼ tsp. table salt
- 2¼ lbs. firm but ripe peaches (4 to 5 peaches), pitted and cut into ¾-inch wedges
- 2 tsp. minced fresh ginger
- 2 tsp. fresh lemon juice
- 2 Tbs. cream or whole milk

  Vanilla ice cream or sweetened whipped cream, for serving (optional)

MAKE THE GALETTE DOUGH

Combine the flour, sugar, ground ginger, and salt in a food processor and pulse to combine. Scatter the chilled butter pieces around the bowl and pulse in 1-second bursts just until the mixture resembles coarse crumbs. Drizzle the water evenly over the crumbs and process just until the dough is moist but still extremely crumbly, about 5 seconds. Turn the dough onto a work surface and press it into a 6-inch disk. Wrap the disk in plastic and refrigerate until well chilled, at least 1 hour.

MAKE THE TOPPING

In a small bowl, combine the chopped hazelnuts, brown sugar, and flour with a fork until blended. Drizzle the melted butter evenly over the mixture and toss with the fork until combined.

FILL AND BAKE THE GALETTE

1. Position an oven rack in the middle of the oven; heat the oven to 425°F. Line a rimmed baking sheet with parchment. Unwrap the galette dough and set it on a lightly floured work surface. Roll out the dough, turning and lightly flouring it and the work surface as necessary, into a round that's about 15 inches in diameter and ⅛ to ¼ inch thick. Trim the excess dough to make a 14-inch round. Loosely roll the dough around the rolling pin and transfer it to the lined baking sheet. The dough will hang over the edges of the pan. Cover and refrigerate the dough.

2. Meanwhile, make the filling. In a large bowl, whisk together the cornstarch, brown sugar, and salt until no lumps remain. Add the peach slices, minced ginger, and lemon juice. Toss until the peaches are well combined with the dry ingredients.

3. Remove the dough from the fridge. If it isn't pliable, let it warm up at room temperature for a few minutes. Give the peach filling a toss and pile it in the center of the dough, leaving a 3-inch rim bare. Fold this border over the filling, pleating the dough as you go. Gently press the pleats to seal. Tuck in any peach slices that stick out. Brush the pleated border with the cream or milk and sprinkle the hazelnut topping on the dough border, pressing on the nuts so they stick.

4. Put the galette in the oven and immediately reduce the heat to 400°F. Bake until the crust is browned on the top and bottom, 45 to 50 minutes. Check the galette after about 30 minutes; if the nuts are darkening too much, cover very loosely with foil.

5. Serve warm or at room temperature with a scoop of vanilla ice cream or a dollop of lightly sweetened whipped cream, if you like.
—Abigail Johnson Dodge

PER SERVING: 400 CALORIES | 5G PROTEIN | 49G CARB | 21G TOTAL FAT | 11G SAT FAT | 7G MONO FAT | 1G POLY FAT | 50MG CHOL | 230MG SODIUM | 2G FIBER

plum and raspberry galette

MAKES 1 GALETTE;
SERVES 6 TO 8

⅓ cup crushed amaretti or almond biscotti (use a food processor or put the cookies in a plastic bag and crush with a blunt object until the texture of coarse sand)

1 Tbs. unbleached all-purpose flour

6 ripe plums (about 1 lb.)

1 disk Sweet Galette Dough (recipe below)

1 Tbs. unsalted butter, melted

2 Tbs. granulated sugar

3 oz. raspberries, rinsed, picked over, and drained

2 Tbs. strained raspberry jam (optional)

Amaretti, very sweet, very light, very crisp almond meringue cookies, are available from Italian and specialty groceries. Almond biscotti work well, too, if you can't find amaretti. Choose plums that are ripe but still a bit firm so they're easy to slice. Red-fleshed plums, such as Elephant Heart, make a dazzling tart. You could also use sliced nectarines or peaches.

1. Adjust an oven rack to the center position and heat the oven to 400°F. Combine the crushed amaretti and the flour and set aside.

2. Cut each plum in half, remove its pit, and cut the flesh into ¼-inch-thick slices.

3. Cover a baking sheet, preferably without sides, with kitchen parchment. (If your baking sheet has sides, flip it over and use the back.)

4. On a lightly floured surface, roll the galette dough into a 15-inch round. Transfer the dough by folding it in half, picking it up, and unfolding it on the lined baking sheet. Sprinkle the crushed amaretti over the dough evenly, leaving a 2-inch border without crumbs. Arrange the plums over the crumbs in concentric circles, overlapping slightly. Lift the edges of the dough and fold them inward over the filling, pleating as you go, to create a folded-over border. Brush the border with the melted butter and sprinkle the entire galette with the sugar. Bake for 30 minutes. Remove from the oven and sprinkle the raspberries over the plums. Return the galette to the oven and bake until the crust is browned and the fruit is cooked and tender, another 15 minutes.

5. Slide the galette off the parchment and onto a cooling rack. Let cool for about 10 minutes before slicing. For a shinier filling, brush on the jam before slicing. —*David Lebovitz*

PER SERVING: 240 CALORIES | 3G PROTEIN | 28G CARB | 14G TOTAL FAT | 8G SAT FAT | 4G MONO FAT | 1G POLY FAT | 35MG CHOL | 75MG SODIUM | 2G FIBER

sweet galette dough

MAKES ENOUGH DOUGH FOR 2 GALETTES ABOUT 11 INCHES IN DIAMETER

11¼ oz. (2½ cups) unbleached all-purpose flour

2 Tbs. granulated sugar

½ tsp. table salt

8 oz. (1 cup) unsalted butter, cut into ½-inch pieces and chilled

5 oz. (about ⅔ cup) ice water

Freeze any unused dough well wrapped in plastic; defrost the frozen dough in the refrigerator for a day before using it.

In a large bowl, mix together the flour, sugar, and salt. Cut in the chilled butter using a stand mixer, a food processor, or a pastry blender until the butter is evenly distributed but still in large, visible pieces. Add the ice water all at once to the flour and butter. Mix the dough just until it begins to come together (if using a stand mixer or a food processor, be especially careful not to overmix the dough). Gather the dough with your hands—don't worry if you see streaks of butter—and shape it into two disks. Wrap the disks in plastic and refrigerate for at least 1 hour.

double-crust jumble berry pie

- **1** cup granulated sugar
- **2** Tbs. cornstarch
- **2** Tbs. quick-cooking tapioca
- **¼** tsp. salt
- **6** cups washed, picked over, and well-dried mix of blackberries, blueberries, raspberries, and quartered strawberries
- **1** recipe Flaky Piecrust (recipe on p. 92)
- **1** Tbs. unsalted butter, cut into small pieces

You can make this pie with only one type of berry if you like, but a mix of blueberries, raspberries, blackberries, and strawberries is delicious. Since all these berries are juicy, using both tapioca and cornstarch will keep the texture of the filling somewhat firm and the juices contained around the fruit. You can use these same measurements for sliced or chunked stone fruit, such as peaches, nectarines, or plums.

1. In a large bowl, mix together the sugar, cornstarch, tapioca, and salt. Add the berries and toss with your hands until the berries are evenly coated.

2. Roll out the pie dough according to the directions in the piecrust recipe on p. 92. Pile the berries into the dough-lined pie pan, sprinkling any remaining dry ingredients on top. Dot the surface with the butter, cover the berry mixture with the top crust, and seal the edges by fluting.

3. Cut five or six slits in the top crust to let steam escape during cooking. Heat the oven to 400°F while you chill the pie in the refrigerator for 15 to 20 minutes. Put the pie on a baking sheet to catch any drips, bake it in the hot oven for 15 minutes, and then reduce the temperature to 350°F. Continue baking until the crust is golden and the filling juices that are bubbling through the vents and edges are thick, glossy, and slow, another 50 to 60 minutes. For the best texture for serving, cool the pie completely (which may take up to 5 hours), and then reheat slices or the whole pie just slightly before serving. (Cooling completely allows the filling juices to firm up, while a quick reheat makes the pastry nice and flaky.) You can serve the pie while it's still warm, but the filling will be slightly liquid; definitely don't serve the pie hot, as the juices will be too fluid. —*Carolyn Weil*

PER SERVING: 510 CALORIES | 5G PROTEIN | 70G CARB | 25G TOTAL FAT | 15G SAT FAT | 7G MONO FAT | 1G POLY FAT | 60MG CHOL | 75MG SODIUM | 1G FIBER

continued on p. 92

continued from p. 91

flaky piecrust

8 oz. (1 cup) chilled unsalted butter

9 oz. (2 cups) all-purpose unbleached flour

¼ cup granulated sugar

¼ tsp. table salt

¼ cup cold water

An all-butter dough and a light touch give you the flakiest crust that's perfectly balanced with its filling.

1. Cut the butter into ½-inch cubes. Dump the flour, sugar, and salt into the bowl of a stand mixer fitted with the paddle attachment (or in a large bowl, if mixing the dough by hand). Mix for a second or two to blend the dry ingredients. Add the butter and then, running the mixer on low (or by hand with two knives or a pastry cutter), work the mixture until it's crumbly and the largest pieces of butter are no bigger than a pea (about ¼ inch).

2. The butter should remain cold and firm. To test it, pick up some butter and pinch it between the thumbs and forefingers of both hands to form a little cube. If the butter holds together as a cube and your fingers are not greasy, then the butter is still cold enough. If your fingers look greasy, put the bowl in the refrigerator for 15 minutes to firm up the butter before adding the water.

3. As the mixer turns on low (or tossing with a fork if mixing by hand), sprinkle the cold water evenly over the flour and butter. Work the dough until it just pulls together as a shaggy mass.

4. Roll out the dough for a double-crust pie. Cut the dough in half and pat each piece into a thick flattened ball. Lightly flour your work surface and tap one of the dough balls down with four or five taps of the rolling pan. Begin rolling from the center of your dough outward. Stop the pressure ¼ inch from the edge of the dough. Lift the dough and turn by a quarter, and repeat the rolling until the dough is at least 12 inches in diameter. Be sure to reflour the work surface if your dough is sticking.

5. Using a pot lid or a circle of cardboard as a template, trim the dough to form a 12-inch round (this should give you a 1½-inch margin all around your 9-inch pie pan). Fold the dough in half, slide the out-spread fingers of both hands under the dough, and gently lift it and transfer it to the pie pan. Unfold and ease the dough round into the bottom of the pie pan without stretching it.

6. Roll out the other dough ball and cut a second 12-inch round to be used as the top crust.

how to add a top crust

Use two hands, fingers wide apart for easy lifting that won't stretch or tear the dough. By first folding the round of dough in half, you can easily gauge where to position it on the filling.

Make a strong seal by pressing the two layers of dough together before you begin to fold. The top layer will extend farther than the bottom one.

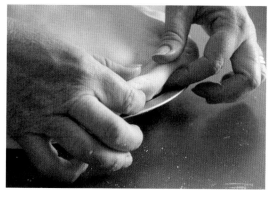

Get a thick, uniform edge by folding the top layer over the bottom one. This double edge will shape up into a pretty flute that will contain the fruit juices during cooking.

Lift up a section of dough and press down on either side to make a graceful vertical flute. The shape will settle down a bit during cooking but will still look nice.

Cut some vents to let off steam. The steam created from the moist fruit during baking needs somewhere to go, so give it an easy escape to avoid unexpected holes and leaks.

Seven Habits of Highly Successful Fruit Pies

Follow these pointers for a perfect pie.

1. Use a metal pie pan. The heat penetrates faster and therefore the bottom crust has a better chance of browning. But be aware that the bottom crust of a double-crust pie will never be crisp—how could it be, sitting under 6 cups of juicy fruit?

2. Use a template to cut nicely round dough circles. Cardboard cake circles work well, but a pot lid is fine, too.

3. Always add a pinch of salt to your fruit fillings. It makes the fruit fruitier and the sweetness sweeter.

4. Don't overfill the pie. It's tempting to pile on the berries, but more fruit releases more juices, and if the level of fruit and juices is higher than the rim of the pan, the juices will leak and spill over.

5. Chill the filled pie for 20 minutes before baking. This lets the butter in the dough set up and the starch in the thickeners start to absorb liquid and swell, so they'll perform better in the oven.

6. Watch the bubbles to see when the pie's done. Juices will probably bubble out of the slits during the latter part of baking. At first the bubbles will be fast, indicating thin juices, but later they'll get lazy and slow, meaning the juices have thickened and the pie is done.

7. Cool the pie completely before slicing. It's tempting to dig right in, but a hot pie will be liquid inside. You need to let the pie come to room temperature so that the juices can set up and cloak the berries properly. The ideal serving method is to cool the pie and then gently heat a slice in the oven to get the butter in the crust warm and toasty.

peach and blueberry galette

SERVES 8 TO 10

FOR THE CRUST

6¾ oz. (1½ cups) unbleached all-purpose flour; more for rolling

1 Tbs. granulated sugar

½ tsp. table salt

5½ oz. (11 Tbs.) chilled unsalted butter, cut into ½-inch dice

1 large egg yolk

3 Tbs. whole milk

FOR THE FILLING

1 lb. peaches, peeled and cut into ½-inch slices (about 2 cups)

2 cups blueberries, rinsed, picked over, and dried

¼ cup light muscovado or light brown sugar

2 Tbs. unbleached all-purpose flour

¼ tsp. ground cinnamon

Pinch of table salt

1 large egg, beaten

2 Tbs. demerara sugar

This rustic fruit tart is the perfect vehicle for ripe summer blueberries and peaches. The crust is freeform—it just gets folded over the filling and then baked. Serve warm with a scoop of vanilla ice cream or a dollop of crème fraîche.

MAKE THE DOUGH

1. Combine the flour, sugar, and salt in a stand mixer fitted with a paddle attachment at low speed. Add the butter to the flour. Mix until the flour is no longer white and holds together when you clump it with your fingers, 1 to 2 minutes. If there are still lumps of butter larger than the size of peas, break them up with your fingers.

2. In a small bowl, beat the egg yolk and milk, and add to the flour mixture. Mix on low speed just until the dough comes together, about 15 seconds; the dough will be somewhat soft. Turn the dough out onto a sheet of plastic wrap, press it into a flat disk, wrap it in the plastic, and let it rest in the refrigerator for 15 to 20 minutes before rolling out.

3. Meanwhile, position a rack in the center of the oven and heat the oven to 350°F. Line a large rimmed baking sheet with parchment paper.

MAKE THE FILLING AND ROLL OUT THE DOUGH

1. In a medium bowl, toss the peaches and blueberries with the muscovado or brown sugar, flour, cinnamon, and salt.

2. Lightly flour a large work surface and roll out the dough to a 12- to 13-inch round. Transfer to the prepared baking sheet. Arrange the fruit in the center of the dough, leaving about 1½ inches of space around the perimeter of the dough empty. Fold the outside edge of the dough over the fruit, making occasional pleats. Brush the crust with the egg. Sprinkle the demerara sugar evenly over the dough and fruit.

3. Bake the galette until the crust turns a light brown and the filling bubbles, about 50 minutes. Let cool for 10 minutes, then cut into wedges and serve warm. *—Tony Rosenfeld*

strawberry crisp

SERVES 8

- 3 pints small ripe strawberries, hulled and halved
- 2½ cups coarse fresh white breadcrumbs
- ½ cup confectioners' sugar
- ½ tsp. finely grated lemon zest
- ¼ tsp. table salt
- ½ cup coarsely chopped hazelnuts
- 2 oz. (4 Tbs.) unsalted butter, melted
- 3 Tbs. granulated sugar

Heavy cream or vanilla ice cream, for serving (optional)

For the breadcrumbs, use firm-textured white bread or a white sourdough, removing the crusts and pulsing cubes of the bread in a food processor until you have large, irregular, coarse crumbs.

1. Position a rack in the middle of the oven and heat the oven to 375°F.

2. In a bowl, toss the strawberries with 1 cup of the breadcrumbs, the confectioners' sugar, the lemon zest, and the salt; scrape into an 8x8-inch Pyrex baking dish. In another bowl, toss the remaining 1½ cups breadcrumbs with the hazelnuts, melted butter, and granulated sugar; sprinkle evenly over the berries. Bake until the berries are bubbling, about 40 minutes. Let cool on a wire rack for about 10 minutes.

3. Spoon the warm crisp into bowls and top with a drizzle of heavy cream or a scoop of ice cream, if you like. *—Lori Longbotham*

PER SERVING: 222 CALORIES | 3G PROTEIN | 31G CARB | 11G TOTAL FAT | 4G SAT FAT | 5G MONO FAT | 1G POLY FAT | 15MG CHOL | 170MG SODIUM | 3G FIBER

how to hull strawberries

Don't mar the strawberries' beauty by cutting straight across their tops to remove the green cap. If you have a strawberry huller, use it. If not, use a sharp paring knife and point it down under the cap at an angle to slice out a cone-shaped piece of the strawberry under the cap.

Handling and Storing Strawberries

Strawberries are delicate, so handle them as little as possible to prevent bruising. When you bring them home, carefully sort out any that are mushy, moldy, or discolored. One bad berry can spoil the whole bowl. Spread the berries in a single layer on a baking sheet or shallow baking dish lined with paper towels. Stored in the refrigerator, they can keep for up to 3 days, but the sooner you eat them, the better.

Don't wash them until you're ready to use them, and then do so very gently and use as little water as possible. Don't hull berries until after you've washed and dried them.

pecan pie
(recipe on p. 108)

pumpkin and nut pies & tarts

pumpkin, sweet potato & coconut pie

MAKES ONE 9-INCH PIE; SERVES 8

- 1¼ lb. sweet potatoes, peeled and cut into 1-inch chunks
- 1 small cinnamon stick, broken into pieces
- 3 whole cloves
- 1 small star anise pod, crumbled
- 1 1-inch piece fresh ginger, peeled and cut into ¼-inch slices
- 1 15-oz. can pure solid-pack pumpkin (not pumpkin pie filling)
- 1 large egg, lightly beaten
- 1 large egg yolk, lightly beaten
- 2 Tbs. unsalted butter, melted and cooled
- ½ cup granulated sugar
- ½ cup packed light brown sugar
- 2 Tbs. unbleached all-purpose flour
- ¾ tsp. table salt
- ½ cup well-stirred canned coconut milk (not coconut cream)
- ½ recipe Tender Piecrust, (recipe on the facing page), chilled
- ¾ cup chilled whipping cream, whipped to soft peaks with 1½ Tbs. granulated sugar

Be sure the pastry is still well chilled when you put the pie in the oven. This helps to ensure that the crust won't darken too much during the long baking time.

1. In a medium saucepan, combine the sweet potatoes, cinnamon stick pieces, cloves, star anise, and ginger slices with enough water to just cover the contents. Bring to a boil over high heat. Reduce the heat and simmer uncovered until the sweet potatoes are very tender when pierced with a fork or skewer, about 10 minutes. Drain the potatoes, reserving the boiling liquid. Return the potatoes to the pot over low heat and toss to dry them a bit. Discard the cinnamon, cloves, and star anise. Force the warm potatoes through a ricer, a food mill, or a sieve. Boil the liquid if needed, until reduced to ¼ cup. Let the sweet potato mash and the liquid cool.

2. Position an oven rack in the lower half of the oven; heat the oven to 350°F. In a large bowl, whisk together the pumpkin and sweet potato purée. Whisk in the egg, egg yolk, melted butter, and reserved spiced liquid. In a separate bowl, stir together the granulated and brown sugars with a wire whisk until any large lumps of brown sugar are gone. Sift the flour and salt over the sugars; stir to blend. Add the sugar-flour mixture to the pumpkin-sweet potato mixture and stir well until no pockets of sugar are visible. Blend in the coconut milk.

3. Scrape the filling into the chilled pie shell; smooth the top. Bake for 1¾ to 2 hours, turning the pie several times so it bakes evenly. The point of a thin-bladed knife should come out clean when inserted into the center of the filling, and the edges of the surface will be unevenly cracked. If the edges of the pastry darken too much before the filling is cooked, cover them with a pie shield or strips of aluminum foil. Transfer the pie to a wire rack and let cool completely before serving with mounds of the lightly sweetened whipped cream. —*Regan Daley*

PER SERVING: 530 CALORIES | 6G PROTEIN | 65G CARB | 28G TOTAL FAT | 13G SAT FAT | 8G MONO FAT | 4G POLY FAT | 110MG CHOL | 400MG SODIUM | 5G FIBER

tender piecrust

- **3** cups (about 13½ oz.) unbleached all-purpose flour
- **1** tsp. table salt
- **1** cup solid vegetable shortening, chilled and cut into small pieces
- **1** large egg
- **2** to 3 Tbs. ice water
- **1** Tbs. white vinegar

Make Ahead

The sweet potatoes and spiced liquid can be prepared up to 3 days ahead and refrigerated. Bring each to room temperature before proceeding with the recipe. Each of these elements can also be frozen for up to 3 months; thaw overnight in the refrigerator before bringing to room temperature.

This recipe makes double the pie dough that you'll need for the pumpkin pie, so freeze half to use another time.

1. Combine the flour and salt in a large mixing bowl or a food processor. Add the shortening and cut it in with a pastry blender or two knives (or pulse the processor) until the largest pieces of shortening are about the size of fat peas. Transfer to a large mixing bowl if using the food processor. In a small bowl, beat together the egg, 2 Tbs. of the ice water, and the vinegar; add this to the flour mixture. Work the liquid evenly through the dough with the tips of your fingers until it can be collected in a rough ball. If the dough is too dry to come together, gradually sprinkle a few drops of the remaining water over it and continue to work gently until it comes together.

2. Cut the dough in half and shape each into a ball. Flatten each ball into a disk and wrap tightly in plastic. Chill for at least 4 hours or up to 3 days. (Freeze one if you like, to save for another purpose.)

3. About 2 hours before baking, remove one of the dough disks from the refrigerator so it can warm up just enough to roll without cracking. Unwrap the dough and roll it between two sheets of waxed paper into a round that's about 12 inches in diameter. Peel off the top sheet of waxed paper. Invert a 9-inch glass pie plate and center it on the dough. Slide one hand under the bottom sheet of waxed paper, position your other hand flat on the pie plate, and quickly flip the plate and dough over. Peel off the waxed paper and gently press the dough down into the plate. With a paring knife, trim the dough to within ¾ inch of the rim of the plate. Fold the dough under and crimp the edges. Use the trimmings to patch any cracks or bare spots. Wrap the shell loosely with plastic wrap and chill for 2 hours or up to 24 hours.

Why Canned Pumpkin?

This recipe calls for canned pumpkin as opposed to fresh. Why? Because pumpkin is one of the few foods that's actually better from a can. It's virtually impossible to get a purée from a sugar pumpkin at home that's as smooth, as consistently flavorful, and as dry as it is from that can in the supermarket. Look for labels that say "pure solid-pack pumpkin." Don't buy canned pumpkin pie filling, which is sweetened, seasoned, and often contains additives.

double ginger pumpkin tart

**MAKES ONE 9½-INCH TART;
SERVES 12**

- **6** oz. cream cheese, at room temperature
- **¾** cup very firmly packed light brown sugar
- **¾** cup solid-pack pumpkin purée (not seasoned pumpkin pie filling)
- **1¼** tsp. ground cinnamon
- **½** tsp. ground ginger
- **¼** tsp. table salt
- **1** large egg yolk
- **1** large egg
- **¾** tsp. pure vanilla extract
- **1** Tbs. finely chopped crystallized ginger; more for garnish (optional)
- **1** Press-In Cookie Crust (recipe on the facing page), baked and cooled (graham cracker or vanilla works well for this tart)
- Whipped cream, for garnish (optional)

Crystallized ginger can be frustrating to chop because it's sticky. To make it easier, coat your knife with vegetable oil or cooking spray. Rather than chopping randomly (which can cause clumping), cut it first into thin strips, then cut across the strips for a fine dice.

1. Position a rack in the center of the oven and heat the oven to 325°F. In a medium bowl, beat the cream cheese and brown sugar with a stand mixer or hand-held mixer on medium speed until smooth and lump-free, about 3 minutes. Add the pumpkin, cinnamon, ginger, and salt and continue beating until well blended, about 1 minute. Add the egg yolk, egg, and vanilla and beat until just incorporated. Sprinkle the chopped crystallized ginger over the batter and stir it in with a rubber spatula.

2. Use the spatula to scrape the filling into the crust and spread it evenly. Bake the tart until the filling just barely jiggles when the tart pan is nudged, 25 to 30 minutes. Transfer the tart to a rack and let cool completely. Refrigerate the tart in the pan until chilled and firm, about 3 hours. Garnish with whipped cream and crystallized ginger, if you like. *—Abigail Johnson Dodge*

press-in cookie crust

MAKES 1 CRUST FOR ONE 9½-INCH TART

1 **cup finely ground cookies (ground in a food processor); choose one from the following: about 25 chocolate wafers, 8 whole graham crackers, or 35 vanilla wafers (Nabisco® Famous Chocolate Wafers, Honey Maid® Grahams, and Nilla® Vanilla Wafers)**

2 **Tbs. granulated sugar**

1½ **oz. (3 Tbs.) unsalted butter, melted**

1. Position a rack in the center of the oven and heat the oven to 350°F. Have ready an ungreased 9 ½-inch fluted tart pan with a removable bottom.

2. In a medium bowl, mix the cookie crumbs and sugar with a fork until well blended. Drizzle the melted butter over the crumbs and mix with the fork or your fingers until the crumbs are evenly moistened. Put the crumbs in the tart pan and use your hands to spread the crumbs so that they coat the bottom of the pan and start to climb the sides (use a piece of plastic wrap over the crumbs as you spread them so they won't stick to your hands). Use your fingers to pinch and press some of the crumbs around the inside edge of the pan to cover the sides evenly and create a wall about a scant ¼ inch thick. Redistribute the remaining crumbs evenly over the bottom of the pan and press firmly to make a compact layer. (I like to use a metal measuring cup with straight sides and a flat base for this task.)

3. Bake the crust until it smells nutty and fragrant (crusts made with lighter-colored cookies will brown slightly), about 10 minutes. Set the baked crust on a rack and let cool. The crust can be made up to 1 day ahead and stored at room temperature, wrapped well in plastic.

how to make a press-in crust

Grind the cookies to crumbs, then add the sugar.

Mix in the butter, then mix with a fork.

Press the crumbs into the pan with plastic wrap over the crumbs so they don't stick to your hands.

bourbon pumpkin tart with walnut streusel

MAKES ONE 10-INCH TART;
SERVES 8 TO 10

FOR THE TART CRUST

- **9** oz. (2 cups) unbleached all-purpose flour
- **⅓** cup granulated sugar
- **1** tsp. finely grated orange zest
- **½** tsp. table salt
- **5½** oz. (11 Tbs.) chilled unsalted butter, cut into ½-inch cubes
- **1** large egg, lightly beaten
- **¼** cup heavy cream; more if needed

FOR THE PUMPKIN FILLING

- **1** 15-oz. can solid-pack pumpkin
- **3** large eggs
- **½** cup granulated sugar
- **¼** cup packed dark brown sugar
- **2** Tbs. unbleached all-purpose flour
- **1** tsp. ground ginger
- **1** tsp. ground cinnamon
- **¼** tsp. ground cloves
- **¼** tsp. table salt
- **½** cup heavy cream
- **¼** cup bourbon

    Lightly sweetened whipped cream, for garnish (optional)

Tarts are as easy to make as pies (and maybe easier) and much easier to cut evenly for serving. This tart tastes best if it's baked a day before you serve it.

MAKE THE CRUST

Using a mixer fitted with a paddle attachment, mix the flour, sugar, orange zest, and salt in a large bowl on low speed for about 30 seconds. Add the butter and combine on low speed until the mixture looks crumbly, with pieces of butter about the size of dried peas, about 3 minutes. Add the egg and cream, mixing on low speed until the dough is just combined. If the dough is too dry to come together, add more cream, 1 Tbs. at a time. Gently mold the dough into a 1-inch-thick disk and wrap in plastic wrap. Refrigerate for at least 1 hour or for up to 1 week; the dough can also be frozen for up to 1 month.

MAKE THE FILLING

Spoon the pumpkin into a large bowl. Whisk in the eggs, one at a time, until thoroughly incorporated. Add both sugars and the flour, ginger, cinnamon, cloves, and salt. Whisk for about 30 seconds. Whisk in the heavy cream and bourbon.

MAKE THE STREUSEL TOPPING

Combine the flour, both sugars, cinnamon, and salt in a food processor fitted with a metal blade. Pulse briefly to mix. Add the butter and pulse until the butter has blended into the dry ingredients and the mixture is crumbly. Remove the blade and stir in the walnuts and crystallized ginger.

ASSEMBLE THE TART

1. Position a rack in the center of the oven and heat the oven to 350°F. Take the tart dough from the refrigerator and let it warm up until pliable, 5 to 15 minutes. Unwrap the dough and set it on a lightly floured work surface. With as few passes of the rolling pin as possible, roll the disk into a 13-inch round about ³⁄₁₆ inch thick. Drape the round into a 10-inch fluted tart pan with a removable bottom, gently fitting it into the contours of the pan. Fold the excess dough into the sides of the pan and press to create an edge that's flush with the top of the pan and about ½ inch thick.

FOR THE STREUSEL TOPPING

- 3½ oz. (¾ cup) unbleached all-purpose flour
- ⅓ cup granulated sugar
- ⅓ cup packed dark brown sugar
- ½ tsp. ground cinnamon
- ½ tsp. table salt
- 4 oz. (½ cup) chilled unsalted butter, cut into ½-inch cubes
- ¾ cup walnut halves, toasted and coarsely chopped
- ¼ cup chopped crystallized ginger

2. Pour the pumpkin mixture into the unbaked tart crust. Scatter the streusel topping evenly over the pumpkin mixture.

3. Bake until the topping is evenly cooked and no longer looks wet in the center, 50 to 65 minutes. Let the tart cool on a rack for at least 2 hours before serving (or wrap it in plastic and refrigerate overnight; before serving, let it sit at room temperature for 1 to 2 hours). Serve warm, at room temperature, or slightly chilled, with lightly sweetened whipped cream, if you like. —*Rebecca Rather*

PER SERVING: 650 CALORIES I 9G PROTEIN I 73G CARB I 35G TOTAL FAT I 19G SAT FAT I 9G MONO FAT I 5G POLY FAT I 165MG CHOL I 340MG SODIUM I 3G FIBER

parsnip buttermilk pie

SERVES 8 TO 10

FOR THE CRUST

- 6 oz. (1⅓ cups) unbleached all-purpose flour; more for rolling
- 4 oz. (½ cup) chilled unsalted butter, cut into small cubes
- 1 tsp. granulated sugar
- ½ tsp. table salt
- 2 Tbs. ice water
- 1 large egg yolk, lightly beaten

FOR THE FILLING

- 2 lb. medium parsnips, peeled, cored, and cut into large chunks
- 1½ cups buttermilk
- ⅔ cup packed dark brown sugar
- 2 large eggs
- ½ tsp. table salt
- ½ tsp. ground cinnamon
- ½ tsp. ground ginger
- ¼ tsp. freshly grated nutmeg
- ⅛ tsp. ground cloves

This may look like pumpkin pie, but it tastes nothing like it—it's sweet and tangy, with a delicate mousse-like texture. Serve with lightly sweetened whipped cream.

MAKE THE CRUST

1. In a stand mixer fitted with the paddle attachment, combine the flour, butter, sugar, and salt and mix on medium speed until the butter blends into the flour and the mixture resembles a coarse meal, about 2 minutes. Mix the ice water with the egg yolk in a small bowl. With the mixer on low speed, add the yolk mixture and mix until just combined. Transfer the dough to a work surface and bring it together with your hands. Shape it into a 1-inch-thick disk, wrap in plastic, and refrigerate for at least 1 hour.

2. Set the dough on a lightly floured surface, sprinkle a little flour over it, and roll it out into a circle that's about 12 inches in diameter and ⅛ inch thick, reflouring the dough and work surface as necessary.

3. Transfer the dough to a 9-inch pie plate and gently fit it into the pan, lifting the edges and pressing the dough into the corners with your fingers. Trim the edges, leaving a ½-inch overhang. Fold the overhanging dough underneath itself and crimp the edges. Prick the dough all over with a fork. Refrigerate for at least 1 hour.

4. Position a rack in the center of the oven and heat the oven to 425°F.

5. Line the dough with foil or parchment, fill with dried beans or pie weights, and bake for 15 minutes. Reduce the oven temperature to 350°F. Carefully remove the foil and weights and continue to bake until the bottom looks dry and the edges are light golden, an additional 5 to 8 minutes. Cool completely before filling.

MAKE THE FILLING

1. Bring a large pot of water to a boil. Add the parsnips and cook until tender when pierced with a fork, 12 to 15 minutes. Drain the parsnips in a colander and let them steam under a clean kitchen towel for about 5 minutes. Return the parsnips to the pot and mash them with a potato masher, keeping the mixture rather rough. Measure 2 cups of the parsnip mash; save any extra for another use.

2. Purée the 2 cups of mashed parsnips and the buttermilk in a blender until smooth. Transfer the purée to a mixing bowl. With a whisk, beat in the sugar, eggs, salt, cinnamon, ginger, nutmeg, and cloves, whisking until the sugar dissolves.

how to core a parsnip

Running down the center of a parsnip is a tough woody core that should be removed before cooking. Here's how to do it.

After trimming the ends and peeling the parsnip, quarter it lengthwise. Hold a sharp paring knife parallel to the cutting board and slowly run the knife between the core and the tender outer part of the parsnip. The core curves with the shape of the parsnip, so you won't be able to get it all, but that's fine—just remove as much as you can without sacrificing too much of the tender part.

BAKE THE PIE
Pour the filling into the piecrust and bake until the top is lightly browned and a toothpick inserted in the center of the filling comes out clean, about 1 hour. Cool on a rack for at least 1 hour. Serve at room temperature. —*David Tanis*

PER SERVING: 310 CALORIES | 6G PROTEIN | 47G CARB | 11G TOTAL FAT | 7G SAT FAT | 3G MONO FAT | 0.5G POLY FAT | 90MG CHOL | 300MG SODIUM | 5G FIBER

More about Parsnips

Grown in cold climates, parsnips are usually harvested in the fall and, like carrots, stored in cool root cellars. However, frost will convert their starches to sugar, concentrating their sweet flavor, so many home gardeners and small growers keep their parsnips in the

ground and dig them as needed through winter and early spring. That's why you're likely to find the sweetest parsnips at a farmstand or farmers' market.

While there are several varieties of parsnips, most markets don't usually indicate which they're selling, mainly because the differences in flavor, texture, and appearance are minimal. Your best bet is to choose what looks freshest.

Choosing
Parsnips should be firm and of uniform color; blemishes can be a sign of decay. Opt for medium parsnips, as very large ones can be woody and bitter.

Storing
Wrap unwashed parsnips in paper towels or newspaper and store them in a loosely closed plastic bag in the crisper drawer of the refrigerator for up to 2 weeks.

pecan pie

MAKES ONE 9-INCH PIE;
SERVES 8 TO 10

FOR THE PIE DOUGH

- 7½ oz. (1⅔ cups) unbleached all-purpose flour; more for rolling
- 2 Tbs. granulated sugar
- 1 tsp. kosher salt
- 6 oz. (¾ cup) chilled unsalted butter, cut into small cubes
- 5 to 7 Tbs. ice water

FOR THE FILLING

- 8 large egg yolks
- 1 tsp. pure vanilla extract
- ⅔ cup packed light brown sugar
- 4 oz. (½ cup) unsalted butter, cut into 4 pieces
- ½ cup light corn syrup
- ½ cup heavy cream
- ½ tsp. kosher salt
- 1½ cups pecan halves, toasted, cooled, and coarsely chopped

This recipe is the perfect formula: flaky, buttery, tender crust; crunchy pecans; and luscious, not-too-sweet filling. Make the classic filling here or mix it up with one of the variations on pp. 111–112.

MAKE THE DOUGH

1. Put the flour, sugar, and salt in a food processor and pulse to combine. Add the butter and pulse until the largest pieces are about the size of corn kernels, 8 to 12 one-second pulses. Drizzle 5 Tbs. of the ice water over the flour mixture and pulse until the mixture becomes a moist, crumbly-looking dough that holds together when squeezed in your hand, 4 to 6 pulses. If the dough is still dry, add another tablespoon or two of ice water and test again.

2. Turn the dough out onto a clean work surface. Gently gather and press the dough into a disk. Wrap the dough in plastic and chill for at least 1 hour or up to 2 days (or freeze for up to 1 month; defrost in the refrigerator overnight before using).

3. Let the dough sit at room temperature to soften slightly (it should be firm but not rock hard), 5 to 20 minutes, depending on how long it was chilled. Roll the dough on a lightly floured work surface with a lightly floured rolling pin until it's about 13 inches wide and ⅛ inch thick.

4. Roll from the center of the dough to the edges and try to use as few passes as possible to avoid overworking the dough. After every few passes, run an offset spatula or a bench knife under the dough to be sure it isn't sticking, and give the dough a quarter turn. Reflour the work surface and rolling pin only as needed—excess flour makes the crust tough.

5. Transfer the dough to a 9-inch pie plate by rolling it around the rolling pin and unrolling it into the plate. You can also fold the dough in half and unfold it into the plate. To fit the dough into the plate, gently lift the edges to create enough slack to line the sides without stretching the dough. Trim off all but ¾ inch of the overhang. Roll the dough under itself to build up the edge of the crust. Crimp the edge of the crust with your fingers. With the tines of a fork, prick the crust all over. Chill for up to 1 hour in the refrigerator or about 30 minutes in the freezer.

6. Position a rack in the center of the oven and heat the oven to 425°F. Line the piecrust with foil and fill with dried beans or pie weights. Bake for 15 minutes. Remove the foil and weights. Reduce the oven temperature to 375°F and continue baking until the bottom looks dry and the edges are golden, 5 to 7 minutes more. Cool on a rack while you prepare the filling. Reduce the oven temperature to 325°F and put a large, rimmed baking sheet on the oven rack.

MAKE THE FILLING

Put the egg yolks in a medium heatproof bowl set on a kitchen towel and add the vanilla. Combine the sugar, butter, corn syrup, cream, and salt in a 1-quart saucepan. Heat over medium heat, stirring often, just until the butter is melted and the mixture is hot but not boiling, 3 to 5 minutes. Whisking vigorously and constantly, very slowly pour the hot sugar mixture into the yolks. Strain through a fine-mesh strainer set over a 1-quart measuring cup.

FILL AND BAKE THE PIE

Spread the toasted pecans evenly in the piecrust. Slowly pour the filling over the pecans. Put the pie on the baking sheet and bake until the center of the pie is slightly firm to the touch and the filling doesn't wobble when the pie is nudged, 35 to 40 minutes. Let cool for at least 1 hour before serving. The pie can be made up to 1 day ahead (store covered with plastic at room temperature), but it's best eaten warm or at room temperature on the day it's made. *—David Guas*

PER SERVING: 590 CALORIES | 6G PROTEIN | 50G CARB | 42G TOTAL FAT | 20G SAT FAT | 15G MONO FAT | 5G POLY FAT | 225MG CHOL | 200MG SODIUM | 2G FIBER

Fresh Pecans Are Key

The star of this pie is the pecans, which we south-erners pronounce pih-KAHNS, not pee-KANS. The oil in pecans can spoil quickly, so be sure to taste them before starting the recipe. If they taste rancid or musty, throw them out and buy fresh ones. To avoid spoilage, store unshelled pecans in an  airtight container in a cool, dry place for up to 1 year, or freeze shelled pecans in an airtight container for up to 2 years.

how to make pecan pie

Test the dough by squeezing a bit in your hand—it should hold its shape without crumbling. If not, add more water 1 Tbs. at a time.

To avoid tough, overworked dough, always roll from the center out toward the edges, making as few passes as possible.

To keep the dough from sticking, run a long offset spatula underneath it every so often.

Try not to stretch the dough as you fit it into the pan—stretched dough shrinks when it's baked.

Rolling the overhanging dough under itself, rather than folding it, creates a thicker crust edge, which makes crimping easier.

For a decorative touch, crimp the dough like this, spacing the flutes about an inch apart.

So the crust doesn't get soggy from the filling, blind bake it first. It's done when the bottom looks dry and the edges are golden.

Constant whisking is my secret to incorporating the hot sugar mixture into the yolks without curdling them. Stabilize the bowl with a towel.

Pour the filling over the pecans in a slow, spiral motion; if you go too fast, the pecans may move, leaving gaps in the finished pie.

Pecan Pie Variations

bacon and cane syrup pecan pie filling

- 8 large egg yolks
- 1 tsp. pure vanilla extract
- ⅔ cup packed light brown sugar
- 4 oz. (½ cup) unsalted butter, cut into 4 pieces
- ½ cup cane syrup, such as Steen's® or Lyle's Golden Syrup®
- ½ cup heavy cream
- ¼ tsp. kosher salt
- 1½ cups pecan halves, toasted, cooled, and coarsely chopped
- ⅓ cup crumbled cooked bacon (3 or 4 strips)

Cane syrup is Louisiana's version of maple syrup, and its sweet, rich flavor goes well with smoky bacon.

1. Put the egg yolks in a medium heatproof bowl set on a kitchen towel and add the vanilla. Combine the sugar, butter, cane syrup, cream, and salt in a 1-quart saucepan. Heat over medium heat just until the butter is melted and the mixture is hot but not boiling, 3 to 5 minutes. Whisking vigorously and constantly, very slowly pour the hot sugar mixture into the yolks. Strain through a fine strainer set over a 1-quart measuring cup.

2. Spread the pecans evenly in the piecrust. Sprinkle the crumbled bacon evenly over the pecans.

3. Add the filling and bake according to the instructions.

chicory coffee pecan pie filling

- ¼ cup ground chicory coffee, such as Café Du Monde® or Community Coffee®
- ½ cup plus 2 Tbs. heavy cream
- 8 large egg yolks
- 1 tsp. pure vanilla extract
- ⅔ cup packed light brown sugar
- 4 oz. (½ cup) unsalted butter, cut into 4 pieces
- ½ cup light corn syrup
- 1 tsp. kosher salt
- 1½ cups pecan halves, toasted, cooled, and coarsely chopped

It's a beloved New Orleans tradition to add roasted, ground chicory root to coffee. The resulting chicory coffee, which you can buy at well-stocked grocery stores, adds a delicious bitter undertone to this pie. If you can't find chicory coffee, use dark-roasted regular coffee.

1. Combine the chicory coffee and cream in a 1-quart saucepan and heat over medium heat just until small bubbles form at the edge of the cream, 3 minutes. Stir, remove from the heat, and steep for 10 minutes. Strain and reserve.

2. Put the egg yolks in a medium heatproof bowl set on a kitchen towel and add the vanilla. Combine the sugar, butter, corn syrup, coffee mixture, and salt in a 1-quart saucepan. Heat over medium heat just until the butter is melted and the mixture is hot but not boiling, 3 to 5 minutes. Whisking vigorously and constantly, very slowly pour the hot sugar mixture into the yolks. Strain through a fine-mesh strainer set over a 1-quart measuring cup.

3. Spread the pecans evenly in the piecrust.

4. Add the filling and bake according to the instructions.

continued on p. 112

Pecan Pie Variations *(continued from p. 111)*

bourbon-chocolate pecan pie filling

- 8 large egg yolks
- 1 tsp. pure vanilla extract
- ⅔ cup packed light brown sugar
- 4 oz. (½ cup) unsalted butter, cut into 4 pieces
- ½ cup light corn syrup
- ½ cup heavy cream
- 3 Tbs. bourbon
- ½ tsp. kosher salt
- 1½ cups pecan halves, toasted, cooled, and coarsely chopped
- ½ cup chopped semisweet or bittersweet chocolate

Bourbon's sweet, toasty flavor is the perfect partner for the dark chocolate in this rich pie filling. Maker's Mark® and Knob Creek® are two good choices—and not just for pie.

1. Put the egg yolks in a medium heat-proof bowl set on a kitchen towel and add the vanilla. Combine the sugar, butter, corn syrup, cream, bourbon, and salt in a 1-quart saucepan. Heat over medium heat just until the butter is melted and the mixture is hot but not boiling, 3 to 5 minutes. Whisking vigorously and constantly, very slowly pour the hot sugar mixture into the yolks. Strain through a fine-mesh strainer set over a 1-quart measuring cup.

2. Spread the pecans evenly in the piecrust. Sprinkle the chopped chocolate evenly over the pecans.

3. Add the filling and bake according to the instructions.

What Is Lyle's Golden Syrup?

A familiar pantry staple in the U.K., Lyle's Golden Syrup is a full-flavored cane sugar syrup that's used as an ingredient in both baking and savory cooking, and as a topping for foods like pancakes and ice cream.

With its rich, caramelly flavor, Lyle's Golden Syrup is an alternative to using corn syrup in some recipes because corn syrup lacks great flavor and often produces a slightly runny filling. Replacing some of the corn syrup with the thicker, sweeter Golden Syrup results in a more stable filling with better flavor.

Store the syrup at cool room temperature. If crystals develop, heat the syrup before using to dissolve them.

gingery cranberry-pear tartlets

MAKES 12 TARTLETS

- **1 cup fresh cranberries**
- **⅓ cup granulated sugar**
- **⅓ cup orange juice**
- **2 medium, slightly underripe pears (I like Anjou), about ¾ lb. total, peeled, cored, and cut into ½-inch chunks**
- **⅓ cup golden raisins**
- **4 tsp. minced crystallized ginger**
- **A few drops of pure vanilla extract**
- **⅓ recipe Sweet Tartlet Dough (recipe on p. 115)**

Make Ahead

You can fill and bake the tartlets up to 1 month ahead and freeze them. Put the cooled tartlets on a shallow pan and freeze until firm, then layer them between waxed paper in an airtight container. Baked tartlets will also keep for 3 days in the fridge, wrapped in waxed paper and then foil (not plastic wrap).

To refresh, bake the tartlets at 325°F until warm, 5 to 7 minutes if refrigerated; 12 to 15 minutes if frozen.

Crystallized ginger accents this filling with sweet pears and tart cranberries. These tarts only require one-third of the dough recipe, so it's easy to double or triple the tarts, making this an ideal recipe for holiday gatherings.

1. In a 3-quart saucepan, cook the cranberries, sugar, and orange juice over medium heat just until the berries begin to pop. Reduce the heat to a simmer, partially cover, and cook for 5 minutes. Add the pears, raisins, and ginger. Cook over low heat with the lid askew until the pears are translucent, stirring gently if necessary, 10 to 12 minutes. Uncover and continue cooking until the liquid is syrupy and has reduced to about 2 Tbs., about 2 minutes. Remove from the heat and gently stir in the vanilla (avoid crushing the pears). Let cool to room temperature; the mixture thickens as it stands.

2. Position a rack in the lower third of the oven and heat the oven to 375°F.

3. Lightly spray a standard-size 12-cup muffin tin with vegetable oil (not necessary for nonstick tins). Using the score lines as a guide, cut off twelve 1-inch pieces of dough (reserve the rest of the dough for another use). Roll each piece into a ball in your palms (lightly flour your hands, if necessary). Put one ball in the center of each muffin cup.

4. If you have a wooden tart tamper, flour it lightly. Press the wider end onto a ball of dough until the dough thins out and begins coming up the sides of the cup, and then twist the tamper slightly to release it. Use the tamper's narrower end to push the dough halfway up the sides and to smooth out the dough where the sides meet the bottom. If you don't have a tart tamper, use a narrow, flat-bottomed glass or your fingers, lightly floured, to press the dough into the cups.

continued on p. 114

continued from p. 113

5. Tilt the muffin tin to see if the dough reaches the same level in all the cups; also check for any holes in the dough (this could cause the tartlet to stick to the pan). Rub your thumb around the rim of the dough in each cup for a clean, smooth edge. Slightly less than ½ inch of each cup should be exposed. Chill for at least 10 minutes to firm the dough.

6. Spoon the cooled filling into the dough-lined muffin cups. Bake until the pastry is golden brown and the fruit is bubbling, about 30 minutes. Let the pan cool on a wire rack for 10 minutes. Run a thin knife around the tartlets to loosen and then let them cool until they're firm enough to handle, about another 15 minutes. Using the tip of a small knife, gently lift the tartlets from the pan and set them on a wire rack to cool.
—Carole Walter

PER SERVING: 140 CALORIES | 1G PROTEIN | 22G CARB | 6G TOTAL FAT | 3G SAT FAT | 2G MONO FAT | 0G POLY FAT | 25MG CHOL | 20MG SODIUM | 1G FIBER

More about Cranberries

Cranberries are the fruit of a low, trailing evergreen vine. These slender vines flower in late summer and produce their distinctively tart, deep red berries in early fall.

Cranberries have a short season, but fortunately, they keep well, so it's easy to stock up. You can store fresh cranberries in the refrigerator's crisper drawer for up to 1 month, but you can also freeze them for up to 1 year. They can be frozen in their original packaging, or you can wash, dry, and pick through the berries first (discard any dark, mushy ones) and then transfer them to a heavy-duty freezer bag.

Use frozen cranberries like fresh cranberries in recipes. There's no need to thaw them—just put them in a colander, rinse in cold water, pat dry with a towel, and use—but you may need to increase cooking time slightly.

sweet tartlet dough

MAKES 3 DOZEN 2-INCH
TARTLETS

10⅛ oz. (2¼ cups) unbleached
all-purpose flour

⅓ cup superfine sugar

¼ tsp. salt

8 oz. (1 cup) chilled unsalted
butter, cut into ½-inch
cubes

1 large egg

1 large egg yolk

1 Tbs. cold water

¾ tsp. pure vanilla extract

This buttery crust is easy to handle, can be made ahead and frozen for up to 1 month, and is a cinch to mold with a wooden tart tamper. I use three standard medium-size muffin tins, each cup measuring 2¾ inches. If you don't have three, bake the tartlets in batches. If you can't find superfine sugar, make your own by processing granulated sugar in a food processor for a few seconds.

Put the flour, sugar, and salt in a food processor. Pulse 3 or 4 times to blend. Distribute the butter in the bowl and pulse 7 or 8 times. Process until the mixture resembles coarse meal, 8 to 10 seconds. In a small bowl, beat together the egg, egg yolk, water, and vanilla with a fork. Pour the egg mixture over the flour mixture and pulse 5 or 6 times. Process until the mixture just begins to form a mass, 8 to 10 seconds. Empty the dough onto a lightly floured surface and knead 6 to 8 times, until the dough is just smooth and malleable. Shape it into an evenly thick 6-inch square. Using a pastry scraper or the dull side of a long knife, score the dough at 1-inch intervals so you get thirty-six 1-inch squares. Cover the dough with plastic wrap and chill for at least 20 minutes.

pecan tartlets

MAKES 12 TARTLETS

⅓ recipe Sweet Tartlet Dough
(recipe on p. 115)

2 large eggs, lightly beaten

1 Tbs. heavy cream

¼ cup packed light brown
sugar

1 tsp. unbleached all-purpose
flour

Pinch of salt

½ cup light corn syrup

1 Tbs. unsalted butter, melted

¾ tsp. vanilla extract

1 cup broken pecans, lightly
toasted in a 325°F oven for
8 to 10 minutes

Make Ahead

Fill and bake the tartlets up
to 1 month ahead and freeze
them. Put the cooled tartlets
on a shallow pan and freeze
until firm, then layer them
between waxed paper in an
airtight container. Baked
tartlets will also keep for
3 days in the fridge, wrapped
in waxed paper and then foil.
Bake the tartlets at 325°F
until warm, 5 to 7 minutes if
refrigerated; 12 to 15 minutes
if frozen.

This version of pecan pie is neither cloyingly sweet nor overly gooey. It's simply crunchy toasted pecans sprinkled over a mouthwatering brown sugar filling.

1. Position a rack in the lower third of the oven and heat the oven to 375°F.

2. Lightly spray a standard-size 12-cup muffin tin with vegetable oil (not necessary for nonstick tins). Using the score lines as a guide, cut off twelve 1-inch pieces of dough (reserve the rest of the dough for another use). Roll each piece into a ball in your palms (lightly flour your hands, if necessary). Put one ball in the center of each muffin cup.

3. If you have a wooden tart tamper, flour it lightly. Press the wider end onto a ball of dough until the dough thins out and begins coming up the sides of the cup, and then twist the tamper slightly to release it. Use the tamper's narrower end to push the dough halfway up the sides and to smooth out the dough where the sides meet the bottom. If you don't have a tart tamper, use a narrow, flat-bottomed glass or your fingers, lightly floured, to press the dough into the cups.

4. Tilt the muffin tin to see if the dough reaches the same level in all the cups; also check for any holes in the dough (this could cause the tartlet to stick to the pan). Rub your thumb around the rim of the dough in each cup for a clean, smooth edge. Slightly less than ½ inch of each cup should be exposed. Chill for at least 10 minutes to firm the dough.

5. In a medium bowl, blend the eggs and cream. In another bowl, combine the brown sugar, flour, and salt. Stir the dry ingredients into the egg mixture, along with the corn syrup and melted butter; don't overmix. Stir in the vanilla. Transfer the filling to a measuring cup with a spout and pour into the dough-lined muffin cups. Sprinkle the pecans evenly over the tops.

6. Bake until the pastry is golden brown, 28 to 30 minutes. Let cool on a wire rack for 10 minutes. Run a thin knife around the tartlets to loosen and then let them cool until they're firm enough to handle, about another 15 minutes. Using the tip of a small knife, gently lift the tartlets from the pan and set them on a wire rack to cool. —*Carole Walter*

PER SERVING: 130 CALORIES | 2G PROTEIN | 13G CARB | 8G TOTAL FAT | 5G SAT FAT | 2G MONO FAT | 0G POLY FAT | 50MG CHOL | 50MG SODIUM | 1G FIBER

coffee-toffee pecan pie

SERVES 8

- 3   oz. (6 Tbs.) unsalted butter
- ¾   cup packed dark brown sugar
- ¾   cup light or dark corn syrup
- ½   cup Lyle's Golden Syrup
- 3   large eggs, at room temperature
- 2   Tbs. bourbon
- 1   Tbs. instant espresso powder
- 1   tsp. pure vanilla extract
- ¾   tsp. table salt
- ⅓   cup very finely chopped toasted pecans
- 2   cups toasted pecan halves
- 1   blind-baked All-Butter Piecrust (recipe on p. 118)
- ½   cup crushed chocolate toffee candy pieces, such as Heath® or Skor®

With notes of butterscotch, espresso, and bourbon, this is a pecan pie like no other.

1. Position a rack in the center of the oven, set a heavy-duty rimmed baking sheet on the rack, and heat the oven to 375°F.

2. In a medium saucepan over medium heat, melt the butter and cook, swirling the pan occasionally, until the butter is brown, 3 to 5 minutes. Immediately whisk in the brown sugar, corn syrup, and Lyle's Golden Syrup until smooth. Remove the pan from the heat and let cool slightly. One at a time, whisk in the eggs. Whisk in the bourbon, espresso powder, vanilla, and salt. Stir in the chopped pecans.

3. Sprinkle half of the pecan halves in the piecrust, followed by the toffee candy pieces, and then the remaining pecan halves. Pour the syrup mixture over all.

4. Put the pie on the heated baking sheet and reduce the oven temperature to 350°F. Bake until set, 45 to 55 minutes, rotating the pan halfway through baking. When the pan is nudged, the center of the pie will no longer wobble, but the whole pie will jiggle just slightly and the filling will bubble at the edges.

5. Transfer to a rack and cool completely before serving. The pie can be stored at room temperature for up to 2 days. *—Nicole Rees*

PER SERVING: 810 CALORIES | 8G PROTEIN | 87G CARB | 49G TOTAL FAT | 17G SAT FAT | 19G MONO FAT | 8G POLY FAT | 135MG CHOL | 430MG SODIUM | 4G FIBER

all-butter piecrust

6 oz. (1⅓ cups) unbleached all-purpose flour

1 tsp. granulated sugar

⅜ tsp. table salt

4 oz. (½ cup) chilled unsalted butter, preferably European style, cut into ¾-inch pieces

3 to 4 Tbs. ice water

This pie dough can be made ahead and refrigerated overnight or frozen (before or after rolling) for up to 3 months. Simply transfer the dough to the refrigerator the night before you plan to make pie, and it'll be ready to go.

MAKE THE DOUGH

1. Put the flour, sugar, and salt in a medium bowl and stir with a rubber spatula or a fork to combine. Add the butter to the bowl. Rub the cold chunks of butter between your fingertips, smearing the butter into the flour to create small (roughly ¼-inch) flakes of fat.

2. Drizzle 3 Tbs. ice water over the flour mixture. Stir with the spatula or fork, adding 1 Tbs. more water if necessary, until the mixture forms a shaggy dough that's moist enough to hold together when pressed between your fingers.

3. With well-floured hands, gently gather and press the dough together, and then form it into a disk with smooth edges. Wrap the dough in plastic and chill for at least 1 hour, but preferably 2 to 4 hours, before rolling.

ROLL THE DOUGH

1. Let the chilled dough sit at room temperature to soften slightly—it should be cold and firm but not rock hard. Depending on how long the dough was chilled, this could take 5 to 20 minutes. When ready to roll, lightly flour the countertop or other surface (a pastry cloth, silicone rolling mat, or parchment on a counter also works great) and position the rolling pin in the center of the dough disk. Roll away from you toward 12 o'clock, easing the pressure as you near the edge to keep the edge from becoming too thin. Return to the center and roll toward 6 o'clock. Repeat toward 3 and then 9 o'clock, always easing the pressure at the edges and picking up the pin rather than rolling it back to the center.

2. Continue to "roll around the clock," aiming for different "times" on each pass until the dough is 13 to 14 inches in diameter and about ⅛ inch thick. Try to use as few passes of the rolling pin as possible. After every few passes, check that the dough isn't sticking by lifting it with a bench knife (dough scraper). Reflour only as needed—excess flour makes a drier, tougher crust. Each time you lift the dough, give it a quarter turn to help even out the thickness.

LINE THE PIE PLATE

1. Gently transfer the dough to a 9-inch pie plate, preferably metal, by folding it in half and unfolding it into the plate. Do not stretch the dough as you line the pan, or it will spring back when baked. Gently lift the outer edges of the dough to give you enough slack to line the sides of the pan without stretching the dough.

2. Trim the overhanging dough to 1 inch from the edge of the pan. Roll the dough under itself into a cylinder that rests on the edge of the pan.

3. To crimp the edge, have one hand on the inside of the edge, and one hand on the outside, and use the index finger of the inside hand to push the dough between the thumb and index finger of the outside hand to form a U or V shape. Repeat around the edge of the pie plate, creating a crimped edge whose individual flutes are about 1 inch apart. As you are going along, if you notice that the edge is not perfectly symmetrical and that the amount of dough you'll have to crimp seems sparse in places, take a bit of trimmed scrap, wet it with a drop or two of water, and attach it to the sparse area by pressing it firmly into place.

4. Prick the sides and bottom of the crust all over with a fork. Refrigerate until firm, about 1 hour or overnight. This will relax the dough and help prevent the edges from caving in.

BLIND BAKE THE CRUST

1. Position a rack in the center of the oven and heat the oven to 425°F. Line the chilled piecrust with foil and fill it with dried beans or pie weights. Bake for 15 minutes; remove the foil and the beans or weights. Reduce the oven temperature to 375°F.

2. Bake until the bottom looks dry but is not quite done and the edges are light golden, 5 to 7 minutes more.

jamaican-spiced pumpkin pie

SERVES 8

1   15-oz. can pure pumpkin purée

1¼ cups unsweetened coconut milk (full fat only, stirred or shaken well before using)

¾   cup packed light brown sugar

1   tsp. ground ginger

¾   tsp. ground cinnamon

½   tsp. table salt

⅛   tsp. freshly grated nutmeg

4   large eggs, at room temperature

2   Tbs. spiced rum, such as Captain Morgan®

1   blind-baked All-Butter Piecrust (recipe on p. 118)

Coconut milk and spiced rum add an unusual and delicious twist to this pumpkin pie.

1. Position a rack in the center of the oven, set a heavy-duty rimmed baking sheet on the rack, and heat the oven to 425°F.

2. In a large bowl, whisk the pumpkin, coconut milk, sugar, ginger, cinnamon, salt, and nutmeg until smooth. Whisk in the eggs and then the rum, until the mixture is smooth. Pour the filling into the piecrust.

3. Put the pie on the heated baking sheet. Bake for 10 minutes and then reduce the oven temperature to 350°F. Bake until the center of the pie no longer wobbles when the pan is nudged (a slight jiggle is fine), an additional 45 to 55 minutes.

4. Transfer to a rack and cool completely before serving. The pie can be stored at room temperature for up to 2 days. *—Nicole Rees*

PER SERVING: 430 CALORIES | 7G PROTEIN | 53G CARB | 22G TOTAL FAT | 15G SAT FAT | 4.5G MONO FAT | 1G POLY FAT | 135MG CHOL | 410MG SODIUM | 6G FIBER

sweet potato pie

FOR THE PIE DOUGH

- **6** oz. (1⅓ cups) unbleached all-purpose flour
- **½** tsp. granulated sugar
- **½** tsp. kosher salt
- **3** oz. (6 Tbs.) chilled unsalted butter, cut into ½-inch pieces
- **1** oz. (2 Tbs.) chilled vegetable shortening, cut into ½-inch pieces
- **3½** Tbs. ice water; more as needed

FOR THE FILLING

- **2** medium-to-large sweet potatoes (12 to 14 oz. each)
- **1** cup half-and-half
- **3** large eggs
- **¾** cup packed light brown sugar
- **2** tsp. dark rum
- **1½** tsp. ground ginger
- **1½** tsp. ground cinnamon
- **1** tsp. pure vanilla extract
- **½** tsp. kosher salt
- **¼** tsp. ground cloves
- Pinch of freshly grated nutmeg
- Pinch of freshly ground black pepper
- Lightly sweetened whipped cream, for serving (optional)

Because of its similar texture, sweet potato is a natural stand-in for pumpkin in this spin on traditional Thanksgiving pie.

MAKE THE DOUGH

1. Combine the flour, sugar, and salt in a large bowl. Add half of the butter. Using your hands, gently toss the butter to coat each piece with flour. Using a pastry cutter or two knives, cut the butter into the flour until the mixture has the texture of coarse oatmeal. Add the remaining butter and the shortening, gently toss, and quickly cut again until the larger pieces are about the size of kidney beans.

2. While tossing the mixture with your hand, sprinkle the ice water on top. Continue to toss between your fingers until moistened evenly. The dough should look shaggy but hold together when gently squeezed in the palm of your hand. If not, add a little more water. Gather the dough into a ball—don't knead it, just squeeze it into one solid mass. Press the dough into a flat disk and wrap tightly in plastic. Refrigerate for at least 2 hours or up to 2 days.

3. On a lightly floured surface, roll out the dough to a round that's 12 to 13 inches in diameter and ⅛ inch thick. Gently fit the dough into a 9-inch pie plate, being careful not to stretch it. Trim the edge to a ½-inch overhang. Fold the overhang under to create a thick edge—if some areas are sparse, use the trimmings to bulk them up. Crimp the edge. Prick the dough all over with a fork. Cover and refrigerate until firm, at least 1 hour or overnight.

4. Position a rack in the center of the oven and heat the oven to 425°F.

5. Line the pie shell with parchment or foil and fill with pie weights or dried beans. Bake until the edges are just beginning to turn golden, about 15 minutes. Carefully remove the parchment and weights and reduce the oven temperature to 375°F. Continue to bake until the bottom of the crust looks dry and is just beginning to turn golden, 10 to 15 minutes more. Cool completely on a wire rack.

MAKE THE FILLING

1. Raise the oven temperature to 400°F. Prick each potato once and roast on a rimmed baking sheet until tender, about 1 hour. Let cool. When the potatoes are cool enough to handle, peel them and cut away any dark spots. Pass the potatoes through a food mill or potato ricer; you'll need 2 cups. (The potatoes can be prepared to this point up to a day ahead. Refrigerate and return to room temperature before continuing with the recipe.)

continued on p. 122

continued from p. 121

2. Put the potato purée, half-and-half, eggs, sugar, rum, ginger, cinnamon, vanilla, salt, cloves, nutmeg, and pepper in a blender and blend until well combined, 1 to 2 minutes. Transfer the sweet potato mixture to a 3-quart saucepan and warm just slightly (to about 100°F) over medium-low heat, stirring constantly, about 2 minutes. Pour the filling into the baked pie shell and bake until just set in the center, 25 to 30 minutes. Transfer to a wire rack and let cool completely. Slice and serve with a generous dollop of whipped cream, if using. —*Tasha DeSerio*

PER SERVING: 310 CALORIES | 5G PROTEIN | 40G CARB | 14G TOTAL FAT | 7G SAT FAT | 4G MONO FAT | 1.5G POLY FAT | 90MG CHOL | 160MG SODIUM | 2G FIBER

honey-spice walnut tart

**MAKES TWO 5X15-INCH TARTS;
SERVES 8 TO 10**

- **4** Tbs. unsalted butter, at room temperature
- **⅓** cup honey
- **2** Tbs. granulated sugar
- **1½** tsp. ground cinnamon
- **1** tsp. ground ginger
- Pinch of salt
- **1** large egg
- **1** cup coarsely chopped walnuts
- **1** sheet (about 9 oz.) frozen puff pastry, thawed

You can make this tart several hours ahead and reheat it in a 400°F oven for a couple of minutes to freshen it up before serving.

1. Heat the oven to 400°F. In a food processor or with a wooden spoon, blend the butter, honey, sugar, cinnamon, ginger, and salt until smooth. Add the egg and process or beat just until blended. Add the nuts all at once and process only until blended. The nuts should be chopped, but not so fine that the mixture becomes a smooth paste; you want some crunch left.

2. Cut the pastry sheet in half to make two strips about 4x9 inches. Roll one strip to 6x15 inches. Prick the entire surface of the strip with the tines of a fork. Slide the sheet onto a parchment-lined or nonstick baking sheet. Spread the center of the strip with half of the nut mixture, to within ½ inch of the long edges and all the way to the edge on the short ends. Fold the bare long edges ½ inch over the nut mixture and press firmly to stick; with the blunt edge of a table knife, make indentations into the long edges about ½ inch apart to crimp the border a bit. Repeat with the second pastry strip and the rest of the nut mixture.

3. Bake until the filling looks slightly dry on top and the pastry is deep golden brown on the edges and underneath, 19 to 21 minutes. Slide the tarts onto a rack to cool. Cut into four or five strips each and serve slightly warm. *—Martha Holmberg*

butterscotch tartlets

SERVES 6

FOR THE TARTLET CRUST

6¾ oz. (1½ cups) unbleached all-purpose flour

2 Tbs. granulated sugar

½ tsp. baking powder

Pinch of salt

2 oz. (4 Tbs.) unsalted chilled butter, cut into small pieces

1 large egg, beaten slightly

1 Tbs. cold water; 1½ tsp. more if needed

FOR THE FILLING

½ cup cashews, well toasted

½ cup sliced almonds, well toasted

½ cup walnut pieces, well toasted

⅓ cup shredded coconut, well toasted

½ cup golden raisins

1¼ cups warm Butterscotch Sauce (recipe on the facing page)

Unsweetened whipped cream or crème fraîche (optional)

You'll need six 4-inch tartlet pans to make these small tarts. If you don't have all the nuts on hand, just use 1½ cups total of what you do have.

MAKE THE CRUST

1. In a large bowl, combine the flour, sugar, baking powder, and salt. Add the butter and cut it into the dough using two knives, a pastry blender, or your fingertips until the dough looks crumbly. Add the egg and 1 Tbs. of the cold water; mix with a fork until the dough just holds together. (If the dough won't come together, add up to another 1½ tsp. water, a tiny bit at a time.) Don't overmix; the dough should feel slightly sticky. Shape the dough into a 6-inch log. Wrap it in plastic and refrigerate until firm, about 1 hour.

2. Heat the oven to 400°F. Cut the chilled dough into six equal pieces. Roll each piece into a round about ⅛ inch thick. Prick the rounds all over with a fork and gently fit them into 4-inch tartlet pans, trimming any excess dough.

3. Line each tartlet with foil and fill with dried beans or pie weights. Bake the tartlet shells for about 15 minutes.

4. Remove the pie weights and the foil and bake for an additional 5 minutes, until golden. Cool on a rack.

FILL AND BAKE THE TARTLETS

Reduce the oven temperature to 350°F. Combine the toasted nuts, coconut, and raisins with the warm butterscotch sauce. Divide the filling among the six tartlet shells. Bake until the filling just starts to bubble, 7 to 9 minutes. Using a wide spatula, carefully transfer the tartlets to a rack. Allow the tartlets to cool for 5 minutes. Carefully remove the tartlets from their pans and serve warm with a dollop of unsweetened whipped cream or crème fraîche, if you like. —*Melissa Murphy*

PER SERVING: 740 CALORIES | 10G PROTEIN | 89G CARB | 41G TOTAL FAT | 18G SAT FAT | 14G MONO FAT | 7G POLY FAT | 95MG CHOL | 430MG SODIUM | 4G FIBER

butterscotch sauce

MAKES 2½ CUPS

- **4 oz. (½ cup) unsalted butter**
- **⅔ cup firmly packed dark brown sugar**
- **⅔ cup granulated sugar**
- **1½ tsp. salt**
- **¾ cup light corn syrup**
- **¾ cup heavy cream**
- **2 tsp. pure vanilla extract**

This sauce is also great drizzled over grilled pineapple, ice cream, or even apple pie. Refrigerated, it will keep for about 2 weeks. Reheat it gently, adding a little cream if it's too thick.

In a medium, heavy-based saucepan, melt the butter. Stir in the two sugars, the salt, 2 Tbs. water, and the corn syrup. Bring the mixture to a boil over medium-high heat, stirring to dissolve the sugars. Let the mixture boil for 5 minutes, stirring often. You'll see big, slow bubbles as it boils. Remove the sauce from the heat. Carefully whisk in the cream and vanilla (the sauce may sputter). Allow the sauce to cool to warm before serving.

tips for making butterscotch

The trick to making butterscotch is to be bold about cooking it. You don't want to burn it, but if you cook it too lightly, you won't create the deep caramelized flavor.

Dark brown sugar gives butterscotch a deep flavor.

A pot of butterscotch will bubble and sputter. Use a long spoon to stir it.

pumpkin praline pie

½ recipe Classic Piecrust
(recipe on the facing page)

FOR THE PRALINE

½ cup packed dark brown
sugar

1 Tbs. unsalted butter,
at room temperature

1 Tbs. finely chopped fresh
ginger

FOR THE FILLING

1⅔ cups canned pumpkin purée

⅔ cup packed dark brown
sugar

4 tsp. unbleached all-purpose
flour

1½ tsp. ground cinnamon

½ tsp. ground ginger

Pinch of ground cloves

Pinch of salt

3 large eggs

1 cup heavy cream

1 tsp. pure vanilla extract

Chill this pie overnight to let the flavors marry and mellow; serve slightly chilled.

Roll out the dough for a one-crust pie, line a 9-inch pie pan, and chill it in the freezer for 30 minutes. Position a rack in the middle of the oven; heat the oven to 425°F. Line the pie shell with foil and fill with weights. Bake until the crust's edge is golden brown, about 10 minutes.

MAKE THE PRALINE
Meanwhile, in a bowl, mix the sugar, butter, and fresh ginger until well blended. Remove the beans and foil from the crust; crumble the praline evenly over the bottom. Bake until the sides of the crust are golden brown and the praline is bubbling and dark brown, about 12 minutes, checking for bubbles (press them down gently with the back of a spoon). Remove from the oven. Reduce the oven heat to 325°F.

MAKE THE FILLING
1. In a bowl, whisk the pumpkin, brown sugar, flour, cinnamon, ground ginger, cloves, and salt until smooth. Add the eggs, cream, and vanilla; whisk until just blended. When the praline has hardened but is still warm, pour the filling into the crust.

2. Bake until the edge of the filling looks slightly dry and the center jiggles slightly when the pan is nudged, 45 to 50 minutes. Cool on a rack. Refrigerate overnight before serving. *—Abigail Johnson Dodge*

PER SERVING: 440 CALORIES | 6G PROTEIN | 54G CARB | 24G TOTAL FAT | 13G SAT FAT | 7G MONO FAT | 2G POLY FAT | 140MG CHOL | 160MG SODIUM | 2G FIBER

classic piecrust

**MAKES ENOUGH DOUGH FOR
ONE 9-INCH DOUBLE-CRUST
PIE**

- **11¼ oz. (2½ cups) unbleached
  all-purpose flour**
- **1 Tbs. granulated sugar**
- **½ tsp. salt**
- **¼ lb. (½ cup) chilled unsalted
  butter, cut into ½-inch
  pieces**
- **¼ cup chilled vegetable shortening, cut into ½-inch pieces**
- **2 tsp. fresh lemon juice**
- **3 oz. (¼ cup plus 2 Tbs.) very
  cold water**

This dough keeps in the freezer for 3 months.

Put the flour, sugar, and salt in a food processor; pulse briefly to combine. Add the butter and shortening; pulse just until coarse crumbs
form, about 30 seconds. Add the lemon juice and water. Pulse just
until moist crumbs form. Turn the dough onto a work surface and
gently shape it into two equal disks 4 or 5 inches in diameter. Wrap in
plastic and refrigerate for at least 1 hour or up to 1 day.

FOR A ONE-CRUST PIE

Roll one disk of dough between two large pieces of lightly floured
parchment. Roll into a 14-inch-diameter round that's ⅛ inch thick.
Remove the top sheet of parchment. Gently roll the dough around
the pin and position the pin over the pie pan. Unroll, gently easing the
dough into the pan, gently but firmly pressing the dough against the
sides and bottom, taking care not to pull or stretch. With scissors, trim
the edge of the dough, leaving a ¾-inch margin from the outer edge of
the pan. Tuck this dough under to shape a high edge crust that rests
on top of the rim. Pinch-crimp the edge of the dough.

FOR BLIND BAKING

Freeze the crust for at least 30 minutes. Heat the oven to 425°F. Line
the frozen crust with a large piece of foil, fill with pie weights (or dried
beans or rice), and bake for 12 minutes. Remove the foil and weights
and continue baking the shell until golden, about 8 minutes longer,
checking for bubbles (push them down gently with the back of a spoon).

FOR A DOUBLE-CRUST PIE

Roll out one disk of dough as for a one-crust pie and line a 9-inch
pie pan, leaving the excess hanging over the side. Cover loosely with
plastic while you roll out the other disk between parchment. Load the
filling into the shell. Brush the edge of the bottom crust with water. Roll
the top crust around the pin and position it over the pie. Gently unroll,
centering the dough over the filling. Press the edges together and,
with scissors, trim both crusts so they're ½ inch larger than the outer
edge of the pie pan. Tuck this dough under to shape a high edge crust
that rests on top of the rim. Pinch-crimp the edge of the dough. With
a paring knife, slash two or three vent holes in the top crust and bake
following the recipe directions.

chocolate-espresso pecan pie

SERVES 8 TO 10

FOR THE CRUST

- **6** oz. (1⅓ cups) unbleached all-purpose flour; more for rolling out the crust
- **1** tsp. granulated sugar
- **¼** tsp. plus ⅛ tsp. kosher salt
- **2** oz. (4 Tbs.) chilled unsalted butter, cut into ½-inch pieces
- **2** oz. (4 Tbs.) vegetable short-ening, chilled and cut into ½-inch pieces (put it in the freezer for 15 minutes before cutting)
- **2** to 4 Tbs. cold water

FOR THE FILLING

- **3** oz. unsweetened chocolate, coarsely chopped
- **2** oz. (4 Tbs.) unsalted butter
- **4** large eggs
- **1** cup light corn syrup
- **1** cup granulated sugar
- **¼** tsp. kosher salt
- **2** Tbs. instant espresso powder (or instant coffee)
- **2** Tbs. coffee liqueur (Kahlúa® or Caffé Lolita)
- **2** cups lightly toasted, coarsely chopped pecans
- About ½ cup perfect pecan halves

This pie tastes best if cooled and then refrigerated for several hours or overnight. Serve it lightly chilled with a dollop of very lightly sweetened whipped cream.

MAKE THE CRUST

1. Pulse the flour, sugar, and salt in a food processor just to blend. Add the butter and shortening and pulse several times until the mixture resembles coarse cornmeal, 8 to 10 pulses. Transfer the mixture to a medium bowl. Tossing and stirring quickly with a fork, gradually add enough of the cold water that the dough just begins to come together. It should clump together easily if lightly squeezed but not feel wet or sticky. With your hands, gather the dough and form it into a ball. Flatten the ball into a disk and wrap it in plastic. Chill the dough for 2 hours or up to 2 days before rolling. The dough can also be frozen for up to 2 months; thaw it overnight in the refrigerator before using.

2. Remove the dough from the refrigerator and let it sit at room tem-perature until pliable, 10 to 15 minutes. On a lightly floured surface with a lightly floured rolling pin, roll the dough into a 13-inch-diameter round that's ⅛ inch thick. Be sure to pick up the dough several times and rotate it, reflouring the surface lightly to prevent sticking. I use a giant spatula or the bottom of a removable-bottom tart pan to move the dough around. Transfer the dough to a 9-inch Pyrex pie pan and trim the edges so there's a ½-inch overhang. Fold the overhang under-neath itself to create a raised edge and then decoratively crimp or flute the edge. (Save the scraps for patching the shell later, if neces-sary.) Chill until the dough firms up, at least 45 minutes in the refrig-erator or 20 minutes in the freezer.

3. Position a rack in the center of the oven and heat the oven to 350°F. Line the pie shell with parchment and fill with dried beans or pie weights. Bake until the edges of the crust are light golden brown, 25 to 30 minutes. Carefully remove the parchment and beans or weights. If necessary, gently repair any cracks with a smear of the excess dough. Transfer the shell to a rack to cool.

MAKE THE FILLING

1. Melt the chocolate and butter in the microwave or in a small metal bowl set in a skillet of barely simmering water, stirring with a rubber spatula until smooth.

2. In a medium mixing bowl, whisk the eggs, corn syrup, sugar, and salt. Dissolve the instant espresso in 1 Tbs. hot water and add to the egg mixture, along with the coffee liqueur and the melted chocolate and butter. Whisk to blend.

continued on p. 130

continued from p. 129

3. Evenly spread the toasted pecan pieces in the pie shell. To form a decorative border, arrange the pecan halves around the perimeter of the pie shell, on top of the pecan pieces, keeping the points of the pecans facing in and the backs just touching the crust. Carefully pour the filling over the pecans until the shell is three-quarters full. Pour the remaining filling into a liquid measuring cup or small pitcher. Transfer the pie to the oven and pour in the remaining filling. (The pecans will rise to the top as the pie bakes.)

4. Bake the pie until the filling puffs up, just starts to crack, and appears fairly set, 45 to 55 minutes. Transfer it to a rack and allow it to cool completely (at least 4 hours) before serving. *—Karen Barker*

PER SERVING: 650 CALORIES | 8G PROTEIN | 66G CARB | 42G TOTAL FAT | 12G SAT FAT | 18G MONO FAT | 8G POLY FAT | 110MG CHOL | 120MG SODIUM | 5G FIBER

how to make a decorative pecan border

Arrange the pecan halves in a ring around the perimeter of the pie shell interior, keeping the points of the pecans facing in and the backs just touching the pie shell.

Carefully pour the filling over the pecans until the shell is three-quarters full. The pecans will rise to the top as the pie bakes.

sugar and spice pumpkin pie with brandied ginger cream

SERVES 8 TO 10

FOR THE CRUST

- ½ tsp. table salt
- ⅓ cup very cold water
- 6¾ oz. (1½ cups) unbleached all-purpose flour
- 5 oz. (10 Tbs.) chilled unsalted butter, cut into 1-inch pieces

FOR THE FILLING

- 1 15-oz. can pure pumpkin
- 2 large eggs
- 1 large egg yolk
- 1 cup heavy cream
- 1 Tbs. brandy
- ¾ cup lightly packed light brown sugar
- 1 tsp. ground ginger
- 1 tsp. freshly ground cinnamon stick (or 1½ tsp. ground cinnamon)
- ½ tsp. table salt
- ⅛ tsp. freshly grated nutmeg
- ⅛ tsp. freshly ground black pepper
- Pinch of freshly ground cloves (or ⅛ tsp. ground cloves)

FOR THE CREAM

- 1 cup heavy cream
- 2 Tbs. packed light brown sugar
- 1 tsp. ground ginger
- 1 tsp. brandy

It's worth freshly grinding the spices for this rich and silky pie; they add a depth and vibrancy you just don't get with the pre-ground variety.

MAKE THE CRUST

1. In a small bowl, stir the salt into the ⅓ cup cold water until dissolved. Put the flour in a food processor and scatter the butter on top. Pulse until the mixture forms large crumbs and some of the butter is in pieces the size of peas, about 8 pulses. Add the saltwater and pulse until the dough begins to come together in large clumps, about 7 pulses; you'll still see some butter pieces. Shape the dough into a 1-inch-thick disk, wrap in plastic, and chill for at least 1 hour or up to overnight.

2. On a lightly floured surface, roll the dough into a circle 16 inches in diameter and ⅛ inch thick. Transfer to a 9-inch ceramic, metal, or glass pie plate, easing the dough into the bottom and sides and then gently pressing into place. For a traditional crimped edge, trim the overhanging dough to ½ inch from the edge of the plate. Fold the overhang under and crimp decoratively. Wrap and refrigerate for at least 30 minutes or up to overnight, or freeze for up to 2 weeks.

BLIND BAKE THE CRUST

Position a rack in the center of the oven and heat the oven to 400°F. Line the chilled pie shell with parchment and fill it with dried beans or pie weights. Bake until the sides have just set and look dry, 16 to 20 minutes (lift the parchment to check). Remove the weights and parchment and bake until the edges are light golden and the bottom is pale and completely dry, about 5 minutes. If the dough starts to bubble while baking, gently push the bubbles down with the back of a spoon. Let the crust cool completely on a wire rack before filling.

MAKE THE FILLING AND BAKE THE PIE

1. Heat the oven to 325°F. In a large bowl, whisk the pumpkin, eggs, egg yolk, cream, and brandy. In a small bowl, mix the brown sugar, ginger, cinnamon, salt, nutmeg, pepper, and cloves. Whisk the sugar mixture into the pumpkin mixture.

continued on p. 132

continued from p. 131

Make Ahead

You can make and freeze the crust up to 2 weeks ahead. The pie may be filled and baked up to 2 days ahead.

2. Pour the filling into the cooled piecrust. Bake until the pie is set around the outside but still slightly wet and jiggly in the center, about 1 hour. The filling will continue to set as it cools. Let the pie cool completely on a wire rack and then refrigerate for at least 2 hours and up to 2 days before serving.

MAKE THE CREAM JUST BEFORE SERVING
Whip the cream with an electric mixer on medium-high speed until it forms very soft peaks, about 2 minutes. Add the sugar, ginger, and brandy and continue whipping until it forms medium-firm peaks, about 30 seconds longer. Dollop in the center of the pie, leaving a band of filling visible around the edge of the pie, or dollop on individual servings. *—Elisabeth Prueitt*

PER SERVING: 420 CALORIES | 5G PROTEIN | 37G CARB | 29G TOTAL FAT | 18G SAT FAT | 8G MONO FAT | 1.5G POLY FAT | 155MG CHOL | 260MG SODIUM | 2G FIBER

More about Nutmeg

This spice comes from the nutmeg tree, which grows in tropical climates and actually yields two spices. The crinkled, hard nutmeg "nut" itself is encased in a lacy scarlet membrane which, when dried and ground, becomes mace.

Although you can buy nutmeg already ground, nutmeg's highly volatile oils have the most punch when you grate whole nutmeg freshly into a dish. Use a Microplane® grater to make fast work of grating nutmeg. You can also buy a nutmeg grater especially for this task.

Most manufacturers and merchants agree that whole and ground spices have a 2-year shelf life once opened, if stored away from heat (under 68°F is best), humidity (no higher than 60 percent), light, and strong odors. It's a good idea to write the date of purchase right on the bag or tin.

creamy orange–ricotta tart
(recipe on p. 144)

creamy pies & tarts

lemon-lime meringue pie

SERVES 10 TO 12

FOR THE CRUST

- 9 oz. (2 cups) unbleached all-purpose flour
- 1 Tbs. granulated sugar
- ¼ tsp. table salt
- 6 oz. (¾ cup) chilled unsalted butter, cut into small pieces
- ¼ tsp. pure vanilla extract
- 1 large egg

FOR THE FILLING

- 6 large eggs
- 1½ cups granulated sugar
- ½ cup fresh lime juice (from 4 to 6 limes)
- ¼ cup fresh lemon juice (from about 2 lemons; grate the zest before juicing)
- 1 cup heavy cream
- 1 Tbs. grated lemon zest

FOR THE MERINGUE

- 1¼ cups firmly packed light brown Domino® pure cane sugar
- ¾ cup granulated sugar
- 1 cup egg whites, at room temperature (from about 8 large eggs)
- ¼ tsp. cream of tartar

You can make the pie filling up to 2 days before serving, but it's best to make the meringue the day the pie is served.

MAKE THE CRUST

1. In a stand mixer fitted with the paddle attachment, combine the flour, sugar, salt, and butter and mix on the lowest speed until a coarse meal texture forms, about 2 minutes. With the mixer running, add 2 Tbs. water and the vanilla; continue mixing on low until the dough clumps together, about 45 seconds. If the dough remains too dry and crumbly to form a cohesive mass, add a bit more water. Gather the dough into a ball and wrap in plastic, pressing on the plastic to flatten the dough into a disk. Refrigerate until the dough is firm enough to roll, about 30 minutes.

2. On a lightly floured surface, roll the dough to an 11-inch circle that's ⅛ inch thick. Transfer to a 9-inch deep-dish pie pan and flute the edges, if you like. Freeze the crust until hard, about 40 minute. Heat the oven to 350°F.

3. When the crust is hard, line it with foil and fill the foil with pie weights or dried beans. Put the pan on a baking sheet, bake for 40 minutes, and then remove the weights and foil and bake until the crust is golden brown and feels dry, another 20 to 30 minutes. Whisk the egg with about 1 tsp. water. Brush the egg on the crust bottom and sides and bake the crust until the egg is set and dry, about 3 minutes.

MAKE THE FILLING

While the piecrust is baking, in a medium bowl, whisk together the eggs and sugar until combined. Add the lime and lemon juices and whisk until smooth. Whisk in the heavy cream and strain the mixture into a pitcher or batter bowl (a large Pyrex measuring cup works well). Stir in the zest. When the crust is done, pour the filling into the crust without removing it from the oven, and reduce the oven temperature to 325°F. Bake the pie until the center is just set, about 50 minutes. Remove the pie from the oven, cool it on a rack, and then refrigerate until cold, at least 6 hours.

MAKE THE MERINGUE

Put the brown sugar and white sugar in a small, deep, heavy-based saucepan and cover with ½ cup water. In a stand mixer fitted with the whip attachment, put the egg whites and cream of tartar. Attach a candy thermometer to the sugar saucepan and boil the sugar over high heat. When the sugar syrup reaches 248°F, start whipping the egg whites on medium-high speed until they're very foamy, white, and have increased in volume, about 45 seconds. Keep whipping the egg whites; when the temperature of the syrup hits 254°F, remove the thermometer, set the mixer to medium speed, and carefully and slowly pour about one-third of the sugar syrup into the mixing egg

whites (it plops out in drops), avoiding the whip. Add the remaining syrup in a faster, steady stream. Increase the speed to high and whip the whites until they have become voluminous and form firm but not stiff peaks, about 3 minutes; the meringue should still be warm.

CREATE THE SPIKY MERINGUE DOME
Scrape the meringue from the bowl onto the chilled pie and, using a rubber spatula, create a smooth dome (avoid pressing on the meringue). With the back of a soupspoon, make decorative peaks in the meringue, working quickly before the meringue cools completely. If you have a kitchen torch, use it to brown the meringue. If not, set a broiler or oven rack to a lower rung and heat the broiler. Set the pie on a baking sheet and put it under the broiler, turning it several times to brown the meringue as evenly as possible.

Store the meringue pie in the refrigerator and serve within a few hours. —*Brigid Callinan*

PER SERVING: 490 CALORIES | 7G PROTEIN | 69G CARB | 22G TOTAL FAT | 13G SAT FAT | 7G MONO FAT | 1G POLY FAT | 180MG CHOL | 105MG SODIUM | 1G FIBER

lemon tart

SERVES 10 TO 12

FOR THE CRUST

- 4½ oz. (1 cup) unbleached all-purpose flour; more for dusting
- ¼ cup confectioners' sugar
- ¼ tsp. table salt
- 3 oz. (6 Tbs.) chilled unsalted butter, cut into ½-inch pieces
- 1 large egg yolk
- 1 Tbs. water

FOR THE FILLING

- ¾ cup granulated sugar
- 1 Tbs. unbleached all-purpose flour
- 1 tsp. finely grated lemon zest

  Pinch of table salt
- ⅔ cup strained fresh lemon juice (from about 3 lemons)
- 3 large eggs, at room temperature
- ¼ tsp. pure vanilla extract

  Strawberry Sauce (optional; recipe on the facing page)

Chill the tart dough for at least 1 hour or up to 2 days. If it has been in the refrigerator overnight, you may need to let it sit at room temperature for about 10 minutes until it's pliable enough to roll. Be sure the finished tart is fully cooled before wrapping well to freeze.

MAKE THE CRUST

1. Combine the flour, confectioners' sugar, and salt in a food processor. Process briefly to blend. Add the chilled butter pieces and pulse until the butter is no bigger than small peas (about ¼ inch). Ad d the egg yolk and drizzle the water over the mixture. Pulse briefly until the dough forms a loose ball. Dump the dough onto a large piece of plastic wrap and shape into a flat disk about 4 inches in diameter. Wrap the dough and refrigerate until well chilled, at least 1 hour or up to 2 days.

2. Lightly dust your work surface and rolling pin with flour. Roll the chilled dough into a 12-inch round. Lift and turn the dough several times as you roll to prevent sticking; dust the work surface and the rolling pin with flour as needed. Use a dough scraper or a spatula to loosen the rolled dough; carefully roll it up around the pin and unroll it over a 9¼-inch tart pan with a removable bottom. Gently fit it into the pan. Using lightly floured fingertips, gently press the dough into the corners and against the sides of the tart pan. Run the rolling pin over the top of the pan to trim the dough so that it's level with the top of the pan. Cover and freeze until the tart shell is very firm, at least 30 minutes.

3. Position a rack in the middle of the oven and heat the oven to 425°F. Line the frozen crust with foil and fill it with pie weights or a mix of raw rice and dried beans. Put the crust in the oven and immediately reduce the oven temperature to 400°F. Bake until the sides are golden and the bottom no longer looks wet, 15 to 20 minutes. Remove the foil, rice, and beans. Prick the bottom of the crust lightly with a fork (but don't pierce through it) and continue to bake until the shell is golden brown, another 5 to 8 minutes. Set the pan on a wire rack to cool while you prepare the filling. Reduce the oven temperature to 325°F.

Make Ahead

Let the tart cool in the pan to room temperature. Put the tart in the freezer for 1 hour to let it firm up, and then wrap it well in plastic and freeze it for up to 1 month. To serve, unwrap the tart, remove it from the pan, and set it on a flat serving plate. Let thaw at room temperature for about 1 hour.

MAKE THE FILLING AND FINISH THE TART

1. In a medium bowl, whisk together the sugar, flour, lemon zest, and salt. Pour in the lemon juice and whisk until blended and the sugar is dissolved. In a small bowl, lightly beat together the eggs and vanilla and then add to the lemon mixture. Whisk until just blended. (Don't overwhisk or the filling will have a foamy top when baked.)

2. Pour the filling into the baked crust. Return the tart to the oven and bake until the filling jiggles slightly when the pan is nudged, about 20 minutes. Let cool on a wire rack until the tart is room temperature, about 1 hour. If not serving right away, chill it for 1 hour and then wrap it in plastic; refrigerate overnight or freeze (see the directions at left). If serving immediately, remove the outer ring and run a long metal spatula under the tart to loosen. Carefully slide the tart onto a flat serving plate and serve with the strawberry sauce, if you like.

—*Abigail Johnson Dodge*

strawberry sauce

6 oz. frozen unsweetened strawberries (about 14 whole berries)

½ cup boiling water

2 to 3 Tbs. granulated sugar

Put the strawberries in a food processor and pour the boiling water over them. Add 2 Tbs. sugar and process until smooth; taste and add the other 1 Tbs. of sugar if desired. Serve immediately or refrigerate until ready to serve.

"key" lime pie

MAKES ONE 9-INCH PIE;
SERVES 8 TO 10

FOR THE CRUST

- 6¾ oz. (1½ cups) unbleached all-purpose flour
- ½ tsp. table salt
- 3 oz. (6 Tbs.) chilled unsalted butter, cubed
- 2 Tbs. chilled vegetable shortening, cubed
- 2½ to 3 Tbs. ice water

FOR THE FILLING

- 2 14-oz. cans sweetened condensed milk
- 2 large egg yolks
- 1 cup fresh lime juice (from about 4 limes)
- 2 tsp. finely grated lime zest (from about 2 limes)

FOR THE GARNISH

- 1 cup heavy cream
- 2 tsp. granulated sugar
- 1 lime, zested into thin strips

To make this version of this creamy-tangy pie, you don't need Key limes, just juicy ones.

MAKE THE CRUST

1. Put the flour and salt in a food processor; pulse to combine. Add the butter cubes and pulse until they're the size of extra-large peas (about 10 quick pulses). Add the shortening and continue pulsing until the largest pieces of butter and shortening are the size of peas (10 to 15 more quick pulses). Sprinkle 2½ Tbs. of the water over the flour mixture and pulse a few times until the mixture just begins to come together. It should look rather crumbly, but if you press some between your fingers, it should hold together. (If it doesn't, sprinkle on another 1½ tsp. of the water and pulse a few more times.) Dump the crumbly mix onto a lightly floured surface and press the dough into a 1-inch-thick disk. Wrap in plastic and chill for 30 minutes.

2. On a lightly floured work surface, roll the dough into a round that's 12 to 13 inches in diameter and ⅛ inch thick. Drape the dough around the rolling pin and ease it into a 9-inch pie pan. With kitchen shears, trim the overhang to ½ inch. Fold the overhang under and crimp it to build up an edge. Prick the crust with a fork in several places. Cover with plastic and refrigerate for 30 minutes. Meanwhile, position an oven rack on the middle rung and heat the oven to 350°F.

BAKE THE CRUST

Grease one side of a sheet of foil with cooking spray, oil, or butter. Line the pie pan with the foil, greased side down, and fill it with pie weights or beans. Bake until the edges of the crust look dry and start to turn golden, 25 to 30 minutes. Carefully remove the foil and weights; continue baking until the entire crust is deeply golden brown, another 15 to 20 minutes. Let cool on a rack.

MAKE THE FILLING

1. In a medium bowl, whisk the condensed milk, egg yolks, lime juice, and grated zest. Pour into the cooled pie crust and bake at 350°F until just set, about 30 minutes. The center may still be a bit jiggly. (Use an instant-read thermometer to double-check the doneness; the center of the pie should be at least 140°F.) Let the pie cool thoroughly on a rack and then cover with plastic and refrigerate to chill completely, at least 3 hours but no longer than 1 day.

2. Just before serving, whip the cream and sugar until stiff peaks form. Spread the cream on top of the pie, garnish with the strips of lime zest strips, and serve. —*Becky Campbell*

PER SERVING: 620 CALORIES | 11G PROTEIN | 79G CARB | 28G TOTAL FAT | 16G SAT FAT | 8G MONO FAT | 3G POLY FAT | 120MG CHOL | 320MG SODIUM | 1G FIBER

Choosing Limes

The limes available in most grocery stores are known as Tahiti or Persian limes. Choose limes that are about 2 inches in diameter, fragrant, and plump, with smooth, medium-green skin. Stay away from those that are rough-skinned, dark green, and hard. If you can find good Key limes, about 1½ inches in diameter with smooth greenish yellow or yellow skin and a lovely lime aroma, buy them—it will be a treat. Whatever you do, avoid bottled Key lime juice: The processing changes the flavor significantly.

chocolate-raspberry tart with gingersnap crust

SERVES 8 TO 10

Vegetable oil, for the pan

About 40 gingersnap wafers (to yield 1½ cups finely ground)

¼ cup melted unsalted butter

3½ cups raspberries, rinsed, picked over, and drained

8 oz. semisweet or bittersweet chocolate, finely chopped

1¼ cups heavy cream

Small pinch of table salt

It's easy to make this simple tart look stunning because the ganache is chilled slightly so the raspberries don't sink into the chocolate layer as you arrange them. An added bonus for entertaining—you can make the tart up to a day ahead.

1. Position a rack in the middle of the oven and heat the oven to 325°F. Oil the sides and bottom of a 9½-inch fluted tart pan with a removable bottom. In a food processor, grind the gingersnaps until they're the texture of sand. Transfer to a bowl, add the melted butter, and work it in by squishing the mixture together with your hands. Press into the sides and bottom of the oiled tart pan. Set the pan on a baking sheet and refrigerate for 20 minutes to firm. Bake the tart crust on the baking sheet until fragrant, about 15 minutes, checking and rotating if needed to make sure the crust doesn't get too dark. Set on a rack to cool.

2. Meanwhile, pass 1 cup of the berries through a food mill fitted with a fine disk or force them through a fine-mesh sieve, mashing with a wooden spoon, into a medium bowl. You'll have about ½ cup purée; set it aside and discard the contents of the sieve.

3. Put the chopped chocolate in a medium bowl. Heat the cream just until boiling. Pour the hot cream over the chopped chocolate; whisk to blend, creating a ganache. Stir in the raspberry purée and the salt. Pour the ganache into the cooled tart shell. Refrigerate until the ganache is fairly firm, about 1 hour. Arrange the remaining raspberries on top of the ganache; they should completely cover the surface. Chill until the ganache is completely firm, about 30 minutes, and serve.

—*Michelle Polzine*

PER SERVING: 350 CALORIES | 3G PROTEIN | 33G CARB | 25G TOTAL FAT | 14G SAT FAT | 7G MONO FAT | 2G POLY FAT | 55MG CHOL | 150MG SODIUM | 7G FIBER

More about Raspberries

Raspberries, the most intensely flavored member of the berry family, are made up of connected drupelets (individual sections of juicy pulp, each with a single seed) surrounding a central core. The most common raspberries are red, but you'll find black, golden, and even pink raspberries at farmers' markets and specialty stores. The differences in flavor are subtle, but a mix is beautiful.

Like most fruit these days, raspberries are available just about year-round, but it's best to take advantage of those few weeks in summer when local raspberries call your name at the farmers' market. Depending on the region, they are available from May through November.

Raspberries love to be paired with lemon, chocolate, ginger, blackberries, blueberries, strawberries, coconut, fresh figs, mint, and stone fruit of all sorts.

creamy orange-ricotta tart

1   15-oz. container whole-milk
    ricotta (about 1½ cups)

3   oz. cream cheese, at room
    temperature

¾   cup granulated sugar

2   Tbs. unbleached all-
    purpose flour

¼   tsp. table salt

3   large egg yolks

1   Tbs. finely grated orange
    zest

1   Tbs. orange-flavored
    liqueur (such as Grand
    Marnier® or Cointreau) or
    orange juice

1   Press-In Cookie Crust
    (recipe on the facing page),
    baked and cooled (vanilla
    or chocolate is delicious in
    this tart)

    Strips of orange zest or seg-
    ments of blood orange, for
    garnish (optional)

Cookie crumbs make a short-cut crust, and a creamy filling makes an impressive but easy dessert.

1. Position a rack in the center of the oven and heat the oven to 350°F. In a medium bowl, combine the ricotta and cream cheese. Using an electric mixer, beat on medium speed until well blended and no lumps remain, about 3 minutes. Add the sugar, flour, and salt and continue beating until well blended, about 1 minute. Add the egg yolks, orange zest, and orange liqueur. Beat until just incorporated. Use a rubber spatula to scrape the filling into the crust and spread the filling evenly.

2. Bake the tart until the filling just barely jiggles when the pan is nudged, 30 to 35 minutes. Let cool completely on a rack. Refrigerate the tart in the pan until chilled and firm, 2 to 3 hours. Serve garnished with strips of orange zest or blood orange segments, if you like.
—*Abigail Johnson Dodge*

---

3 Tools to Remove Orange Zest

Orange zest adds a floral accent to dishes like this tart. Choose one of these three tools to remove the zest.

• A **rasp-style grater** gives feathery, moist threads (and no pith).

• Use a **vegetable peeler** to cut wide sections of skin. Trim away the white pith by laying the strips flat and holding a sharp knife at a nearly flat angle. Slice the piece into thin strips if desired.

• A **citrus zester** has five small holes for peeling thin shreads of zest.

press-in cookie crust

1 cup finely ground cookies (ground in a food processor); choose one from the following: about 25 chocolate wafers, 8 whole graham crackers, or 35 vanilla wafers (like Nabisco FAMOUS Chocolate Wafers, Honey Maid Grahams, and Nilla Wafers)

2 Tbs. granulated sugar

1½ oz. (3 Tbs.) unsalted butter, melted

1. Position a rack in the center of the oven and heat the oven to 350°F. Have ready an ungreased 9½-inch fluted tart pan with a removable bottom.

2. In a medium bowl, mix the cookie crumbs and sugar with a fork until well blended. Drizzle the melted butter over the crumbs and mix with the fork or your fingers until the crumbs are evenly moistened. Put the crumbs in the tart pan and use your hands to spread the crumbs so that they coat the bottom of the pan and start to climb the sides (use a piece of plastic wrap over the crumbs as you spread them so they won't stick to your hands). Use your fingers to pinch and press some of the crumbs around the inside edge of the pan to cover the sides evenly and create a wall about a scant ¼ inch thick. Redistribute the remaining crumbs evenly over the bottom of the pan and press firmly to make a compact layer. (A metal measuring cup with straight sides and a flat base works well for this task.)

3. Bake the crust until it smells nutty and fragrant (crusts made with lighter-colored cookies will brown slightly), about 10 minutes. Set the baked crust on a rack and let cool. The crust can be made up to 1 day ahead and stored at room temperature, wrapped well in plastic.

To remove a tart from the pan, set the pan on a wide can and let the outside ring fall away. If it's stubborn, grip the ring with your fingers to coax it off. Slide a long, thin metal spatula between the pan base and the crust and ease the tart onto a flat serving plate.

banana-toffee tart

SERVES 12

- 1 can (14 oz.) sweetened condensed milk (preferably Eagle®)
- 6 oz. (1⅓ cups) unbleached all-purpose flour
- ¼ cup plus 2 tsp. granulated sugar
- ½ tsp. table salt
- 4 oz. (½ cup) unsalted butter, cut into ⅜-inch dice and chilled well
- 2 cups heavy cream
- 1 large egg yolk
- 4 ripe bananas
- ¼ tsp. instant coffee granules
- ½ tsp. pure vanilla extract

For tips on how to make this dessert in advance, see the sidebar on p. 148. If you don't have a tart pan with a removable bottom, use a 9-inch springform pan.

MAKE THE TOFFEE

Fill the base pan of a double boiler (or a medium saucepan) halfway with water. Bring to a boil and then reduce heat to medium for an active simmer (just shy of a boil). Pour the sweetened condensed milk into the double boiler's top insert (or into a stainless-steel bowl that fits snugly on top of the saucepan) and set over the simmering water. Every 45 minutes, check the water level in the pot and give the milk a stir. Replenish with more hot water as needed. Once the milk has thickened to the consistency of pudding and has turned a rich, dark caramel color, 2½ to 3 hours, remove from the heat, cool, and cover.

MAKE THE CRUST

1. Meanwhile, combine the flour, ¼ cup of the sugar, and salt in a food processor. Pulse to combine. Add the butter pieces and gently toss to lightly coat with flour. Blend the butter and flour mixture with about five 1-second pulses (count "one one-thousand" with each pulse) or until the mixture is the texture of coarse meal with some of the butter pieces the size of peas. In a small bowl, whisk together 2½ Tbs. of the cream and the egg yolk and pour this over the flour mixture. Process continuously until the mixture turns golden in color and thickens in texture yet is still crumbly, about 10 seconds.

2. Transfer the mixture to a medium-large bowl and press the mixture together with your hand until it comes together into a ball. Shape the dough into an 8-inch-wide disk and put it in the center of an 8½- to 9-inch fluted tart pan with a removable bottom. Beginning in the center of the dough and working out toward the edges, use your fingertips to gently press the dough evenly into the bottom and up the pan sides. The edges should be flush with the top edge of the pan. If you find a spot that's especially thick, pinch away some of the dough and use it to bulk up a thin spot. Cover with plastic wrap and freeze for 1 hour.

BAKE THE CRUST

Heat the oven to 400°F. Right before baking, line the dough with aluminum foil and cover with pie weights or dried beans. Bake on the lower oven rack for 20 minutes. Carefully lift the foil (along with the weights) out of the tart pan, lower the oven temperature to 375°F, and bake until the crust is deep golden brown, about 15 minutes. Transfer the tart pan to a wire rack to cool to room temperature.

continued on p. 148

continued from p. 146

ASSEMBLE THE TART

1. Spread the caramel over the crust using a rubber spatula or offset spatula. If the caramel has cooled and is too firm to spread easily, reheat it over simmering water in the double boiler until loosened but not hot. Slice each banana in half lengthwise and arrange the halves on top of the caramel in a circular pattern. To fit the banana halves snugly in the center of the pan, cut them into smaller lengths.

2. Put the coffee granules in a small zip-top bag. Press a rolling pin back and forth over the granules to crush them into a powder.

3. In a chilled medium stainless-steel mixing bowl, beat the remaining heavy cream, the vanilla, and the remaining 2 tsp. sugar with an electric mixer at medium-high speed until it holds soft peaks when the beaters are lifted. (If you overbeat the cream, fold in 1 Tbs. cream to relax it.) Spoon the whipped cream over the bananas, sprinkle with the coffee powder, remove the pan sides, and serve immediately. The tart can be held for 30 minutes in the refrigerator, though it's best not to sprinkle on the coffee powder until just before serving.
—*Maryellen Driscoll*

PER SERVING: 420 CALORIES | 6G PROTEIN | 44G CARB | 26G TOTAL FAT | 16G SAT FAT | 7G MONO FAT | 1G POLY FAT | 105MG CHOL | 160MG SODIUM | 1G FIBER

Make Ahead

Up to 3 days ahead
• Make the caramel; cover tightly and refrigerate.

1 day ahead
• Bake the crust; once cooled, wrap tightly in plastic wrap or an extra-large zip-top bag.

A few hours before serving
• Reheat the caramel in a double boiler (or in a heatproof bowl over simmering water) just long enough to soften; spread the caramel in the crust; cover tightly with plastic wrap.
• Whip the cream to soft peaks; transfer to a large mesh sieve set over a bowl to catch any liquid that settles; chill, uncovered.
• Put the coffee granules in a small zip-top bag.

Right before serving
• Slice the bananas and arrange on top of the caramel.
• Spoon on the whipped cream.
• Crush the coffee granules with a rolling pin and sprinkle on top.

how to make a banana-toffee tart

Cut the butter into the flour with five quick pulses of the food processor.

Add the yolk and cream and blend for 10 more seconds. The dough will look like coarse meal.

Pat and press the mixture in a bowl until it forms a cohesive ball.

Skip the rolling pin and press the dough by hand.

Spread the toffee over the crust.

After the bananas are added, spoon on the whipped cream, lifting up some of the cream as you pull the spoon away.

Add a sprinkling of crushed coffee granules to melt into the cream.

chocolate truffle tart with whipped vanilla mascarpone topping

MAKES ONE 9½-INCH TART;
SERVES 12 TO 16

FOR THE FILLING

- 12 oz. bittersweet chocolate, finely chopped
- 1 cup whole milk
- 2 oz. (4 Tbs.) unsalted butter, cut into 4 pieces
- 1 tsp. pure vanilla extract
- ¼ tsp. table salt

- 1 Press-In Cookie Crust (recipe on p. 145), baked and cooled (graham cracker is nice for this tart)

FOR THE TOPPING

- 8 oz. mascarpone, at room temperature
- ¾ cup heavy cream
- ¼ cup granulated sugar
- ½ tsp. pure vanilla extract

Cookie crumbs make a shortcut crust, and with the creamy filling, this makes an impressive—but easy—dessert.

MAKE THE FILLING

1. Melt together the chocolate, milk, and butter in a medium bowl in a microwave or in a double boiler over medium heat. (For information on how to melt chocolate, see the sidebar on p. 162.) Add the vanilla and salt. Whisk the mixture until well blended and smooth. Set aside, whisking occasionally, until room temperature and slightly thickened, about 1 hour. (For faster cooling, refrigerate the filling until thickened to a pudding consistency, about 30 minutes, whisking and scraping the sides of the bowl with a rubber spatula every 5 minutes.)

2. With a rubber spatula, scrape the mixture into the crust and spread evenly, taking care not to disturb the edge of the crust. Let cool completely, cover, and refrigerate until the filling is set, about 4 hours and up to 8 hours, before proceeding with the recipe.

MAKE THE TOPPING

1. In a medium bowl, combine the mascarpone, cream, sugar, and vanilla. Using an electric mixer, beat on low speed until almost smooth, 30 to 60 seconds. Increase the speed to medium high and beat until the mixture is thick and holds firm peaks, another 30 to 60 seconds. Don't overbeat.

2. With a rubber or metal spatula, spread the topping over the chocolate filling, leaving lots of swirls and peaks. Serve the tart right away or cover loosely and refrigerate, in the pan, for up to 4 hours.
—*Abigail Johnson Dodge*

More about Mascarpone

Mascarpone is a thick and buttery double- to triple-cream cow's milk cheese (containing over 60 percent and often over 75 percent milk fat). It's slightly sweet with a faint yellow hue and spans dishes from starters to sweets.

Try mixing mascarpone into pasta with asparagus and mushrooms, or fold it into polenta. For simple desserts, serve mascarpone with fresh figs, pears, or berries, or dollop a spoonful alongside fruit pies or tarts.

chocolate-glazed peanut butter tart

MAKES ONE 9½-INCH TART; SERVES 12

FOR THE FILLING AND CRUST

- 1½ cups whole milk
- ¼ tsp. table salt
- 3 large egg yolks
- ⅓ cup very firmly packed light brown sugar
- 4 tsp. unbleached all-purpose flour
- ½ cup creamy peanut butter (preferably natural, made with only peanuts and salt)
- ½ tsp. pure vanilla extract
- 1 Press-In Cookie Crust (recipe on p. 145), baked and cooled (chocolate or graham cracker is delicious for this tart)

FOR THE GLAZE

- 3 oz. bittersweet chocolate, finely chopped
- 2 oz. (4 Tbs.) unsalted butter, cut into 6 pieces
- 1 Tbs. light corn syrup

You'll need to plan ahead for this rich dessert, but for peanut butter and chocolate lovers, it's worth it. The easy cookie crust must be baked and cooled before filling, and the filling must be chilled before glazing.

MAKE THE FILLING

1. In a medium saucepan, bring the milk and salt to a simmer over medium heat, stirring occasionally. Meanwhile, in a small bowl, whisk the egg yolks, brown sugar, and flour until well blended. Slowly add the hot milk, whisking constantly. Pour the mixture back into the saucepan. Cook over medium heat, whisking constantly, until it thickens and comes to a full boil, about 3 minutes. Continue to cook, whisking constantly, for 1 minute. Remove the pan from the heat and add the peanut butter and vanilla; whisk until well blended.

2. Pour the hot peanut butter mixture into the crust and spread evenly with a rubber or offset spatula. Gently press a piece of plastic wrap directly on the filling's surface to prevent a skin from forming. Refrigerate the tart until cold, about 2 hours, before proceeding with the recipe.

MAKE THE GLAZE

Melt the chocolate in a small bowl in a microwave or in a double boiler over medium heat. (For information on how to melt chocolate, see the sidebar on p. 162.) Add the butter and corn syrup and whisk until the butter is melted and the mixture is smooth, about 1 minute. Carefully remove the plastic wrap from the top of the chilled filling. Drizzle the glaze over the filling and spread it evenly to cover the tart completely. Refrigerate the tart in the pan until the glaze sets, about 30 minutes or up to 12 hours. —*Abigail Johnson Dodge*

More about Bittersweet Chocolate

Whether a chocolate is called unsweetened, bittersweet, or semisweet depends mostly on the percentage of cacao the chocolate contains. As the cacao percentage increases, the chocolate itself will taste more intensely chocolaty and less sweet. Bittersweet chocolate generally contains less sugar than semisweet and is called for in recipes where deep, intense chocolate flavor is desired. But the distinction between the two types becomes hazy among different brands.

Today, supermarkets and specialty shops offer semisweet and bittersweet chocolates that range from 54 percent to more than 70 percent cacao. Chocolate with radically different cacao percentages can produce radically different results. Unless a recipe specifies a very high-percentage chocolate, stick with bittersweet chocolate in the 54 to 60 percent cacao range.

Well wrapped and stored in a cool, dry place, dark chocolate has an indefinite shelf life. However, its high fat content means it can easily pick up other flavors, so be careful of what you store near it.

triple chocolate ice cream pie

6 oz. (about 30) chocolate wafer cookies

2½ oz. (5 Tbs.) unsalted butter, melted; more for greasing the pan

2 pints chocolate ice cream, slightly softened

Quick Hot Fudge Sauce (recipe on p. 156), at room temperature

1 pint coffee ice cream, slightly softened

1 pint vanilla ice cream, slightly softened

This pie features a chocolate crust, chocolate ice cream, and choco-late sauce, with a few scoops of coffee and vanilla added for contrast.

1. Position a rack in the middle of the oven and heat the oven to 350°F. Butter a 9-inch Pyrex or metal pie plate.

2. Put the cookies in a zip-top bag and crush them with a rolling pin (or process in a food processor) until you have fine crumbs. Measure 1½ cups of crumbs (crush more cookies, if necessary) and put them in a bowl. Add the melted butter and stir until the crumbs are evenly moistened. Transfer to the pie plate and, using your fingers, press the mixture evenly into the bottom and sides (but not on the rim). Bake for 10 minutes. Let cool completely on a wire rack.

3. Scoop 1 pint of the chocolate ice cream into the cooled crust and spread it evenly with a rubber spatula. Place in the freezer to firm up for about 30 minutes. Remove the pie from the freezer and, working quickly, drizzle ½ cup of the room-temperature fudge sauce over the ice cream. Using a small ice cream scoop (1½ inches in diameter), scoop round balls of the chocolate, coffee, and vanilla ice creams and arrange them over the fudge sauce layer (you may not need all of the ice cream). Drizzle with about ¼ cup of the remaining fudge sauce, using a squirt bottle if you have one. Freeze until the ice cream is firm, about 2 hours. If not serving right away, loosely cover the pie with waxed paper and then wrap with aluminum foil. Freeze for up to 2 weeks.

4. To serve, let the pie soften in the refrigerator for 15 to 30 minutes (premium ice cream brands need more time to soften). Meanwhile, gently reheat the remaining fudge sauce in a small saucepan over medium-low heat. Pry the pie out of the pan with a thin metal spatula. (If the pie doesn't pop out, set the pan in a shallow amount of hot water for a minute or two to help the crust release.) Set the pie on a board, cut into wedges, and serve drizzled with more hot fudge sauce, if you like. —*Lori Longbotham*

PER SERVING: 495 CALORIES | 7G PROTEIN | 48G CARB | 34G TOTAL FAT | 20G SAT FAT | 6G MONO FAT | 1G POLY FAT | 90MG CHOL | 190MG SODIUM | 3G FIBER

continued on p. 156

continued from p. 154

quick hot fudge sauce

MAKES 1½ CUPS

1   **cup heavy cream**

2   **Tbs. light corn syrup**

   Pinch of table salt

8   **oz. bittersweet chocolate, finely chopped (to yield about 1⅓ cups)**

This sauce will keep for at least 2 weeks in the refrigerator and for several months in the freezer.

Bring the cream, corn syrup, and salt just to a boil in a medium-size heavy saucepan over medium-high heat, whisking until combined. Remove the pan from the heat, add the chocolate, and whisk until smooth. Let cool to a bit warmer than room temperature before using in the ice cream pie. The sauce thickens as it cools; you want it warm enough to drizzle but not so warm that it melts the ice cream.

More Ice Cream Pie Ideas

• **Ginger ice cream pie.** Make a simple gingersnap crust, fill with vanilla ice cream, and top with scoops of ginger ice cream. Dust the top with chopped crystallized ginger.

• **Refreshing sorbet pie.** Fill an amaretti cookie or graham cracker crust with vanilla ice cream and top with scoops of sorbet. Mango, pineapple, and coconut are luscious with a sprinkle of toasted coconut flakes. Or try raspberry and strawberry sorbets topped with mixed berries.

• **Peachy ice cream pie.** Fill a graham cracker or gingersnap crust with peach ice cream, top with scoops of peach sorbet, sprinkle with toasted almonds, and serve with sliced ripe peaches.

• **Banana split pie.** Try chocolate, vanilla, and strawberry ice cream in a chocolate cookie crust. Serve with chocolate, strawberry, or caramel sauces and garnish with thinly sliced bananas.

• **Mango ice cream pie.** Use mango or vanilla ice cream as the base layer in a crushed shortbread cookie crust and top with scoops of mango sorbet. Serve with sliced fresh mangos and raspberry sauce.

chocolate-caramel-almond tart

SERVES 8

FOR THE CRUST

4½ oz. (1 cup) unbleached all-purpose flour; more for rolling the dough

3 Tbs. granulated sugar

Pinch of table salt

3 oz. (6 Tbs.) chilled unsalted butter, cut into ½-inch pieces

2 Tbs. ice-cold water

FOR THE CARAMEL-ALMOND LAYER

¾ cup blanched whole almonds

1 recipe Basic Caramel (recipe on p. 159)

½ cup heavy cream

1 oz. (2 Tbs.) unsalted butter

1 tsp. pure vanilla extract

¼ tsp. table salt

FOR THE CHOCOLATE LAYER

2 oz. bittersweet chocolate, coarsely chopped

⅓ cup heavy cream

½ oz. (1 Tbs.) unsalted butter, cut into 3 pieces

½ tsp. pure vanilla extract

Lightly sweetened whipped cream or vanilla ice cream, for serving (optional)

Lightly sweetened whipped cream is the perfect counterpoint to chocolate and caramel.

MAKE THE CRUST

1. Put the flour, sugar, and salt in a food processor and pulse a few times to combine. Add the butter pieces and pulse until the mixture is the texture of coarse meal with some pea-size butter pieces, five to seven 1 second pulses. Sprinkle the ice-cold water over the flour mixture and process until the dough just begins to come together in small, marble-size clumps. Don't overprocess; the dough should not form a ball.

2. Turn the dough out onto a work surface and shape it into a thick 4-inch-diameter disk. Wrap the dough in plastic and chill until firm enough to roll, about 30 minutes.

3. On a lightly floured surface, roll the dough into an 11-inch circle, lifting and rotating it often while lightly dusting the work surface and the dough with flour as necessary. Transfer the dough to a 9½-inch fluted tart pan with a removable bottom. Gently press the dough into the bottom and up the sides of the pan. Roll the pin over the top of the pan to trim the excess dough. Lightly prick the bottom of the dough with a fork at ½-inch intervals. Refrigerate for 20 minutes to firm it up.

4. Meanwhile, position a rack in the center of the oven and heat the oven to 350°F.

continued on p. 158

continued from p. 157

5. Line the dough with aluminum foil and fill it with pie weights or dried beans. Put the tart pan on a baking sheet and bake for 20 minutes. Carefully lift the foil (and the weights) out of the tart pan and bake the crust until golden brown along the top edge and in some spots on the bottom, 13 to 17 minutes. Transfer the tart pan to a wire rack and cool completely. Raise the oven temperature to 375°F.

MAKE THE CARAMEL-ALMOND LAYER

1. Toast the almonds on a baking sheet in the oven until golden, 5 to 10 minutes. Let cool briefly and then chop coarsely.

2. Make the Basic Caramel then immediately remove the pan from the heat and carefully add the heavy cream. The mixture will bubble up furiously. Once the bubbling has subsided, add the butter and stir until completely melted. Whisk in the vanilla, salt, and almonds until the nuts are completely coated. Pour the hot caramel mixture into the cooled tart shell, using a heatproof spatula to scrape the pot clean and distribute the nuts evenly in the shell. Let cool for 30 minutes and then refrigerate until the caramel is completely chilled, about 1 hour.

MAKE THE CHOCOLATE LAYER

Put the chocolate and cream in a small saucepan over low heat and stir occasionally until the chocolate is melted, 3 to 5 minutes. Add the butter and stir until melted and the mixture is smooth. Stir in the vanilla. Pour over the caramel layer and tilt the pan as needed to smooth the chocolate into an even layer that covers the caramel. Refrigerate until the chocolate is set, at least 1 hour and up to 1 day. Serve the tart with whipped cream or vanilla ice cream, if you like. —*Tish Boyle*

PER SERVING: 470 CALORIES | 6G PROTEIN | 47G CARB | 30G TOTAL FAT | 15G SAT FAT | 11G MONO FAT | 2.5G POLY FAT | 65MG CHOL | 125MG SODIUM | 3G FIBER

basic caramel

MAKES ⅔ CUP

1 cup granulated sugar

¼ tsp. fresh lemon juice

The caramel will harden quickly upon cooling.

1. Fill a 1-cup measure halfway with water and put a pastry brush in it; this will be used for washing down the sides of the pan to prevent crystallization.

2. In a heavy-duty 2-quart saucepan, stir the sugar, lemon juice, and ¼ cup cold water. Brush down the sides of the pan with water to wash away any sugar crystals. Bring to a boil over medium-high heat and cook, occasionally brushing down the sides of the pan, until the mixture starts to color around the edges, 5 to 8 minutes. Gently swirl the pan once to even out the color and prevent the sugar from burning in isolated spots. Continue to cook until the sugar turns medium amber, about 30 seconds more. (Once the mixture begins to color, it will darken very quickly, so keep an eye on it.)

5 Tips for Perfect Caramel

One of two things can go wrong when making caramel: The caramel burns or sugar crystals form, so the caramel goes from liquid and smooth to crystallized and solid. Follow these pointers for making a perfectly smooth caramel every time.

• **Watch bubbling caramel like a hawk.** Caramel cooks quickly and will turn from bold amber to a smoking mahogany in seconds. Burnt caramel has an unpleasantly bitter taste.

• **Use clean utensils.** Sugar crystals tend to form around impurities and foreign particles.

• **Acid helps.** Adding lemon juice to the sugar and water helps break down the sucrose molecules and prevents sugar crystals from forming.

• **Swirl, don't stir.** Stirring tends to splash syrup onto the sides of the pan, where sugar crystals can form. So once the sugar is completely dissolved in water, just gently swirl the pan to caramelize the sugar evenly.

• **A pastry brush is your friend.** Keep a pastry brush and some water next to the stove; you'll need it to wash off any crystals that might form on the sides of the pan.

bittersweet chocolate tart with salted caramelized pistachios

SERVES 12 TO 14

FOR THE TART SHELL

- **4** oz. (½ cup) unsalted butter, melted
- **¼** cup granulated sugar
- **1** tsp. finely grated orange zest
- **¾** tsp. pure vanilla extract
- **⅛** tsp. table salt
- **4½** oz. (1 cup) unbleached all-purpose flour

FOR THE FILLING

- **1** cup half-and-half
- **2** Tbs. granulated sugar
- Pinch of table salt
- **7** oz. semisweet chocolate (up to 64% cacao), coarsely chopped
- **1** large egg, lightly beaten
- **1** recipe Salted Caramelized Pistachios (recipe on p. 162)
- Fleur de sel or other flaky sea salt

This buttery shortbread tart crust is filled with rich, dark chocolate and garnished with salty-sweet caramelized nuts and sea salt.

MAKE THE TART SHELL

1. In a medium bowl, combine the butter, sugar, zest, vanilla, and salt. Add the flour and mix just until well blended. If the dough seems too soft to work with, let it sit for a few minutes to firm up. Press the dough into a 9½-inch fluted tart pan with a removable bottom. Start with the sides, making them about ¼ inch thick, and then press the remaining dough evenly over the bottom, pressing well into the corners. Let rest at room temperature for 30 minutes or chill until ready to bake (you can make the crust up to 3 days ahead).

2. Position a rack in the lower third of the oven and heat the oven to 350°F. Put the pan on a baking sheet and bake until the crust is a deep golden brown, 20 to 25 minutes, checking after about 15 minutes to see if the dough has puffed. Press the dough down with the back of a fork and prick a few times if necessary.

MAKE THE FILLING

1. In a small saucepan, bring the half-and-half, sugar, and salt to a simmer. Move the pan off the heat, then add the chocolate and stir with a whisk until completely melted and smooth. Cover to keep warm.

2. Just before the crust is ready, whisk the egg thoroughly into the chocolate mixture. When the crust is done, lower the oven temperature to 300°F. Pour the filling into the hot crust. Return the tart (still on the baking sheet) to the oven and bake until the filling is set around the edges but still jiggles a little in the center when you nudge the pan, 10 to 15 minutes. Cool on a rack.

3. Serve at room temperature or slightly cool. Garnish each slice with crushed Salted Caramelized Pistachios and a light sprinkling of fleur de sel.

4. The tart is best on the day it's made but may be refrigerated for 2 to 3 days. Once the tart is completely chilled, cover it, but make sure no plastic wrap touches the surface by first putting the tart pan in a larger cake pan. Or cover the tart with an overturned plate. —*Alice Medrich*

PER SERVING: 260 CALORIES | 4G PROTEIN | 31G CARB | 15G TOTAL FAT | 8G SAT FAT | 5G MONO FAT | 1G POLY FAT | 40MG CHOL | 95MG SODIUM | 2G FIBER

continued on p. 162

continued from p. 161

salted caramelized pistachios

MAKES 1 CUP

½ **cup salted whole roasted shelled pistachios**

½ **cup granulated sugar**

⅛ **tsp. fine sea salt**

You can make these up to 1 week in advance. Store in an airtight container while still warm to prevent the caramel from becoming sticky.

1. Line a baking sheet with foil.

2. Microwave the nuts on high for 1 minute so they will be warm when you add them to the caramel. Alternatively, heat them in a 200°F oven while you make the caramel.

3. Pour ¼ cup water into a heavy 3-quart saucepan. Pour the sugar and salt in the center of the pan and pat it down just until evenly moistened (there should be clear water all around the sugar). Cover the pan and cook over medium-high heat until the sugar dissolves, 2 to 4 minutes. Uncover and cook without stirring until the syrup begins to color slightly, about 1 minute. Reduce the heat to medium and continue to cook, swirling the pot gently if the syrup colors unevenly.

4. When the caramel is a pale to medium yellow, less than 1 minute more, add the warm nuts. With a heatproof silicone spatula, stir gently and slowly to coat the nuts with caramel. Continue to cook until a bead of caramel dribbled onto a white plate is reddish amber, about 1½ minutes more. Immediately scrape the mixture onto the baking sheet and spread it as thin as you can before it hardens. When the caramel is slightly cooled, slide the foil with the caramel nuts into a zip-top plastic bag and seal the bag. Cool completely. Chop or crush.

Melting Chocolate

The goal of melting chocolate is to make it fluid and warm (or very warm, depending on the recipe) to the touch without overheating or scorching it.

While most recipes call for a double boiler (a bowl set over a pan of simmering water), you can also use a wide, shallow skillet of water with a stainless-steel bowl of chocolate sitting directly in it. The open bath allows you to see and then adjust the water if it begins to boil or simmer too actively (the water in a double boiler is usually out of sight and trickier to monitor). Just as chocolate in a double boiler will scorch if the cook is inattentive, chocolate in an open bath must also be watched carefully, stirred frequently, and removed from the bath when melted.

chocolate-cherry cheesecake tart

SERVES 8 TO 10

- **6** oz. chocolate wafers, finely crushed (1⅓ cups)
- **⅓** cup plus 2 Tbs. granulated sugar
- **2½** oz. (5 Tbs.) unsalted butter, melted
- **1** cup pitted fresh or frozen sweet cherries, puréed
- **3** Tbs. cherry preserves
- **1** Tbs. kirsch
- **12** oz. cream cheese, at room temperature
- **4** oz. sour cream (⅓ cup plus 1 Tbs.), at room temperature
- **1** Tbs. unbleached all-purpose flour
- **1** tsp. pure vanilla extract
- **½** tsp. kosher salt
- **2** large eggs, at room temperature

Black forest cake was the inspiration for this tart, which has a chocolate crust, cherry-swirled topping, and subtly tangy cream cheese filling.

1. Position a rack in the center of the oven and heat the oven to 350°F.

2. In a small bowl, mix the crushed wafers with 2 Tbs. of the sugar. Add the melted butter and toss with your fingers until evenly moistened. Transfer the crumbs to a 9½-inch fluted tart pan with a removable bottom. With your fingers, gently pack the crumbs into the bottom and up the sides to form the crust. Bake on a rimmed baking sheet until set, 10 to 12 minutes. Set aside to cool. Reduce the oven temperature to 325°F.

3. Meanwhile, in a 1-quart saucepan over medium heat, bring the cherry purée to a simmer. Whisk in the cherry preserves and continue to simmer until the mixture thickens slightly, 3 to 5 minutes. Stir in the kirsch and continue to cook for 30 seconds more. Remove from the heat and let cool.

4. In a stand mixer fitted with the paddle attachment, beat the cream cheese and remaining ⅓ cup sugar on medium-low speed until the mixture is smooth and fluffy, about 3 minutes. Add the sour cream, flour, vanilla, and salt and beat until well combined, about 1 minute more. Add the eggs one at time, beating until just combined, about 15 seconds for each egg (do not overbeat).

5. Pour the batter into the crust and distribute evenly. Dot the batter with the cherry mixture and gently drag a butter knife through the filling to form decorative swirls.

6. Bake until the tart is just set but still slightly moist in the center, 18 to 24 minutes. Cool on a wire rack. Refrigerate for at least 4 hours. Serve cold. *—Samantha Seneviratne*

PER SERVING: 350 CALORIES | 5G PROTEIN | 31G CARB | 23G TOTAL FAT |
13G SAT FAT | 6G MONO FAT | 1.5G POLY FAT | 95MG CHOL |
310MG SODIUM | 1G FIBER

blueberry-vanilla cream cheese pies

MAKES 12 PIES

- 2 **17.3-oz. packages frozen puff pastry**
- 3 **oz. cream cheese, at room temperature**
- 7 **Tbs. granulated sugar**
  Seeds scraped from ½ vanilla bean (or ½ tsp. pure vanilla extract)
- 2 **large egg yolks**
- 1 **cup blueberries, rinsed, picked over, and dried**
- 2 **tsp. cornstarch**
- 2 **tsp. crème de cassis**
- ⅛ **tsp. kosher salt**
  Confectioners' sugar, for sprinkling

These portable pies are like mini blueberry cheesecakes wrapped in puff pastry. They are best served within a few hours of baking.

1. Thaw three sheets of puff pastry overnight in the refrigerator.

2. Position racks in the top and bottom thirds of the oven and heat the oven to 375°F.

3. In a medium bowl, combine the cream cheese, 3 Tbs. of the sugar, the vanilla bean seeds or extract, and 1 of the egg yolks. Mix with a wooden spoon until well combined and smooth.

4. Combine the blueberries, 2 Tbs. of the sugar, the cornstarch, crème de cassis, and salt in another medium bowl and mix gently.

5. On a lightly floured surface, roll each pastry sheet into a 10-inch square. Using a 4-inch round cutter (or a small plate as a guide), cut out four rounds from each sheet. Arrange them on two parchment-lined rimmed baking sheets.

6. In a small bowl, beat the remaining egg yolk with 1 tsp. water. Brush the outer edge of each pastry round with the egg wash. Dollop ½ Tbs. of the cream cheese mixture in the center of each round. Top with 1 Tbs. of the blueberry mixture. Fold in half to form a half-moon shape and pinch the edges together to seal them. Lightly brush each pie with egg wash and sprinkle with ½ tsp. of the remaining sugar. With the tip of a paring knife, cut a steam vent in the center of each pie.

7. Bake until golden brown, about 25 minutes, swapping and rotating the baking sheets' positions about halfway through. Cool slightly on the baking sheets and then transfer to a rack to cool completely. Before serving, sprinkle the pies with confectioners' sugar.
—Karen Barker

PER SERVING: 110 CALORIES | 2G PROTEIN | 13G CARB | 6G TOTAL FAT | 2.5G SAT FAT | 2G MONO FAT | 0G POLY FAT | 45MG CHOL | 80MG SODIUM | 1G FIBER

rosemary-lemon tartlets with pine nut shortbread

MAKES FIFTY 2-INCH TARTLETS

FOR THE LEMON CURD

- **1** cup granulated sugar
- **½** cup plus 2 Tbs. freshly squeezed lemon juice (from about 3 medium lemons)
- **2** Tbs. finely grated lemon zest (from about 2 medium lemons)
- **1** Tbs. very finely chopped fresh rosemary
- **8** large egg yolks
- **¼** tsp. kosher salt
- **4** oz. (½ cup) chilled unsalted butter, cut into pieces

FOR THE SHORTBREAD DOUGH

- **7** oz. (1½ cups) unbleached all-purpose flour
- **2** oz. (½ cup) confectioners' sugar, sifted
- **½** cup pine nuts, very finely chopped
- **½** tsp. kosher salt
- **6** oz. (¾ cup) unsalted butter, at room temperature

FOR THE GARNISH

- **2** tsp. extra-virgin olive oil
- **¼** cup pine nuts

  Kosher salt

This recipe uses 2-inch tartlet molds (you'll need 25), which turn out elegant, two-bite tarts.

MAKE THE LEMON CURD

1. Bring 2 inches of water in a 3-quart saucepan to a simmer over medium heat. In a stainless-steel bowl that fits snugly in the saucepan without touching the water, combine the sugar, lemon juice, lemon zest, and rosemary. Set the bowl over the saucepan, whisk in the egg yolks, and continue to whisk until the mixture thickens and registers 160°F on an instant-read thermometer, 5 to 10 minutes.

2. Turn off the heat, leaving the bowl over the water. Add the salt and then whisk in one piece of butter at a time, whisking until smooth between each addition. Strain through a fine-mesh sieve into a medium bowl and cover with plastic wrap, pressing it directly on the surface of the curd. Refrigerate until well chilled, 3 hours or up to 2 days.

MAKE THE SHORTBREAD DOUGH

Put the flour, confectioners' sugar, pine nuts, and salt in a stand mixer fitted with the paddle attachment, and mix on low speed to combine. Add the butter and continue to mix on low speed until the dough is smooth, about 1 minute. Divide the dough in thirds, wrap each piece in plastic, and press into flat disks. Refrigerate for at least 2 hours or overnight.

BAKE THE SHELLS IN TWO BATCHES

1. Spray twenty-five 2-inch flared or fluted tartlet molds with cooking spray. Working with one round of the shortbread dough at a time, roll the dough between two pieces of parchment to a ⅛-inch thickness. Using a 2½-inch round cutter, cut the dough into circles—you'll need 25 circles for the first batch. Gather any scraps and refrigerate for rerolling. Using a metal spatula, transfer the rounds to the tartlet pans and press the dough into the pans. Trim the tart dough so that it's flush with the pan by pressing along the rim of the pan with your thumb. Prick each tartlet shell several times with a fork, arrange on a rimmed baking sheet, and refrigerate until chilled, about 30 minutes.

2. Meanwhile, position a rack in the center of the oven and heat the oven to 350°F.

continued on p. 166

continued from p. 165

3. Bake the tartlet shells until they're deep golden brown, 10 to 15 minutes. Transfer the shells to a rack to cool. Remove the shells from the pans and store in a sealed container at room temperature for up to 2 days.

4. Repeat rolling and cutting the remaining dough and scraps, which you can reroll once, to yield 25 more circles. Bake, cool, and store as directed.

MAKE THE GARNISH

Heat the oil in an 8-inch skillet over medium heat. When the oil shimmers, add the pine nuts. Toss the nuts until browned, 30 seconds to 1 minute. With a small slotted spoon, transfer the nuts to a paper-towel-lined plate. Sprinkle with a pinch of salt, and cool. Store in an airtight container for up to 2 days.

ASSEMBLE THE TARTLETS

Put the lemon curd in a pastry bag fitted with a ½-inch plain tip (Ateco #806). Pipe the curd into the tartlet shells and top each with 3 pine nuts. (Reserve any remaining curd for another use.) The tartlets may be assembled up to 4 hours ahead. *—Tasha DeSerio*

PER SERVING: 100 CALORIES | 1G PROTEIN | 9G CARB | 6G TOTAL FAT | 3.5G SAT FAT | 2G MONO FAT | 0.5G POLY FAT | 45MG CHOL | 25MG SODIUM | 0G FIBER

chocolate silk pie

SERVES 8 TO 10

- 3 oz. unsweetened chocolate, finely chopped
- 8 oz. (1 cup) unsalted butter, at room temperature
- 1 cup superfine sugar
- ½ tsp. pure vanilla extract
- ½ tsp. almond extract
- ½ tsp. table salt
- 3 large eggs
- 1 baked Classic Piecrust (recipe on p. 127)
- 1 recipe Cacao-Nib Whipped Cream (recipe below)

  Semisweet or bittersweet chocolate shavings, for garnish

You can probably find this old-fashioned pie in your mother's recipe box, but with its intense filling, this version feels as sophisticated as any trendy ganache-based tart, especially when you use a good-quality chocolate. Here we've added a touch of almond extract and a hint more salt than is traditional, to give the filling an extra flavor boost. The longer you beat the mixture after each egg is added, the fluffier the filling will be, so make it dense and rich or light and moussey, as you like. Top with cacao-nib whipped cream to add another layer of chocolate nuance.

1. Melt the chocolate in a medium metal bowl set over a pan of simmering water (don't let the bowl touch the water); let cool slightly.

2. Put the butter and sugar in a mixing bowl and beat with an electric mixer until light and fluffy and the sugar doesn't feel grainy anymore, about 2 minutes. Slowly beat in the cooled melted chocolate, the vanilla and almond extracts, and the salt. Beat in the eggs one at a time, adding the next egg only once the mixture is smooth again.

3. Scrape the filling into the prepared piecrust and chill until firm, at least 2 hours or overnight.

4. To serve, dollop some Cacao-Nib Whipped Cream on each slice and sprinkle with some chocolate shavings. —*Martha Holmberg*

cacao-nib whipped cream

MAKES ABOUT 2 CUPS

- 1 cup heavy cream
- 2 tsp. cacao nibs, coarsely chopped if large
- 2 tsp. granulated sugar

1. Bring the cream and cacao nibs to a boil in a small saucepan. Remove from the heat, cover, and let steep for 20 minutes. Strain the cream, pressing on the nibs to extract any additional liquid, and chill until very cold, at least 4 hours in the refrigerator (alternatively, you can use an ice bath).

2. In a large bowl, whip the cream to soft peaks; sprinkle in the sugar and whip for another few seconds to blend. Use right away.

> **The filling contains raw eggs, so if you're concerned, use pasteurized eggs or ¾ cup of egg substitute.**

mushroom-fontina tart
(recipe on p. 191)

savory pies, tarts & turnovers

upside-down apple-cheddar tarts with frisée and toasted walnuts

SERVES 8

Unbleached all-purpose flour, as needed for rolling

1 9½-oz. sheet frozen puff pastry, thawed overnight in the refrigerator

4 medium Fuji apples

2 oz. (4 Tbs.) unsalted butter

8 thin slices sharp white Cheddar (about 3 inches square and ⅛ inch thick)

1 small head frisée, torn into small pieces (4 cups)

½ cup toasted walnuts, coarsely chopped

2 Tbs. extra-virgin olive oil

1 Tbs. balsamic vinegar

Kosher salt and freshly ground black pepper

This savory twist on a tarte tatin makes a delicious appetizer. If you can't find Fuji apples, use another sweet apple variety instead, such as Gala or Braeburn.

1. Position a rack in the center of the oven and heat the oven to 350°F. On a lightly floured surface, roll out the pastry to a 12x15-inch rectangle.

2. With a 3½- to 4-inch round cookie cutter, cut out eight disks of puff pastry. Prick each disk all over with a fork. Arrange them on a rimmed baking sheet lined with a nonstick baking mat or parchment and bake until puffed and golden, about 25 minutes. Set aside to cool.

3. Peel and core the apples with an apple corer. Cut off about ½ inch from both ends to create two flat surfaces, and then cut the apple in half along the equator. You should have eight ½- to ¾-inch-thick apple rings. If the rings are wider than 3 inches, use a 3-inch round cookie cutter to trim them down.

4. Heat 2 Tbs. of the butter in a 12-inch ovenproof skillet over medium heat. Cook four of the rings until light golden brown on the bottom, about 3 minutes. Transfer to a plate. Repeat with the remaining 2 Tbs. butter and four apple rings. Flip the apples in the pan and add the first batch of apples to them, browned side up. Bake the apples at 350°F until soft and slightly caramelized, 40 to 45 minutes.

5. Put 1 slice of the cheese on top of each apple and bake until slightly melted, 3 to 4 minutes. Place a disk of puff pastry over the cheese and bake until heated through and the cheese has fully melted, about 3 minutes. Transfer the tarts with a spatula to individual salad plates, turning them over so the apple is on top.

6. In a large bowl, toss the frisée with the walnuts. Whisk the olive oil and balsamic vinegar in a small bowl. Toss the salad with the dressing and season to taste with salt and pepper. Distribute the salad among the plates and serve. *—François Payard*

PER SERVING: 390 CALORIES | 7G PROTEIN | 26G CARB | 30G TOTAL FAT | 10G SAT FAT | 12G MONO FAT | 6G POLY FAT | 30MG CHOL | 310MG SODIUM | 3G FIBER

olive tapenade tart
with caramelized red onions

**SERVES 6 AS A STARTER OR
4 AS A LIGHT LUNCH**

- 2 Tbs. extra-virgin olive oil
- 1 Tbs. unsalted butter
- 3 oil-packed anchovy fillets, drained and finely chopped

  Pinch of crushed red pepper flakes
- 1 tsp. fennel seeds, crushed
- 2 medium red onions, halved lengthwise and sliced cross-wise ¼ inch thick (7⅓ cups)

  Kosher salt
- 2 Tbs. chopped fresh flat-leaf parsley
- 1 Tbs. chopped fresh thyme

  Freshly ground black pepper
- 1 cup rinsed, pitted, and coarsely chopped jarred brined olives
- 1 medium clove garlic, minced
- 2 tsp. fresh lemon juice
- 1 tsp. finely grated lemon zest

  Unbleached all-purpose flour, for rolling
- 1 sheet frozen all-butter puff pastry (about 9 oz.), thawed
- ⅓ cup whole-milk ricotta
- 1 large egg

Tapenade is a savory condiment most often made from olives, capers, anchovies, lemon, and olive oil. Here, it's used to delicious effect in a riff on the Provençal onion-olive-anchovy pizza called pissaladière.

1. Position a rack in the center of the oven and heat the oven to 425°F.

2. In a 12-inch skillet, heat 1 Tbs. of the oil with the butter over medium heat. Add the anchovies, pepper flakes, and fennel seeds and cook, stirring, until fragrant and the anchovies begin to break down, about 30 seconds. Add the onions and a generous pinch of salt and cook, stirring occasionally, until they begin to caramelize, 15 to 18 minutes. Transfer to a bowl, let them cool slightly, and then gently stir in the parsley and 1½ tsp. of the thyme. Season to taste with salt and pepper.

3. In a small food processor, pulse ¾ cup of the olives, the garlic, lemon juice, zest, and the remaining 1 Tbs. oil and 1½ tsp. thyme into a coarse paste. Set the tapenade aside.

4. On a lightly floured surface, roll the puff pastry into a 9x12-inch rectangle. Transfer to a rimmed baking sheet lined with parchment. Dock the pastry by pricking it all over with a fork, leaving a 1-inch border along the edges. Spread the olive tapenade evenly on the pastry within the border. Top with the onions, dollops of the ricotta, and the remaining ¼ cup olives.

5. In a small bowl, beat the egg with ½ tsp. water. Brush the pastry border with the egg wash and bake the tart until the pastry is puffed, deep golden brown on the edges, and light golden brown on the bottom, 20 to 25 minutes. Let cool briefly and serve warm.

—Melissa Pellegrino

PER SERVING: 220 CALORIES | 10G PROTEIN | 8G CARB | 16G TOTAL FAT | 4.5G SAT FAT | 9G MONO FAT | 1.5G POLY FAT, 50MG CHOL | 1,370MG SODIUM | 2G FIBER

swiss chard, sweet potato & feta tart

SERVES 8

FOR THE CRUST

5½ oz. (1 cup) teff flour

4½ oz. (1 cup) unbleached all-purpose flour

¾ tsp. table salt

6 oz. (¾ cup) chilled unsalted butter, cut into ½-inch pieces

4 to 5 Tbs. ice water

FOR THE FILLING

1½ lb. sweet potatoes (2 medium)

3 Tbs. extra-virgin olive oil

2 medium red onions, peeled, halved, and sliced lengthwise into ¼-inch-thick slices (4 cups)

Sea salt

2 Tbs. balsamic vinegar

3 medium cloves garlic, chopped

1 large bunch Swiss chard (15 oz.), thick stems removed, greens coarsely chopped (8 cups)

8 oz. feta, crumbled (1⅓ cups)

Crushed red pepper flakes

2 large eggs

Freshly ground black pepper

Adding teff flour to this tart's crust gives it the texture of shortbread and a rich, nutty flavor. (For information on teff, see the sidebar on p. 175.) The filling is vegetable heaven—chard, sweet potatoes, and red onions—topped off with a salty sprinkle of feta. Serve with a green salad to round out the meal.

MAKE THE CRUST

1. Combine both flours and the salt in a food processor; pulse to combine. Add the butter and pulse until it breaks down to the size of small peas. Sprinkle 4 Tbs. of the ice water over the mixture and pulse again until the pastry just holds together (if it's too dry to hold together, pulse in tiny amounts of the remaining water until it holds). Transfer the dough to a large sheet of plastic wrap, and using the plastic as an aid, shape it into a thick disk. Wrap the dough in the plastic and refrigerate for about 30 minutes.

2. Meanwhile, position a rack in the center of the oven and heat the oven to 375°F.

3. Unwrap and roll the dough on a lightly floured surface into a 14-inch circle. (If the pastry cracks, just press it back together.) Wrap the pastry around the rolling pin and unroll it over an 11-inch fluted tart pan with a removable bottom. Without stretching the dough, very gently work it into the pan, pressing the pastry against the sides. Roll the pin over the pan to trim the excess dough. Use the scraps as needed to make the edge even and about ¼ inch thick (at the narrowest points). Press gently all around the edge so the dough comes up slightly above the rim of the pan.

4. Prick the bottom of the crust all over with a fork, line with parchment, and fill with dried beans or pie weights. Put the tart pan on a baking sheet and bake until the edge looks dry, about 10 minutes. Carefully remove the beans and parchment and bake until the bottom is just set and looks dry, 5 to 7 minutes more. Cool on the baking sheet on a wire rack.

MAKE THE FILLING

1. Scrub the sweet potatoes, poke them once or twice with a fork, and put them on a small foil-lined baking sheet. Roast until tender when pierced, 50 to 60 minutes. Cool, peel, and cut into ¾-inch dice.

2. While the sweet potatoes are roasting, heat 2 Tbs. of the olive oil in a 12-inch nonstick skillet over medium-high heat. Add the onions and a generous pinch of salt; cook, stirring, until the onions wilt and develop dark brown charred spots, about 10 minutes. Reduce the heat to

continued on p. 174

continued from p. 173

medium-low, cover the pan, and stir frequently, until softened and caramelized, 8 to 9 minutes more. Add 1 Tbs. of the balsamic vinegar and stir until it evaporates and glazes the onions.

3. Transfer the onions to a small bowl and wipe out the pan. Heat the remaining 1 Tbs. olive oil in the pan over medium-low heat. Add the garlic and cook until fragrant and just beginning to color, 1 to 2 minutes. Increase the heat to medium-high, add the chopped chard and a pinch of salt, and toss over medium-high heat until the chard is completely wilted, about 4 minutes. Sprinkle the remaining 1 Tbs. balsamic vinegar over the chard and toss it until the vinegar cooks away, about 1 minute. Transfer to a large bowl.

4. Add the diced sweet potatoes, about three-quarters of the cheese, and a pinch of crushed red pepper to the chard; toss gently. In a small bowl, whisk the eggs with a pinch of salt and pepper and add the eggs to the chard mixture.

BAKE THE TART
1. Spread the filling evenly in the tart shell and scatter the remaining cheese on top. Bake the tart on the baking sheet until the cheese is nicely browned, 25 to 30 minutes.

2. Spoon the balsamic onions over the top of the tart, allowing bits of cheese to peek through here and there. Let the tart cool slightly, about 10 minutes; then remove the rim of the pan. Slice and serve the tart warm or at room temperature. —*Anna Thomas*

PER SERVING: 490 CALORIES | 12G PROTEIN | 44G CARB | 31G TOTAL FAT | 16G SAT FAT | 10G MONO FAT | 1.5G POLY FAT | 125MG CHOL | 1,270MG SODIUM | 6G FIBER

More about Teff

Teff is the smallest grain in the world. Native to Africa and an integral part of Ethiopian cuisine (it's used to make their national bread, injera), it can be white, red, or even purple. The most common variety is chocolate-brown. It's a nutritional powerhouse, full of iron and protein, and a good source of fiber and calcium.

Teff's rich, distinctive flavor is reminiscent of hazelnuts to some and artichokes to others. Its toasty-nutty flavor goes well with ingredients both sweet and savory, like apples, winter squash, root vegetables, chicken, onions, corn, and brown sugar. It can also stand up to spicy foods.

Teff can be found at many supermarkets, in health food stores, and online.

Whole teff can be cooked into a dark brown polenta, which can be sweetened and eaten with fruit as a breakfast porridge. You can also let it set up, cut it into wedges, and grill or sauté it to serve with savory foods. Teff flour, which is gluten-free, imparts its nuttiness and dusky cocoa shade to piecrusts, waffles, and other baked goods.

Storing
Store whole teff in an airtight container in a cool, dry place for up to 1 year. Teff flour will keep in an airtight container at room temperature for up to 3 months or frozen for up to 6 months.

classic chicken potpies

FOR THE CRUST

9 oz. (2 cups) unbleached all-purpose flour

¾ tsp. table salt

6 oz. (¾ cup) chilled unsalted butter, cut into 10 pieces

3 Tbs. cold water

FOR THE FILLING

5 Tbs. olive oil

2½ lb. boneless, skinless chicken thighs or breasts

Kosher salt and freshly ground black pepper

8 oz. medium cremini mushrooms, quartered (2 cups)

1½ cups frozen pearl onions, thawed and patted dry

4 medium carrots, peeled and sliced ½ inch thick (1½ cups)

3 medium cloves garlic, minced

2 oz. (4 Tbs.) unsalted butter, cut into 3 pieces

2¼ oz. (½ cup) unbleached all-purpose flour

3 cups lower-salt chicken broth

1 cup half-and-half or heavy cream

1¾ lb. red potatoes, cut into ½-inch dice (5 cups)

1 cup frozen petite peas, thawed

¼ cup dry sherry

¼ cup chopped fresh flat-leaf parsley

2 Tbs. chopped fresh thyme

1½ Tbs. Dijon mustard

You can assemble the potpies and refrigerate them, covered, for up to 1 day before baking and serving.

MAKE THE CRUST

1. Put the flour and salt in a food processor and pulse to blend. Add the butter and pulse until the butter pieces are the size of peas, 10 to 12 pulses. Drizzle 3 Tbs. cold water over the mixture. Pulse until the dough forms moist crumbs that are just beginning to clump together, 8 or 9 pulses more.

2. Turn the crumbs onto a large piece of plastic wrap and gather into a pile. With the heel of your hand, gently smear the dough away from you until the crumbs come together (two or three smears should do it). Shape the dough into a 4-inch square, wrap tightly in the plastic, and refrigerate until firm, at least 2 hours or up to 2 days. (The dough can also be frozen for up to 1 month. Thaw in the refrigerator overnight or at room temperature for about 1 hour before rolling.)

MAKE THE FILLING

1. Heat 2 Tbs. of the oil in a 7- to 8-quart Dutch oven over medium-high heat until very hot. Generously season the chicken with salt and pepper. Working in two batches, brown the chicken well on both sides, 4 to 5 minutes per side, adding 1 Tbs. oil with the second batch. Transfer the chicken to a cutting board and cut into ¾- to 1-inch pieces (it's fine if the chicken isn't fully cooked; it will finish cooking later). Put the chicken in a large bowl.

2. Add 1 Tbs. oil to the pot and heat over medium-high heat until hot. Add the mushrooms. Cook without stirring for 1 minute. Continue cooking, stirring occasionally, until well browned, 3 to 4 minutes. Transfer the mushrooms to the bowl of chicken.

3. Reduce the heat to medium and add the remaining 1 Tbs. oil and then the onions and carrots to the pot. Cook, stirring occasionally, until the edges are browned, 8 to 9 minutes. Add the garlic and stir constantly until fragrant, about 30 seconds more. Scrape the vegetables into the bowl of chicken and mushrooms.

4. Melt the butter in the same pot over low heat. Add the flour and cook, whisking constantly, until the texture, which will be clumpy at first, loosens and smooths out, about 4 minutes. Slowly whisk in the chicken broth and half-and-half. Bring to a boil over medium-high heat, whisking to scrape up any browned bits from the bottom of the pan. Reduce the heat to low and add the potatoes, chicken, and vegetables (and any accumulated juice), and a generous pinch each of salt and pepper. Partially cover the pot and simmer gently (adjusting the heat as necessary), stirring occasionally, until the potatoes and carrots are just tender, 15 to 18 minutes. Stir in the peas, sherry, parsley, thyme, and mustard. Season to taste with salt and pepper. (At this point, the filling can be cooled and refrigerated for up to 8 hours before proceeding with the recipe.)

ASSEMBLE THE POTPIES

1. Distribute the filling evenly among six ovenproof bowls or ramekins that are 2 to 3 inches deep and hold at least 2 cups.

2. Let the dough soften slightly at room temperature, about 20 minutes. On a lightly floured surface, roll the dough into a ⅛-inch-thick rectangle. With a round cookie cutter (or using a plate as a guide), cut six dough circles that are slightly wider than the inner diameter of the bowls (reroll the scraps if necessary). Cut one small X in the center of each circle.

3. Top each bowl of stew with a dough round. With your fingertips, gently press the dough down into the edge of the stew so that it flares up the sides of the bowl.

BAKE THE PIES

Position a rack in the center of the oven and heat the oven to 425°F. Put the potpies on a foil-lined rimmed baking sheet. Bake until the filling is bubbling and the crust is deep golden brown, about 45 minutes. Cool on a rack for 20 to 30 minutes before serving.

—Abigail Johnson Dodge

PER SERVING: 860 CALORIES | 45G PROTEIN | 64G CARB | 47G TOTAL FAT | 20G SAT FAT | 19G MONO FAT | 4.5G POLY FAT | 195MG CHOL | 770MG SODIUM | 7G FIBER

slow-cooker steak and guinness pie

SERVES 4

- 1⅛ oz. (¼ cup) unbleached all-purpose flour; more for rolling

  Kosher salt and freshly ground black pepper

- 2 lb. boneless beef chuck, trimmed of excess fat, cut into 1-inch pieces

- 2 large carrots, cut into ¼-inch-thick rounds

- 1 large yellow onion, coarsely chopped

- 3 large cloves garlic, minced

- 2 sprigs fresh thyme

- 1 12-oz. bottle Guinness (or other stout)

- 1 cup lower-salt beef broth

- 2 large russet potatoes (about 1½ lb.), washed and cut into 1-inch cubes

- 1 sheet frozen puff pastry (about 9 oz.), thawed overnight in the refrigerator

This simple version of the classic Irish dish has the distinctive bitter flavor of Guinness® stout. Although it's slow-cooked, the hearty beef stew requires minimal prep time. When it's ready, the puff pastry "tops" are baked separately and served alongside.

1. In a large bowl, combine the flour, 2 tsp. salt, and 1 tsp. pepper. Toss the beef in the flour mixture to coat. Transfer the mixture (including excess flour) to a 6-quart slow cooker and then add the carrots, onion, garlic, and thyme. Slowly pour in the Guinness and then stir in the beef broth. Cover and cook on low for 6 to 7 hours or on high for 4 to 5 hours. Add the potatoes and continue cooking until the meat and the potatoes are fork-tender, about 1 hour more.

2. Position a rack in the center of the oven and heat the oven to 375°F. Coat a large rimmed baking sheet with the cooking spray. On a lightly floured surface, roll the puff pastry sheet into a 10x14-inch rectangle. Put it on the prepared baking sheet and bake until golden brown, 15 to 18 minutes. Remove from the oven, let cool slightly on a rack, and cut into quarters.

3. To serve, lay the puff pastry quarters in four wide, shallow bowls and spoon the stew over the pastry. —*Julissa Roberts*

PER SERVING: 880 CALORIES | 58G PROTEIN | 79G CARB | 34G TOTAL FAT | 7G SAT FAT | 9G MONO FAT | 15G POLY FAT | 80MG CHOL | 860MG SODIUM | 5G FIBER

More about Puff Pastry

Puff pastry is a rich, multilayered dough. This traditional French pastry is known as a "laminated" dough because it alternates layers of fat (usually butter) with dough. It's used to make a variety of classic French pastries like croissants, napoleons, and palmiers.

Puff pastry is made by placing a block of chilled fat between layers of pastry dough, then rolling it out, folding it in thirds, and letting it rest. This process, usually repeated six to eight times, produces hundreds of layers of dough and butter. When baked, the butter melts, creating gaps between the dough layers; the water in the dough and in the butter turns to steam, filling the gaps and forcing the dough to puff and separate into hundreds of flaky layers. Because the process is labor-intensive (and because frozen puff pastry is delicious and simple), most home cooks don't make their own. But if you do, the results are well worth the effort.

Puff pastry is not to be mistaken for phyllo dough, which is also commonly sold frozen. Both are flaky and crisp, but puff pastry is incredibly buttery, soft, and of course, puffy, where phyllo dough is not. The two are generally not interchangeable.

tomato, corn & cheese galette with fresh basil

MAKES 1 GALETTE; SERVES 4 AS LUNCH OR 8 AS AN APPETIZER

- 2 Tbs. olive oil
- 1 large white onion, thinly sliced

  Salt and freshly ground black pepper
- 2 cloves garlic, finely chopped
- ½ bunch basil, washed, dried, and coarsely chopped, (to yield about ½ cup); plus 10 whole basil leaves

  Kernels from 1 ear of corn (about 1 cup)
- 1 recipe Cornmeal Galette Dough (recipe on the facing page)
- 1 large or 2 medium ripe tomatoes (about 12 oz. total) cut into ⅓-inch slices, drained on paper towels
- 3 oz. Comté or Gruyère, shredded
- 1 large egg yolk mixed with 1 tsp. milk or cream

Because this dough has the added crunch and texture of cornmeal, it's a bit more difficult to roll out, so be a little more generous when flouring your work surface. If the dough tears, just pinch it back together. Olives may be used in place of corn for a delicious variation.

1. Heat the olive oil in a sauté pan, preferably nonstick, over medium heat. Add the sliced onion and cook, stirring frequently, until lightly browned, about 10 minutes. Season with salt and pepper. Add the garlic, chopped basil, and corn and cook for 30 seconds. Transfer the mixture to a bowl and set aside to cool.

2. Adjust an oven rack to the center position and heat the oven to 375°F. Line a baking sheet, preferably one without sides, with kitchen parchment. (If your baking sheet has sides, flip it over and use the back.)

3. Roll the dough on a floured surface into a 15-inch round, lifting the dough with a metal spatula as you roll to make sure it's not sticking. If it is, dust the surface with more flour. Transfer it by rolling it around the rolling pin and unrolling it on the lined baking sheet.

4. Spread the onion and corn mixture over the dough, leaving a 2-inch border without filling. Arrange the tomatoes in a single layer over the onions and season them with salt and pepper. Sprinkle the cheese over the tomatoes. Lift the edges of the dough and fold them inward over the filling, pleating as you go, to form a folded-over border. Pinch together any tears in the dough. Brush the egg yolk and milk mixture over the exposed crust.

5. Bake until the crust has browned and the cheese has melted, 35 to 45 minutes. Slide the galette off the parchment and onto a cooling rack. Let cool for 10 minutes. Stack the remaining 10 basil leaves and use a sharp knife to cut them into a chiffonade. Cut the galette into wedges, sprinkle with the basil, and serve. *—David Lebovitz*

PER SERVING: 330 CALORIES | 7G PROTEIN | 27G CARB | 22G TOTAL FAT | 9G SAT FAT | 10G MONO FAT | 2G POLY FAT | 60MG CHOL | 480MG SODIUM | 3G FIBER

cutting a chiffonade

Making chiffonade is a method of shredding. When working with basil, stack leaves atop one another and roll into a tight tube. (For smaller leaves, bunch as tightly together as possible before cutting.) Cut the rolled leaves using a single swift, smooth stroke for each slice. The width is up to you.

cornmeal galette dough

- **5** oz. (1¼ cups) all-purpose flour
- **1½** oz. (⅓ cup) fine yellow cornmeal
- **1** tsp. sugar
- **1¼** tsp. salt
- **3** oz. (6 Tbs.) chilled unsalted butter, cut into ½-inch pieces
- **3** Tbs. olive oil
- **2** oz. (¼ cup) ice water

The texture of this dough makes it a little more prone to tearing, especially as you fold it up and over a filling. If this happens, simply pinch the dough together and move on.

In a medium bowl, mix together the flour, cornmeal, sugar, and salt. Cut in the chilled butter using a stand mixer, a food processor, or a pastry blender until it's evenly distributed but still in large, visible pieces. Add the olive oil and ice water and mix until the dough begins to come together. Gather the dough with your hands and shape it into a disk. Wrap the disk in plastic and refrigerate for at least 1 hour.

spinach, goat cheese & chive quiche

SERVES 4 TO 6

10	oz. fresh spinach, stemmed and washed
2	large eggs
2	large egg yolks
1½	cups heavy cream
	Salt and freshly ground black pepper
½	cup semi-dry finely crumbled goat cheese, such as Bucheron
2 to 3	Tbs. finely snipped fresh chives
1	Tbs. finely minced fresh thyme
⅓	cup freshly grated Parmigiano-Reggiano
1	recipe Basic Quiche Dough, partially baked in a 10-inch porcelain quiche pan or a 10½- to 11-inch metal tart pan (recipe on the facing page)

Serve this quiche accompanied by a salad of baby spinach leaves dressed with a shallot vinaigrette. You can substitute a good sheep's milk cheese like Brin d'Amour for the goat cheese, if you like.

1. Heat the oven to 375°F. In a large saucepan, bring 1 cup water to a boil. Add the spinach and cook until just wilted, 2 to 3 minutes. Drain and set aside. In a bowl, combine the eggs, yolks, and heavy cream. Season the mixture with salt and pepper and whisk until thoroughly blended. Add the finely crumbled goat cheese, chives, thyme, and Parmigiano-Reggiano.

2. Put the spinach in a kitchen towel and squeeze out all the moisture; you should have a ball measuring about ⅔ cup. Mince the spinach and add it to the custard mixture. Blend well.

3. If using a tart pan with a removable bottom, put it on a baking sheet. Pour the spinach and goat cheese custard into the prepared tart shell, being careful that it doesn't overflow. Put the tart on a baking sheet and bake until the filling is nicely puffed and browned, 40 to 50 minutes. Let cool for at least 15 to 20 minutes before serving.
—*Perla Meyers*

PER SERVING: 630 CALORIES | 16G PROTEIN | 28G CARB | 51G TOTAL FAT | 31G SAT FAT | 15G MONO FAT | 2G POLY FAT | 300MG CHOL | 490MG SODIUM | 2G FIBER

basic quiche dough

FOR ONE 10- TO 11-INCH TART SHELL

6¾ oz. (1½ cups) unbleached all-purpose flour

¼ tsp. plus a pinch of salt

4½ oz. (9 Tbs.) unsalted butter, cut into small pieces and chilled

4 Tbs. ice water

FOR ONE 12- TO 12½-INCH TART SHELL

9 oz.(2 cups) unbleached all-purpose flour

½ tsp. salt

6 oz. (¾ cup) unsalted butter, cut into small pieces and chilled

6 Tbs. ice water

Before making the dough, check your filling recipe for the size shell you'll need. To make enough dough for a 10-inch porcelain quiche dish or a 10½- or 11-inch metal tart pan with removable bottom, measure your ingredients using the first list. To make enough dough for a 12-inch porcelain quiche dish or a 12½-inch metal tart pan with removable bottom, use the second ingredient list. The method is the same for both.

MAKE THE DOUGH

In a food processor, combine the flour, salt, and butter. Using short pulses, process until the mixture resembles oatmeal. Add the ice water and pulse quickly until the mixture begins to come together—don't let it actually form a ball. Transfer the mixture to a lightly floured surface and gather it into a ball with your hands. Gently flatten the ball into a smooth disk about 1½ inches thick and wrap it in plastic or foil. Refrigerate until firm enough to roll, at least 1 hour.

ROLL AND SHAPE THE SHELL

Roll the dough on a lightly floured surface into a circle about ⅛ inch thick. Roll the dough over your rolling pin and lift it over the tart pan. Unroll it loosely over the tart pan and gently press the dough into the pan without stretching it. Fold a bit of the excess dough inward to form a lip. Roll the rolling pin back and forth over the pan. Remove the severed dough from the outside of the pan. Unfold the lip of dough and press it down into the sides of the pan to form a double thickness. Prick the bottom of the shell all over with a fork, cover with aluminum foil, and freeze for at least 30 minutes and as long as overnight. At this point, the shell can also be wrapped and kept frozen for up to 2 weeks.

PARTIALLY BAKE THE SHELL

Arrange a rack in the center of the oven and heat the oven to 425°F. Remove the foil, line the frozen shell with parchment or fresh foil, fill it with dried beans or pie weights, and put it on a baking sheet. Bake until the sides are set, about 12 minutes. Remove the parchment and weights and continue to bake until the dough is just beginning to brown lightly, another 6 to 8 minutes. Cool on a wire rack until needed.

continued on p. 184

continued from p. 183

how to make a quiche crust

Turn the tart dough out of the food processor when the dough is just holding together but hasn't quite formed a ball.

Unroll the dough over the pan and press it in without stretching it. Pull some of the overhang inward to form a ½-inch lip.

Roll the rolling pin back and forth over the pan. This will sever the excess dough from the outside of the pan.

Unfold the dough lip and press it into the pan's sides with two fingers to create a double layer around the sides of the shell.

Quiche Crust Tips

• Do keep your flour, water, and butter very cold; leave them in the refrigerator until the very last minute.

• Do cut the butter into tiny cubes; you will be less likely to overwork the dough.

• Don't overwork the dough; process until it's just beginning to form a ball.

• Don't mash the dough into a ball; flatten it gently into a disk and wrap in plastic wrap—it will be much easier to roll out.

• Do let the dough rest for at least an hour in the refrigerator before rolling; this allows the gluten to relax and makes for a flakier crust.

• Do keep your work surface cold when rolling; rub ice packs or ice-filled plastic bags on it if you don't have a marble pastry board.

• Do use a straight French rolling pin instead of a standard pin; the French pin lets you control the dough better.

sweet potato cottage pie

SERVES 4 TO 6

FOR THE TOPPING

- **2** large sweet potatoes (about 2 lb. total)
- **½** cup whole milk
- **¾** oz. (¼ cup) finely grated Parmigiano-Reggiano
- **1** oz. (2 Tbs.) unsalted butter, at room temperature

   Kosher salt and freshly ground black pepper

FOR THE FILLING

- **2** Tbs. olive oil
- **2** medium celery stalks, cut into ¼-inch dice (about ¾ cup)
- **1** large carrot, cut into ¼-inch dice (about ¾ cup)
- **1** medium onion, finely chopped (about 1½ cups)

   Kosher salt

- **3** medium cloves garlic, minced
- **2** tsp. ground cumin
- **2** tsp. chopped fresh oregano or ½ tsp. dried oregano
- **1** tsp. ancho chile powder or other pure chile powder
- **¼** tsp. ground cinnamon
- **1½** lb. ground beef (85% lean)
- **1** 14-oz. can whole peeled tomatoes, with their juice
- **½** cup coarsely chopped pimento-stuffed green olives
- **⅓** cup coarsely chopped raisins or dried cranberries

A cottage pie is like a shepherd's pie, except that it's made with beef, not lamb. Here, a hearty filling of ground beef, salty olives, savory tomatoes, and warming spices like chile powder, cumin, and cinnamon rein in the sweetness of the creamy sweet potato topping.

PREPARE THE TOPPING

1. Position a rack in the center of the oven and heat the oven to 425°F. Line a heavy-duty rimmed baking sheet with foil.

2. Slice the sweet potatoes in half lengthwise and set them cut side down on the baking sheet. Roast until very tender, about 30 minutes.

3. When cool enough to handle, scoop the flesh into a medium mixing bowl. Add the milk, cheese, butter, 1 tsp. salt, and ½ tsp. pepper and beat with an electric hand-held mixer on low speed until smooth and creamy, about 1 minute. Set aside.

PREPARE THE FILLING

1. Heat the oil in a 12-inch sauté pan over medium-high heat. Add the celery, carrot, onion, and 1 tsp. salt. Reduce the heat to medium and cook, stirring frequently, until the vegetables are soft, fragrant, and starting to turn golden, 10 to 15 minutes. Add the garlic, cumin, oregano, chile powder, and cinnamon and cook for 30 seconds. Add the beef, season with 2 tsp. salt, and cook until no longer pink, about 5 minutes. Tilt the pan and spoon off all but about 1 Tbs. of the fat; return the pan to the heat.

2. Pour the tomatoes and their juice into a small bowl and crush them with your hands or a fork. Add the tomatoes to the meat and cook, uncovered, until thick, 10 to 12 minutes. Add the olives and raisins or cranberries and cook for another minute; season to taste with salt.

ASSEMBLE AND BAKE THE PIE

1. Transfer the beef mixture to a 9x9-inch baking dish. Spread the sweet potatoes over the top in an even layer. Bake until bubbling around the edges, about 30 minutes. Switch the oven to a high-broil setting and position the rack about 6 inches from the broiler element. Broil the pie until the sweet potatoes are a bit browned, 2 to 4 minutes.

2. Let cool for at least 15 minutes before serving. —*Martha Holmberg*

PER SERVING: 460 CALORIES | 27G PROTEIN | 36G CARB | 23G TOTAL FAT | 9G SAT FAT | 11G MONO FAT | 1.5G POLY FAT | 85MG CHOL | 1,340MG SODIUM | 6G FIBER

rustic beefsteak tomato tart

SERVES 8 TO 10

FOR THE CRUST

- **9** oz. (2 cups) unbleached all-purpose flour
- **¼** cup freshly grated Parmigiano-Reggiano (about ½ oz.)
- **1** Tbs. chopped fresh thyme
- **¼** tsp. table salt
- **¼** tsp. freshly ground black pepper
- **⅛** tsp. ground cayenne
- **5½** oz. (11 Tbs.) chilled unsalted butter, cut into ½-inch cubes
- **5** to 6 Tbs. ice water

FOR THE FILLING

- **1½** lb. ripe beefsteak tomatoes
- Kosher salt
- **1½** cups freshly grated Parmigiano-Reggiano (about 3 oz.)
- **4** Tbs. coarsely chopped pitted oil-cured black olives or Kalamata olives
- **12** large fresh basil leaves, thinly sliced
- **2** tsp. capers, drained and patted dry, coarsely chopped if large
- Freshly ground black pepper
- **2** Tbs. extra-virgin olive oil

Use the best-tasting, locally grown beefsteak tomatoes you can find.

PREPARE THE CRUST AND TOMATOES

1. Combine the flour, cheese, thyme, table salt, pepper, and cayenne in a food processor and pulse to blend thoroughly. Add the butter and pulse until the pieces are about the size of rice grains. Add the ice water through the feed tube, 1 Tbs. at a time, while pulsing in short bursts until the dough starts to come together. It may still look crumbly, but if you press it with your fingers, it should become compact. Don't add more water than is necessary to get the dough to cling together. Turn it out onto a clean work surface and, using your hands, press and gather the dough into a ball. Put the ball on a sheet of waxed paper, gently shape it into a flat disk, and wrap it tightly. Refrigerate for at least 45 minutes.

2. Meanwhile, core (but don't peel) the tomatoes and slice them ¼ inch thick. Sprinkle with ½ tsp. salt, stack them in a colander set over a bowl, and let drain for at least 45 minutes and up to 1 hour. Every 15 minutes, turn the slices gently and tilt the colander to let drain.

ASSEMBLE AND BAKE

1. Position a rack in the center of the oven and heat the oven to 425°F. Cut parchment to fit a rimmed baking sheet and chill the baking sheet in the freezer. Take the dough out of the fridge and let it warm until pliable, about 10 minutes. Sprinkle the parchment with flour, then roll the dough into a 14-inch round that's ⅛ inch thick. Transfer the parchment and dough to the baking sheet and refrigerate for 15 minutes.

2. Remove the dough from the refrigerator and let it sit at room temperature for about 5 minutes to keep it from cracking. When filling the dough, work steadily without delays. Sprinkle two-thirds of the cheese over the center of the dough, leaving a 2-inch band around the edges. Scatter half the olives and half the basil over the cheese and arrange the tomatoes on top so they overlap slightly. Sprinkle on the remaining basil and olives, the capers, and the rest of the cheese. Season with pepper and drizzle the olive oil over the filling. Fold the edges of the pastry over the edge of the filling, pleating as you go so it forms a neat edge. Bake until the dough is lightly browned, turning the pan halfway through, about 40 minutes total. Transfer the tart from the parchment to a rack and let it rest for at least 30 minutes before cutting.
—Ruth Lively

PER SERVING: 270 CALORIES | 5G PROTEIN | 22G CARB | 18G TOTAL FAT | 9G SAT FAT | 6G MONO FAT | 1G POLY FAT | 35MG CHOL | 230MG SODIUM | 2G FIBER

cottage pie with beef and carrots

SERVES 6 TO 8

FOR THE BEEF STEW

- 1¾ cups lower-salt beef broth (one 14-oz. can)
- ½ oz. dried porcini mushrooms
- 2 to 3 Tbs. olive or vegetable oil
- 2½ lb. thin-cut chuck steaks, preferably top blade (or flat iron), ½ to ¾ inch thick, trimmed of any excess fat or gristle
- Kosher salt and freshly ground black pepper
- 3 medium carrots, peeled and cut into ½-inch dice (about 1⅓ cups)
- 2 celery stalks, cut into ½-inch dice (about 1 cup)
- 2 small onions, cut into ½-inch dice (about 2 cups)
- 1½ tsp. fresh thyme leaves or ½ tsp. dried thyme
- 2 Tbs. tomato paste
- 3 Tbs. unbleached all-purpose flour
- ¾ cup dry white wine or dry vermouth

FOR THE TOPPING

- 2 lb. russet potatoes (3 to 4 medium), peeled and cut into 1½- to 2-inch chunks
- Kosher salt
- 5 Tbs. unsalted butter (at room temperature, cut into 3 pieces) plus 2 tsp. (chilled, cut into small bits); more for the baking dish
- ½ cup whole milk, light cream, or half-and-half, warmed
- Freshly ground black pepper

Cottage pie originated as a way to use up leftover beef stew, but why wait for leftovers? Here's how to make the ultimate comfort meal from scratch.

MAKE THE BEEF STEW

1. Position a rack in the center of the oven and heat the oven to 350°F.

2. Pour the broth into a small saucepan and add the mushrooms. Bring to a simmer over medium-high heat. Remove from the heat, cover, and steep for at least 15 minutes.

3. Meanwhile, heat 2 Tbs. of the oil in a heavy stew pot or shallow 5-quart Dutch oven over medium-high heat. Pat the steaks dry, season lightly with salt and pepper, and put only as many in the pan as will fit without crowding. Sear the steaks, flipping once, until nicely browned, 3 to 4 minutes per side. Set aside on a platter, and repeat with the remaining steaks.

4. Lower the heat to medium, and if the pan looks dry, add the remaining 1 Tbs. oil. Add the carrots, celery, onions, and thyme. Season with salt and pepper and cook, stirring occasionally, until the vegetables begin to soften, about 7 minutes. Stir in the tomato paste and cook for a few minutes. Add the flour, stirring to blend, and cook for another minute. Add the wine, bring to a simmer, and reduce the heat to low. With a slotted spoon, scoop the mushrooms from the broth and transfer to a cutting board. Coarsely chop the mushrooms and add them to the vegetables. Slowly add the broth, being careful to hold back the last few tablespoons, which may contain grit from the mushrooms.

5. Cut the steaks into ½- to ¾-inch cubes and add to the pot, along with any juices. Cover tightly and transfer to the oven. Cook, stirring once or twice, until the meat is tender, about 1 hour. Season to taste with salt and pepper. Set the stew in a warm place and increase the oven temperature to 375°F. (Or if making ahead, let cool, then cover and refrigerate.)

MAKE THE TOPPING

1. About 30 minutes before the stew is ready, put the potatoes in a large saucepan and cover by an inch with cold water. Add 1 tsp. salt. Bring to a simmer over medium heat, partially cover, and simmer until the potatoes are easily pierced with a skewer, about 20 minutes. Drain, and return the potatoes to the saucepan. Put the pan over low heat and shake or stir the potatoes until a floury film forms on the bottom of the pot, 1 to 2 minutes.

continued on p. 188

continued from p. 187

Make Ahead

The beef stew can be made several days ahead and kept, covered, in the refrigerator; just reheat before proceeding with the recipe. You can also fully assemble the pie 1 day ahead: Dot the top with the 2 tsp. butter, cool the pie, cover with plastic, and refrigerate until ready to bake.

2. Using a ricer, food mill, or potato masher, mash the potatoes. Stir in the 5 Tbs. of butter with a broad wooden spoon. Once the butter is thoroughly absorbed, add the milk or cream in three parts, stirring vigorously between additions. Season to taste with salt and pepper.

ASSEMBLE AND BAKE

Lightly butter a shallow 3-quart baking dish. Spoon the stew into the baking dish. Spread the potatoes on top in an even layer—you don't need to spread them all the way to the edge. Dot the top with the remaining 2 tsp. butter. Bake at 375°F until the stew is bubbling around the sides, and the top is lightly browned, 35 to 45 minutes (45 to 55 minutes if the pie has been refrigerated). —*Molly Stevens*

PER SERVING: 490 CALORIES | 25G PROTEIN | 29G CARB | 29G TOTAL FAT | 12G SAT FAT | 12G MONO FAT | 1.5G POLY FAT | 85MG CHOL | 780MG SODIUM | 4G FIBER

Tips for Storing Potatoes Properly

• Refrigerating russets turns their starches to sugars. Instead, store them in a cool, dark, well-ventilated place—in a paper bag in a low cupboard, for instance.

• Don't wash russets before storing. Dampness can cause decay. Remove any rotten spots, as they'll cause the other potatoes to spoil.

• Avoid storing russets near onions, which will cause both to spoil sooner.

shepherd's pie

SERVES 6 TO 8

FOR THE LAMB FILLING

- 3   **Tbs. olive oil**
- 2   **medium onions (10 oz. total), finely chopped**
-     **Salt**
- 3   **lb. ground lamb**
-     **Freshly ground black pepper**
- 3   **cloves garlic, minced**
- ⅔   **cup red wine**
- ⅔   **cup homemade or lower-salt canned chicken broth**
- 1   **14-oz. can whole peeled tomatoes, drained and crushed**
- 3   **Tbs. tomato paste**
- 1   **4-inch sprig fresh rosemary**
- 6   **stems fresh flat-leaf parsley**
- ½   **cup chopped fresh flat-leaf parsley leaves**

FOR THE POTATO TOPPING

- 3   **lb. russet potatoes, peeled and cut into 2-inch chunks**
- ½   **cup whole milk**
-     **Kosher salt**
- 5   **Tbs. unsalted butter**
-     **Freshly ground black pepper**

Though these days it's often made with beef, classic shepherd's pie is made with a rich filling of ground (or leftover) lamb in gravy beneath a blanket of buttery mashed potatoes.

MAKE THE FILLING

1. In a large, deep skillet or Dutch oven, heat the oil over medium-high heat, add the onions, season with a pinch of salt, and cook, stirring frequently, until the onions are soft and light golden brown, about 10 minutes. Add the meat and cook, stirring occasionally, until the meat has lost its pink color. Season with 1 tsp. salt and ¼ tsp. freshly ground pepper. Add the garlic and the wine. Raise the heat if necessary so that the wine simmers vigorously and reduces down slightly (the meat will be giving off juices, too). Add the chicken broth, tomatoes, tomato paste, rosemary, and parsley stems. Adjust the heat until you have a lively simmer and cook the meat, stirring occasionally, until the liquid has reduced to a sauce consistency and cloaks the meat, like a bolognese sauce.

2. Remove from the heat, let the meat cool slightly, remove the herb stems, and then stir in the parsley leaves. Taste and adjust salt and pepper.

MAKE THE TOPPING

Boil the potatoes in a large pot of salted water until they're very tender when poked with a knife. Drain them and return them to the pot. Put the pot over low heat and dry out a little more moisture from the potatoes by shaking them over the heat for a minute or two. Remove from the heat and mash with a hand masher or wooden spoon. Gradually beat in the milk and 1½ tsp. salt and then the butter. When the potatoes are smooth, season with pepper, taste, and add more seasoning or milk, if necessary. The consistency should be fairly thick because the potatoes will soak up liquid from the meat filling during cooking.

ASSEMBLE THE DISH

Heat the oven to 375°F. Spread the meat filling in a 9x13-inch baking dish. Drop large spoonfuls of potatoes evenly over the surface of the meat and gently spread to get an even layer; it shouldn't be perfectly smooth. Bake for 30 to 40 minutes, until the potatoes are golden brown and the filling is bubbling around the edges. Let cool for at least 15 minutes before serving. *—Martha Holmberg*

greek spinach and feta pie (spanakopita)

MAKES ONE 9X13X2-INCH PIE;
SERVES 8

FOR THE FILLING

- 2 lb. fresh spinach, washed, dried, trimmed, and coarsely chopped
- 3 Tbs. extra-virgin olive oil
- 1 bunch scallions (about 3 oz. or 10 small), white and light green parts only, trimmed and finely chopped
- 2 cups crumbled feta (10 oz.)
- ½ cup finely grated Greek kefalotyri cheese or Parmigiano-Reggiano
- 2 large eggs, lightly beaten
- ½ cup finely chopped fresh dill
- ⅓ cup finely chopped fresh flat-leaf parsley
- ¼ tsp. freshly grated nutmeg
- Kosher or fine sea salt

FOR THE ASSEMBLY

- ⅓ cup extra-virgin olive oil, for brushing; more as needed
- 18 9x14-inch sheets frozen phyllo dough, thawed and at room temperature
- 2 tsp. whole milk

Make Ahead

You can make the pie up to 4 hours ahead. Keep warm, if desired, or serve at room temperature.

Instead of fresh spinach, you may use 1 lb. frozen chopped spinach. Thaw overnight or in a colander under warm running water. Squeeze out the liquid and skip the pan-wilting step.

Position a rack in the center of the oven and heat the oven to 375°F.

MAKE THE FILLING

1. Heat a 10-inch straight-sided sauté pan over medium-high heat. Add a few large handfuls of spinach and cook, tossing gently with tongs. As the spinach starts to wilt, add the rest a handful at a time. Cook until all spinach is wilted and bright green, about 4 minutes. With a slotted spoon, transfer to a colander. Let cool slightly and squeeze with your hands to extract as much of the remaining liquid as you can.

2. Wipe the pan dry with a paper towel, then heat the oil over medium heat. Add the scallions and cook until soft, about 4 minutes. Stir in the spinach, turn off the heat, and let cool for 5 minutes. Then stir in the cheeses, eggs, dill, parsley, nutmeg, and ½ tsp. salt and mix thoroughly.

ASSEMBLE THE PIE

1. Lightly coat the bottom and sides of a 9x13x2-inch dish with oil. Working quickly, lightly oil one side of a phyllo sheet and lay it in the pan, oiled side up and off center, so that it partially covers the bottom and reaches halfway up one long side of the pan (the edge on the bottom of the pan will be about 1 inch from the side). Lightly oil the top of another phyllo sheet and lay it oiled side up and off center so it reaches halfway up the other long side of the pan. (If your pan has sloped sides, the sheets may be slightly longer than the bottom of the pan; if so, let the excess go up one short side of the pan and then alternate with subsequent sheets.) Repeat with four more phyllo sheets.

2. Next, lightly oil the tops of three phyllo sheets and layer them, oiled side up and centered, in the pan. Spread the filling evenly over the last layer.

3. Repeat the oiling and layering of the remaining nine phyllo sheets over the filling in the same way you layered the previous nine. Push the edges of the phyllo down around the sides of the pan to enclose the filling.

4. With a sharp knife, score the top phyllo layer into 24 rectangles; don't cut all the way through to the filling. Brush the milk along the score marks (this will keep the phyllo from flaking up along the edges of the squares). Bake until the top crust is golden brown, 35 to 45 minutes. Let cool until just warm. Cut out the rectangles along the score marks and serve. —*Susanna Hoffman*

PER SERVING: 400 CALORIES | 13G PROTEIN | 28G CARB | 27G TOTAL FAT | 9G SAT FAT | 14G MONO FAT | 2.5G POLY FAT | 90MG CHOL | 790MG SODIUM | 3G FIBER

mushroom-fontina tart

SERVES 8 AS AN APPETIZER

- **1 Tbs. olive oil**
- **1 Tbs. unsalted butter**
- **1 lb. mixed fresh mushrooms (I like to use 4 oz. shiitakes and 6 oz. each cremini and white mushrooms), trimmed and sliced ¼ inch thick, to yield 5½ to 6 cups**
- **2 cloves garlic, minced**
- **½ tsp. kosher salt**
- **2 Tbs. chopped fresh flat-leaf parsley**
- **Freshly ground black pepper**
- **1 sheet frozen puff pastry (about 9 oz.)**
- **Unbleached all-purpose flour, for dusting**
- **1 large egg, beaten**
- **½ cup finely grated Fontina (1¾ oz.)**

For reliable, ready-made frozen puff pastry, try Pepperidge Farm brand.

1. Heat the oil and butter in a 12-inch sauté pan or skillet over medium heat until the butter foams. Add the mushrooms and garlic. Like sponges, the mushrooms will immediately absorb all the fat in the pan. Sprinkle with the salt and stir with a wooden spoon until the mushrooms start to release their moisture and begin to shrink, 2 to 3 minutes. Increase the heat to medium-high so that you hear a steady sizzle; stir occasionally. In about 5 minutes, when the liquid evaporates and the mushrooms start to brown, give just an occasional sweep with the spoon (about once a minute) to allow the mushrooms to brown nicely, cooking them for another 2 to 4 minutes. Resist the inclination to stir too often. Turn off the heat and toss the mushrooms with the parsley and pepper to taste, adding more salt if needed.

2. Thaw the frozen puff pastry at room temperature until pliable, 30 to 45 minutes. Set aside.

3. Position a rack in the center of the oven and heat the oven to 425°F. Lightly dust a work surface with flour. Unfold the pastry sheet and roll it into a rectangle that's about 10x15 inches and about ¹⁄₁₆ inch thick. Slide it onto a baking sheet lined with parchment. With the exception of about a 1-inch border around the rectangle, prick the pastry all over with a fork. With a pastry brush, brush the beaten egg over the border (you won't need all of it). Bake until the pastry begins to puff and the surface feels dry, about 5 minutes.

4. Scatter the mushroom sauté onto the pastry, leaving the inch or so border uncovered. Bake until the crust border is puffed and deeply golden brown, about 10 minutes. Scatter the cheese over the mushrooms and continue baking until the cheese melts, another 2 to 3 minutes. Let cool briefly on a rack before slicing and serving.
—*Lynne Sampson*

PER SERVING: 110 CALORIES | 4G PROTEIN | 5G CARB | 9G TOTAL FAT | 4G SAT FAT | 4G MONO FAT | 1G POLY FAT | 45MG CHOL | 230MG SODIUM | 0G FIBER

goat cheese, lemon
& chive turnovers

4 oz. fresh goat cheese (about ½ cup), at room temperature

¼ cup thinly sliced fresh chives

¼ cup minced yellow onion

1 tsp. finely grated lemon zest

Kosher salt and freshly ground black pepper

Unbleached all-purpose flour, for dusting

1 sheet frozen puff pastry (about 9 oz.), thawed overnight in the refrigerator

Make Ahead

The turnovers may be filled and shaped up to 2 hours ahead of cooking. Cover tightly with plastic wrap or brush with melted butter before refrigerating.

These turnovers are perfect for a party or a casual "small-plate" dinner, where guests can sample multiple recipes.

1. Position a rack in the center of the oven and heat the oven to 400°F.

2. In a medium bowl, mash the goat cheese with a fork. Add the chives, onion, lemon zest, ½ tsp. kosher salt, and ¼ tsp. pepper. Stir until well combined.

3. On a lightly floured surface, unfold the pastry sheet and lightly dust with flour. Use a rolling pin to roll the sheet into a 12-inch square. Cut the dough into nine squares. Put equal amounts of the filling (about 1 Tbs.) onto the center of each square. Moisten the edges of a square with a fingertip dipped in water. Fold the dough over to form a triangle, gently pressing to remove air pockets around the filling and pressing the edges of the dough together. Use the tines of a fork to crimp and seal the edges of the turnover. Repeat this process with the other dough squares.

4. Arrange the turnovers on a cookie sheet and bake until the turnovers are puffed and golden all over, 15 to 18 minutes. Let them cool on a rack for a few minutes and serve warm. *—Jessica Bard*

PER SERVING: 60 CALORIES | 3G PROTEIN | 2G CARB | 4G TOTAL FAT | 2G SAT FAT | 1.5G MONO FAT | 0G POLY FAT | 0MG CHOL | 1300MG SODIUM | 0G FIBER

METRIC EQUIVALENTS

LIQUID/DRY MEASURES	
U.S.	METRIC
¼ teaspoon	1.25 milliliters
½ teaspoon	2.5 milliliters
1 teaspoon	5 milliliters
1 tablespoon (3 teaspoons)	15 milliliters
1 fluid ounce (2 tablespoons)	30 milliliters
¼ cup	60 milliliters
⅓ cup	80 milliliters
½ cup	120 milliliters
1 cup	240 milliliters
1 pint (2 cups)	480 milliliters
1 quart (4 cups; 32 ounces)	960 milliliters
1 gallon (4 quarts)	3.84 liters
1 ounce (by weight)	28 grams
1 pound	454 grams
2.2 pounds	1 kilogram

OVEN TEMPERATURES		
°F	GAS MARK	°C
250	½	120
275	1	140
300	2	150
325	3	165
350	4	180
375	5	190
400	6	200
425	7	220
450	8	230
475	9	240
500	10	260
550	Broil	290

CONTRIBUTORS

John Ash is the founder and chef of John Ash & Co., in Santa Rosa, California. He teaches at the Culinary Institute of America at Greystone and is an award-winning cookbook author.

Jessica Bard is a food stylist, food writer, and recipe tester who teaches cooking classes at Warren Kitchen and Cutlery in Rhinebeck, New York.

Karen Barker is a pastry chef and cookbook author. She co-owns Magnolia Grill in Durham, North Carolina. She won the James Beard Outstanding Pastry Chef Award in 2003.

Rose Levy Beranbaum is a cooking instructor, cookbook author, and baker extraordinaire. She is the author of nine cookbooks, including *The Cake Bible* and, most recently, *Rose's Heavenly Cakes*.

Tish Boyle is the editor of *Dessert Professional* magazine. She studied at La Varenne in Paris and has been a pastry chef, caterer, food stylist, recipe developer, and cookbook author.

Brigid Callinan is a cookbook author and the pastry chef at Mustards Grill restaurant in the Napa Valley. She co-authored *Mustards Grill Napa Valley Cookbook* with Cindy Pawlcyn.

Becky Campbell has taught and lectured extensively on cooking with tropical fruits.

Joanne Chang is the pastry chef and owner of Flour Bakery + Café, which has two locations in Boston.

Regan Daley is a food writer from Toronto, Canada. Her cookbook, *In the Sweet Kitchen*, won several awards, including the IACP's Award for Best Baking and Dessert Book and Best Overall Book.

Tasha DeSerio is a caterer, cooking teacher, and food writer. Her latest book is *Salad for Dinner*.

Abigail Johnson Dodge, a former pastry chef, is a food writer and instructor, as well as the author of numerous cookbooks, including *Desserts 4 Today* and *Mini Treats & Hand-Held Sweets*.

Maryellen Driscoll is a *Fine Cooking* contributing editor. She and her husband own Free Bird Farm in upstate New York.

Gale Gand is a pastry chef, restaurateur, and cookbook author. She was recognized in 2001 as Outstanding Pastry Chef by The James Beard Foundation and Pastry Chef of the Year by *Bon Appétit* magazine.

Dabney Gough is a frequent contributor to FineCooking.com and a former recipe tester for the magazine.

Dorie Greenspan has written 10 cookbooks and won six James Beard and IACP awards for them. She won the IACP Cookbook of the Year Award for *Desserts by Pierre Herme* and, most recently, for *Around My French Table*.

David Guas is the chef and owner of DamGoodSweet, a pastry consulting company, the owner of Bayou Bakery, and author of *DamGoodSweet*.

Janie Hibler is an award-winning cookbook author, cooking teacher, and magazine contributor. She was a founder of the International Association of Culinary Professionals.

Susanna Hoffman is an anthropologist and food writer. Her most recent book is *The Olive and The Caper: Adventures in Greek Cooking*.

Martha Holmberg is a food writer, cookbook author, and the former editor in chief of *Fine Cooking*.

Wendy Kalen is a food writer who has contributed recipes to *Fine Cooking, Cooking Light, Food and Wine*, and many other magazines.

Jeanne Kelley is a food writer, recipe developer, and food stylist based in Los Angeles, California. She is also the author of *Blue Eggs and Yellow Tomatoes*.

David Lebovitz is a pastry chef, cookbook author, and blogger. His latest book is *Ready for Desert: My Best Recipes*.

Ruth Lively trained at La Varenne in France, was senior editor at *Kitchen Gardener* magazine, and is the editor of the cookbook *Cooking from the Garden*.

CONTRIBUTORS (CONTINUED)

Lori Longbotham is a recipe developer and cookbook author whose books include *Luscious Coconut Desserts* and *Luscious Creamy Desserts.*

Kimberly Y. Masibay is a *Fine Cooking* contributing editor.

Frank McClelland is a James Beard chef and author of *Wine Mondays.* His L'Espalier has been a perennial "best" of America's restaurants for three decades, earning top accolades from *Zagat, Forbes, Food & Wine, Bon Appétit, Frommer's,* and *Condé Nast Traveler.*

Alice Medrich is a three-time Cookbook of the Year Award winner and teacher. Alice's most recent book, *Pure Dessert*, was named one of the top cookbooks of 2007.

Perla Meyers teaches cooking at workshops around the country and has cooked in restaurants throughout Italy, France, and Spain.

Melissa Murphy is the executive chef and owner of Sweet Melissa Patisserie and Sweet Melissa Cremerie.

François Payard is a James Beard Award-winning pastry chef. He headed up the sweet side of the kitchen at Manhattan's Le Bernardin and Daniel before opening his own restaurant, Payard, first in New York City and then in Las Vegas, Japan, and South Korea.

Liz Pearson is a food writer and recipe developer based in Austin, Texas.

Melissa Pellegrino is a former assistant food editor at *Fine Cooking* and author of *The Italian Farmer's Table.*

Michelle Polzine is a pastry chef at Range Restaurant in San Francisco. She was named 2010's Best Pastry Chef by *San Francisco Weekly.*

Elisabeth Prueitt is pastry chef and co-owner of San Francisco's Tartine Bakery and a contributing editor to *Fine Cooking.*

Jeanne Quan is a San Francisco Bay-area retailer and cooking teacher.

Rebecca Rather is a baker and owner of the Rather Sweet Bakery cafe in Fredericksburg, Texas. She is the author of *The Pastry Queen.*

Nicole Rees, author of *Baking Unplugged* and co-author of *The Baker's Manual and Understanding Baking,* is a food scientist and professional baker.

Julissa Roberts is assistant food editor for *Fine Cooking* magazine.

Tony Rosenfeld, a *Fine Cooking* contributing editor, is also a food writer and restaurant owner in the Boston area. His second cookbook, *Sear, Sauce, and Serve,* was published in spring 2011.

Lynne Sampson, formerly a chef at The Herbfarm restaurant near Seattle, is a food writer and cooking teacher.

Samantha Seneviratne is former associate food editor and food stylist at *Fine Cooking.*

Molly Stevens is a contributing editor to *Fine Cooking.* She won the IACP Cooking Teacher of the Year Award in 2006. Her book *All About Braising* won James Beard and IACP awards.

David Tanis is head chef at Chez Panisse, as well as the author of *A Platter of Figs and Other Recipes.*

Anna Thomas is a food writer and author of *The Vegetarian Epicure.* Her cookbook *Love Soup,* won the James Beard Foundation Book of the Year, Healthy Focus award in 2010.

Julia M. Usher is a pastry chef, writer, and stylist whose work has appeared in *Vera Wang on Weddings, Bon Appétit,* and *Better Homes and Gardens.*

Carole Walter is a master baker, cooking instructor, and cookbook author; her most recent book is *Great Coffee Cakes, Sticky Buns, Muffins & More.*

Joanne Weir, a cooking teacher, James Beard Award-winning cookbook author, executive chef of Copita restaurant in northern California, and the host of "Joanne Weir's Cooking Confidence" on public television. Her latest book is *Joanne Weir's Cooking Confidence.*

Carolyn Weil, a former pastry chef, is a food writer and teacher.

INDEX

If you like this cookbook then you'll love everything about *Fine Cooking* magazine

Fine Cooking magazine is the choice for people who love to cook. And there's even more beyond our award-winning pages: With our apps, e-newsletters, interactive web tools, and online recipe search, we're ready to help you cook great food every day.

Discover all that *Fine Cooking* has to offer.

Subscribe today at
FineCooking.com/more